100 THINGS PIRATES FANS
SHOULD KNOW & DO
BEFORE THEY DIE

Steve Ziants
and the

TRIUMPH
BOOKS

Library of Congress Cataloging-in-Publication Data

Ziants, Steve.
  100 things Pirates fans should know & do before they die / Steve Ziants.
     pages cm
  One hundred things Pirates fans should know & do before they die
  Includes bibliographical references.
  ISBN 978-1-60078-925-0 (pbk.)
  1. Pittsburgh Pirates (Baseball team)—History. 2. Pittsburgh Pirates (Baseball team)—Anecdotes. I. Ziants, Steve. II. Title. III. Title: One hundred things Pirates fans should know & do before they die.

GV875.P5Z53 2014
796.357'640974886—dc23

                              2013050913

This book is available in quantity at special discounts for your group or organization. For further information, contact:
  Triumph Books LLC
  814 North Franklin Street
  Chicago, Illinois 60610
  (312) 337-0747
  www.triumphbooks.com

Printed in U.S.A.
ISBN: 978-1-60078-925-0
Design by Patricia Frey
Photos courtesy of the *Pittsburgh Post-Gazette* unless otherwise indicated

For my brother, Mike, who always believed I would do this one day.

And for my wife, Kris, who made sure that I had that day.

Contents

Foreword

In the eighth grade at Charlotte Junior-Senior High School in Rochester, New York, my assignment was to write a vocational booklet. I chose sports broadcasting. I knew then that I wanted to be a Major League Baseball announcer. At the age of 13, I could not have known that one day I would make my dream a reality, that one day I would become a member of the Pirates family, and that one day Pittsburgh would become my home.

When I began my tenure as a Pirates broadcaster in 1976, the scary part was that nearly everybody listening to me knew more about the history of the Pirates than I did. I never saw Roberto Clemente play. I never saw a game at Forbes Field. Shucks, growing up in upstate New York, I was rooting for the Yankees in the 1960 World Series. Now look at me—nearly four decades later, I am writing a foreword to a book about what a Bucco fan should know and do before he or she dies.

I sincerely believe I am qualified because from Day 1 as a Pirates announcer, I committed myself to learning all I could about this storied franchise. I witnessed 33 years of baseball in the great city of Pittsburgh.

I had a front-row seat as Willie Stargell, Kent Tekulve, Chuck Tanner, and the Fam-A-Lee celebrated a championship. From the 1979 season, etched in my mind are the numerous clutch home runs that Pops hit. I reveled in seeing one of my earliest baseball friends, Teke, record save after save. I was there in San Francisco in late August 1979 when Tanner told Tekulve to play left field. He did for one batter and that batter, Darrell Evans, hit a fly ball to Kent who caught it for the final out of the first game of a doubleheader. (Side note: Teke's wife, Linda, is godmother to our daughter, Megan.)

I was there for the improbable three consecutive titles of the early 1990s orchestrated by Jay Bell, Doug Drabek, Barry Bonds, and company. In my resume of more than 5,000 Pirates games announced, my favorite is the division title–clinching game in 1990. Drabek out-dueled Joe Magrane. The final out was a ground ball to second baseman Jose Lind. Boy, did we party that day.

Fortunately for me, I was invited into the inner sanctum of Jim Leyland's leadership committee and developed a strong friendship with Jim, Gene Lamont, trainer Kent Biggerstaff, and Dr. Jack Failla. These are friendships that I cherish to this day. I am proud that Jim and Katie asked me to be the godfather of their son, Patrick.

My other favorites from three-plus decades of living my dream: John Candelaria's no-hitter against the Dodgers; the Francisco Cordova–Ricardo Rincon no-hitter ended by a Mark Smith home run; and the Pirates coming back from a seven-run deficit with two outs in the ninth inning thanks in part to a Brian Giles grand slam.

I am deeply indebted to my predecessor, Bob Prince. Even though I am one of the individuals who replaced Bob and Nellie King following the 1975 season, Bob was a remarkable mentor of mine. He was always willing to provide me with valuable advice. He lectured me on the necessity to be more than a voice on the air. "Go out and meet your listeners," he said. Bob told me to develop a home-run call, and eventually I did: "Go ball, get out of here."

Later I felt the strong urge to pay tribute to Bob. He always said after Pirates wins, "We had 'em all the way." My tribute to the Gunner was, "There was no doubt about it."

I owe a great deal to the fans of the Pirates. They welcomed me into their homes and into their hearts. They shared their summertime memories with me. Many have told me I was their voice of summer.

I now teach at Waynesburg University. I am sharing my love for sports broadcasting with my students, mentoring the next generation of communicators. It is my hope that some of them will have the opportunity to experience the joy of being part of a major league family and to cherish the friendship and memories that I do.

—Lanny Frattare
November 2013

Introduction

Twenty years of losing dulled the memory of how long and rich and textured has been the history of the Pittsburgh Pirates Baseball Club. Dulled, yes. But erased, no. Never erased. The team's roots run too deep, its glories are too ingrained, its narrative too intertwined, not just in the fabric of the city's sports community but in the city itself. The 2013 season helped bring that all back into focus like a good shower after a long and fitful sleepless night that made the mind actually wonder if the sun would ever come up and if its shadows wouldn't actually win. But it did, and with it came the stories and the memories cascading back in a rush so swift that they were experienced more than seen in the way a warm April breeze through a fluttering curtain will let you know spring has arrived. So swift and so powerful you might not have even recognized what was happening. But it was. The Pirates of 2013 did not just win in those six months of summer; that team helped us relive and remember. Other summers. Other teams. Other magic. Other names.

I'm a lot like many of you. I was born 16 days after Maz's home run. I grew up tapping my sneakers and twitching my neck like Clemente. I saw my first game at Forbes Field. I missed Bob Gibson's no-hitter at Three Rivers Stadium by one night but was fortunate enough to have been there the Saturday afternoon Roberto tipped his cap for the 3,000th and final time. In so many memories of my father, Bob Prince's is the voice I hear in the background. I knew an 11-year-old's joy when the Pirates won on a Sunday afternoon in Baltimore in '71 and I was sitting on my college dorm room floor, typing an English paper, eight years later on the night when Stargell homered in that same stadium to rally the Pirates to their fifth world championship. Even the first baseball game I covered as a newspaperman was Pirates-Reds at Cincinnati's Riverfront Stadium in 1986.

Even though I was born in Florida, my roots are Pennsylvania roots, born to a father from Windber and a mother from Johnstown. I spent a lot of my growing up in places on the outer fringes of a Pirates hold like Youngstown, Ohio; Shadyside, Ohio; and Beaver Falls, Pennsylvania. And it was perhaps on the back porch of my grandparents' house in Windber that the seed of this book—or any stories I've written down over the years—may have been planted. If not, well, it still makes for a good story. It was summer. It was late July. Maybe 1968. Maybe 1969. It was dark. And my grandfather made mention that he had once met Babe Ruth. And Miller Huggins. And Bob Meusel. And a couple of other New York Yankees I can't clearly recall. Met them in Florida during spring training in the 1920s. At their hotel, I think. At a party, I think. I think, because I never really asked the good follow-up question. I was likely too awed. Or, just as likely, I was eight. My grandfather died in 1989. And I never did ask the good follow-up questions. Was he spinning a tale to impress his grandson? Maybe. Was he exaggerating? I don't think so. Did he really meet The Babe? I'll never really know.

But it is one of the reasons we write down stories. So we never have to wonder. So our children and grandchildren know us just a little bit better. So we know ourselves just a little better. The Pittsburgh Pirates have penned a wealth of good grandfather stories in more than 125 years. If I didn't know just how many before I began this book, I do now. Many are, to paraphrase Claude Rains in *Casablanca*, a roundup of the usual suspects. October 13, 1960. Harvey Haddix's night in Milwaukee. A New Year's morning that broke our hearts. But the further down you go on this list of 100 things, the more surprises you're likely to find. Chief Wilson. Frank Killen. Bing Crosby (yes, that Bing Crosby). A bar and restaurant that isn't there anymore.

Argue with the rankings. Scratch your head over who and what didn't figure more prominently (Bob Friend, Kiki Cuyler, Andy

Van Slyke, the teams of the early 1990s) or if they even figured at all. But enjoy the debate. And enjoy remembering again. Who knows. Like me in compiling the list, in researching it and in writing it and discovering the men who originally recorded these tales, even the most die-hard Pirates fan is likely to be prompted into remembering at least one thing he probably forgot he knew. One thing that fills in a little piece of the puzzle, that answers the question gone unasked.

That good shower after a bad night, that breeze through a curtain, that story, even half-told, by a grandfather on a back porch in a childhood summer, can be a wondrous experience indeed.

1 3:36 PM, October 13, 1960

If you were alive and a Pirates fans, you remember where you were. If you had not yet been born, you learned it along with your ABC's. And if you were there, it still might not seem real. That's hardly unexpected. Even the protagonist in that day's storybook tale had a hard time wrapping his mind around the blow he struck on an unseasonably warm October Thursday afternoon that charged a city and changed a man's life, and he's been living that life every day for more than half a century. "Fifty years later, I don't think it's sunk in yet," Bill Mazeroski told Robert Dvorchak in a wonderful story written in 2010 to mark the 50th anniversary of the moment voted the greatest in Pittsburgh sports history and, arguably, the greatest in World Series history.

Game 7 of the 1960 World Series between the Pirates and New York Yankees had already given the 36,683 at Forbes Field that day their fill of drama and theater as had the six games that preceded it. The vaunted big-city Yankees, winners of seven of the previous 11 World Series and 18 overall, had outscored the Pirates by a combined 38–3 in their three wins, including 12–0 in Game 6. They had outhit the Pirates (78–49), out-homered them (8–1) and, with a 2.38 earned run average to the Pirates' 6.79, outpitched them. The mill-town Pirates, who had not been to a World Series in 33 years, not won one in 35, finished last or next-to-last in the National League eight times in the previous 10 years, and had won 23 games in their final at-bat during the season just to get to October, had scratched out 6–4, 3–2, and 5–2 wins in Games 1, 4, and 5.

That afternoon, the Pirates had seen a 4–0 lead after three innings become a 5–4 deficit after six, a 9–7 lead after eight, and

1

then a 9–9 tie after 8½. For a few minutes, maybe 10, it seemed that Hal Smith, a journeyman catcher, would be the game's hero and the player who would be remembered 50 years later after his three-run home run in the eighth inning put the Pirates ahead 9–7 and turned Forbes Field into "an outdoor insane asylum." But the Yankees rallied for two runs off Bob Friend in the top of the ninth, runs that elbowed Smith from eternal hero to historical footnote and made way for the 24-year-old son of an Eastern Ohio coal miner with soft hands, a legendary turn at second base, and 49 major league home runs to write his way not just into Pittsburgh history but into the very cement and steel and sky of the city itself.

Earlier in the game, Mazeroski had singled and scored in the second inning. Earlier in the Series, he had hit a two-run homer for what proved to be the winning runs in Game 1. But, like Smith, they became footnotes to the one at-bat that was to come, to the one swing that met a Ralph Terry "slider that didn't slide," to the one hit that would never get old, and to the one and only home run ever to end a World Series Game 7. "For a second there, I didn't know what to do," Mazeroski "wrote" in his Series diary that appeared the next day in the *Pittsburgh Press*. "But the message finally got to my legs, and I set sail." It wasn't until he approached second base that he realized it was a home run; that the ball that he hit toward left field had carried up and out, past Yankees left fielder Yogi Berra, past the Longines scoreboard clock, and ultimately over the piece of the Forbes Field brick wall that measured 406' from home plate.

Three-thirty-six in the afternoon of October 13, 1960. The game was over. The Series was over. The wait for Pittsburgh was over. "From second to home, I never touched the ground," Mazeroski said in 2010—the year the Pirates unveiled a statue in his honor. By second base, he'd pulled off his hat. Between second and third, he waved his arms and his steps found new altitude. By the time he hit third, he'd been joined by seemingly half the fans

Forbes' Last Day

Call it cosmic. Call it poetic. Call it an homage to coincidence. Not quite 10 years after Bill Mazeroski struck the most famous blow in the 61-year history of Forbes Field, the old park hosted its last games on June 28, 1970—a doubleheader against the Chicago Cubs. The Pirates collected their last hit in the seventh inning of the nightcap. The owner of that last hit? William Stanley Mazeroski. Maz—fittingly, seeing as he was the game's best-fielding second baseman more than he was a home-run hitter—also made the park's last play, a grounder to second by Chicago's Don Kessinger that he turned into a force out of Willie Smith at second.

in Forbes Field. By the time he touched home plate, the rest of Pittsburgh had joined them.

"It was V-E Day, V-J Day, New Year's Eve, and the Fourth of July all rolled up in one," wrote Vince Johnson of the *Post-Gazette*. "It elevated the status of a shot-and-a-beer industrial city trying to remake itself from its sooty past," wrote Dvorchak. "Emotionally, nothing quite like it had happened in Pittsburgh since 1758 when Gen. John Forbes clobbered the French," wrote Joe Williams in the *Press*. "All hell broke loose," wrote Al Gioia of the *Post-Gazette*. One estimate put the celebrating crowd in Pittsburgh's Golden Triangle at 300,000. Entryways into the city were shut down by mid-evening. Confetti piled up knee deep in parts of the city. Pittsburgh has celebrated six Super Bowls, three Stanley Cups, and two more World Series since that night. None of those celebrations approached that level of spontaneity or tapped the vein of pure joy of Mazeroski's homer.

"I just figured it was another home run to win a ballgame," said Mazeroski in a story that appeared the morning his statue was dedicated. "But here we are 50 years later, and it's bigger now than it was then. The longer and longer it went, the bigger and bigger it got."

It was a good quote uttered in typical Mazeroski raised-on-a-dirt-road humility. But also not necessarily honest. For no matter how much time passes or how many times the events of October 13, 1960, are re-told, the product of human memory and recollection can never be bigger than the storybook ending that he wrote that afternoon. It just isn't possible. Not in Pittsburgh. Not in baseball.

2 The Perfect Loss

There was no reason to believe that Harvey Haddix, a 5'9" left-hander from Ohio farm country, would do what he did that night in Milwaukee. He had given up 10 hits to the St. Louis Cardinals in his previous start. He was fighting a cold. Rain threatened. The winds were picking up. And he was on the road facing the two-time defending National League champion Milwaukee Braves, against whom he was 1–5 with a 4.47 earned run average over the previous two-plus seasons. But then, the impossibly amazing wouldn't be so if it were expected or scheduled. Then it would be the everyday, the routine, the ordinary.

To be sure, there was no trace of ordinary in what Haddix did from the mound of Milwaukee's County Stadium the night of May 26, 1959. On that Tuesday night, beginning just after 8:00 and stretching over the next 2 hours, 54 minutes, and 12-plus innings, he authored arguably the greatest game ever pitched.

And he lost.

He lost.

Therein lies the tug of his story. He lost. The other men in baseball history who had pitched perfect games had all won. But

Pitcher Harvey Haddix (left) and catcher Smoky Burgess on May 28, 1959.
(*Pittsburgh Post-Gazette*)

on this night, in the 13th inning, after setting down 36 consecutive Braves batters, including Hall of Famers Eddie Mathews and Hank Aaron four times each, Haddix lost. "A note so despairing," wrote Lester J. Biederman in the next day's *Pittsburgh Press*, "that the boxscore might have been compiled by William Shakespeare, who realized that defeat at the brink of heroic victory is the essence of tragedy."

This was sporting tragedy, for Haddix had given great theater.

For 12 innings—three innings longer than any pitcher in baseball history—he had set the Braves down 1-2-3; the definition of the perfect game and then some, spilling out into the margins of the book where no pens had before written. Even his pitch count was perfect, particularly in the light of twenty-first century standards in which so many pitchers need 100 pitches just to get through six innings. Against the Braves that night, Haddix threw just 115 in 12⅔. Eighty-two for strikes. No more than 14 in any inning. "The greatest game in the history of baseball," was said or written more than once in the hours and days afterward. History has done little to negate that instant analysis. But he lost. Because his Pirates teammates, despite collecting 12 hits—all singles—could not score against Milwaukee pitcher Lew Burdette.

And so 0–0 it went into the bottom of the 13th inning. Milwaukee fans, all 19,194 realizing they'd been blessed to witness something no one had seen before or likely would again, gave him standing ovations after the ninth, 10th, 11th, and 12th innings. But there would be no ovation after the 13th.

Felix Mantilla led off the Braves' bottom half of the inning with a routine grounder to third baseman Don Hoak. Hoak fielded it cleanly, but his throw to first was in the dirt. Milwaukee's first-base runner was aboard on a throwing error. The perfect game was gone. Still, the no-hitter remained. How important was a single run on this night? Mathews, who would lead the National League with 46 home runs that summer, laid down a sacrifice bunt to move Mantilla to second. Haddix walked Aaron intentionally, bringing up Joe Adcock. After throwing a ball on the first pitch, Haddix hung a slider that Adcock swung at—and hit deep to right-center field. Center fielder Bill Virdon ran hard to the wall. "I never jumped so high in my life," Virdon said. "I never wanted to catch a ball so much in my life." But it dropped over. Not far out of reach. But far enough, perhaps defining the distance Shakespeare had in mind.

The final score would not go down as 3–0, however. In a messy scoring twist to a clean night, Aaron, thinking the game was over once Mantilla crossed home plate, headed for the dugout after touching second base. Adcock kept running and passed him. Aaron did not score. Adcock was ruled out. The final score would go down as 1–0. Not that it mattered.

"A man pitches a perfect game like this once in a lifetime—once in baseball history—and we can't win it for him," Virdon bemoaned, reflecting the sentiments of the Pirates' clubhouse.

Everyone except for Haddix. He didn't sleep that night, walking the streets of Milwaukee until dawn. But he cast no blame—at Hoak or the Pirates offense. He begged no sympathy. His only regret was that the Pirates lost the game, not that he lost his chance at immortality. Funny thing about that, though. The immortality he might have thought lost was, in fact, paradoxically enhanced by the way the game played out. Even baseball's decision later to rule that what Haddix did that night was not a perfect game could in no way diminish what he did, what players on both teams saw, what the 19,194 in the stadium witnessed, and what writers for generations have tried to explain.

"It's like a good story with that final twist in the end," Haddix would later say.

Could Shakespeare have said it better?

3 The First World Series

In a mostly vacant professional team sports landscape, decades before national all-consuming events like the Super Bowl and college basketball's March Madness and just seven years after the return of the Olympic Games, Pirates owner Barney Dreyfuss had an idea. It wasn't a new idea, but it was the version that history most remembers because it was the idea that endured. It was 1903 and professional baseball was emerging from a decade of labor wars in which teams and leagues fought for players, fans, and their very survival. Earlier that year the National League had acknowledged the two-year-old American League as its equal. The American, in turn, promised to cease raiding National League rosters for players. But labor peace alone wouldn't be enough to re-invigorate the imagination of fans for the sport.

Dreyfuss, then 38, envisioned something greater—a season-ending series of games between the champions of the two leagues. A series that would channel the enmity and rivalry built up on the labor front, spark interest among fans wearied by the bickering, and—oh, by the way—make a few dollars along the way. In a sport that wouldn't have a commissioner or centralized administration for nearly 20 years, Dreyfuss was free to act on his vision. In August, with his team headed to a third consecutive National League pennant, he wrote to Henry Killilea, owner of the Boston Americans (forerunner of the Red Sox), who were running away with the AL pennant behind manager and star third baseman Jimmy Collins. "We would create great interest in baseball, in our leagues and in our players," Dreyfuss wrote. "I also believe it would be a financial success." On September 18—less than two weeks before the first game would be played—Dreyfuss and Killilea met in Pittsburg (no 'h' yet) to sign the agreement for a best-of-nine "Great World's Series."

It would be a Series we might find difficult to recognize in a twenty-first century of specialists, pitch counts, and schedules dictated by television. Not only was it best-of-nine instead of best-of-seven, there were other elements unique to its day.

- Pirates 25-game winner Deacon Phillippe started five of the eight games played, won three, and pitched 44 innings.

- The Boston duo of Cy Young and Bill Dinneen proved even more durable, combining to pitch 69 of a possible 71 innings.
- The teams combined for 25 triples, a number inflated by overflow crowds allowed to ring the outfield in both Pittsburgh's Exposition Park and Boston's Huntington Avenue Grounds, a decision that forced a ground rule whereby any ball hit into those fans was an automatic triple.
- Losing players earned a bigger series check than winning players (Dreyfuss pitched in his own share of the gate), meaning each Pirates' player share was $1,316.25, and each Americans' player share was $1,182.
- Betting was a big part of the series and figured prominently in daily newspaper coverage. Dreyfuss reportedly lost $7,000 betting on the Pirates. He was not alone.

The two-time defending National League champion Pirates, led by Honus Wagner, Ginger Beaumont, and player/manager Fred Clarke, were decided favorites. For four games, they looked the part. Beginning with the first game in World Series history— October 1, 1903, at Boston's Huntington Avenue Grounds, a 7–3 Pirates victory that included the first pitch in Series history (by Boston's Cy Young to Beaumont), first hit (Pittsburg's Tommy Leach), first run (Leach), first RBI (Wagner), and first home run (Pittsburg's Jimmy Sebring off Young)—they won three of the first four games with Phillippe earning the win in all three. But with Clarke lacking a dependable arm other than Phillippe because of illness (Ed Doheny would be committed to an insane asylum before the end of the year and never pitch again) and injury (Sam Leever hurt his shoulder in a trap-shooting contest days before the start of the Series), the Americans rallied behind Young and Dinneen to win Games 5–8 and win the Series 5–3. They limited the Pirates to eight runs over those last four games, with Young pitching a four-hit, 3–0 shutout in the deciding Game 8 on October 13, 1903, in

Boston. Wagner was the most noteworthy victim of Young and Dinneen, going just 1-for-14 in those last four games.

Despite the fact his Pirates lost, Dreyfuss' vision was fulfilled. Although ticket prices were raised to 50 cents and $1, more than 100,000 fans bought tickets, including 7,600 for Game 4 on October 6 at Exposition Park—the first World Series game played in Pittsburg. Even reporters covering the games were forced to pay their way in. As evidence of the Series' quick popularity, their editors didn't balk. Newspapers from all over the country covered this new championship. The *Pittsburg Press* hailed it as "the greatest series of ball games in the history of the national pastime."

Ironically, the Pirates losing may actually have contributed to that greatness and to the future growth of the Series. Had the favored Pirates of the more established National League won, or worse, won handily, would there have been interest in a second? Would it have faded as the long-forgotten Telegraph Series and Temple Cup had over the previous 20 years? It's said that the Super Bowl only became the Super Bowl after Joe Namath's New York Jets of the upstart American Football League defeated the heavily favored Baltimore Colts of the tradition-rich NFL in Super Bowl III in 1969. The same argument could be made for the Americans' win against the Pirates 66 years before. It bestowed validity on the little brother and gave the older reason to return and even the score, which they have every October but two for more than a century.

The Great One

Thirty-seven years. Eighteen seasons. Two-thousand, four-hundred and thirty-three major league games. Millions of fans. One heroic death. An infinite legacy. To condense into a few hundred words the life, the talent, the complexity, and the impact of Roberto Clemente on a baseball team, its city, and his native Puerto Rico—all of Latin America, really—would require the eye of the man who can count the angels that can dance on the head of a needle and at the same time the dexterity of word and pen to pass the Biblical camel through its eye.

Who was Roberto Clemente?

He was a career .317 hitter and the only player to collect 3,000 hits in the uniform of the Pirates. He owned a right arm that invariably was said to possess the thunder of one form of military weapon or another. He won 12 Gold Gloves, more than any outfielder save for Willie Mays. He won four National League batting titles, including three of the four from 1964–67 and in the year he didn't win—1966—he was named the NL Most Valuable Player after manager Harry Walker suggested Clemente concentrate more on his power numbers. He played in 14 World Series games and had a hit in all 14. He was MVP of the 1971 World Series. He was "a ballgame in himself," said one Orioles scout during that '71 Series.

Clemente was also proud and misunderstood and at times labeled a hypochondriac and a malingerer for not playing when others might have. He was a pioneer and a role model for so many Latin American players who followed. He was The Great One and the player for whom longtime Three Rivers Stadium organist Vince Lascheid queued up the theme from *Jesus Christ Superstar* as he stepped to the plate. He was power and style and grace and "[played] a kind of baseball that none of us had ever seen before," wrote noted baseball author Roger Angell, "throwing and running and hitting at something close to the level of absolute perfection." He was the player countless 12-year-olds growing up throughout Western Pennsylvania wanted to be, right down to the flick of the neck and twist of the shoulders when it was their "ups" in their schoolyard Forbes fields. Clemente was a humanitarian and ultimately he was a hero in death, dying on a mission of mercy when his plane, overloaded with relief supplies bound for earthquake-stricken Nicaragua, crashed into the Atlantic Ocean on New Year's Eve 1972.

So much should be included. So much must be left out.

Yet perhaps there is a way—within these spatial limitations— to bring into focus who Roberto Clemente was. And to do so by falling back on the game's common and comfortable language that has spanned generations: the language of numbers. Not the statistics previously mentioned or those that sabermetricians have created, but three numbers that, in order, convey the respect Clemente earned within the game, the enduring quality of his life and career, and the impact of that life long after his death.

3–21–34.

A code. A shorthand. A combination.

3: Days after Clemente's death, on January 3, 1973—a mere 72 hours after his plane went down—the board of directors of the National Baseball Hall of Fame voted to waive the customary five-year waiting period and allow him to be considered for induction immediately. Against baseball's glacial standards, the swiftness with which they acted was stark. Consider that disgraced all-time hits leader Pete Rose filed for reinstatement—and the chance for Hall of Fame consideration—in 1992 and again in 1999. As of the end of the 2013 season, commissioner Bud Selig had yet to formally rule on Rose's application. Clemente was named on 393 of 420 ballots cast (92 percent) that March. The waiting period has been waived for only one other player—Yankees immortal Lou Gehrig.

21: Feet high, PNC Park's right-field wall was designed in honor of Clemente's uniform No. 21. Nine other numbers have been retired by the franchise. Three other players have statues that stand at its gates. But can the symbolism of enduring meaning to the franchise be any greater than to have the number so long associated with him consciously built into the team's existence in mortar, brick and stone?

And finally …

34: Years after Clemente last played an inning, TV cameras captured tears running down the cheeks of fiery American League manager Ozzie Guillen during a tribute to Clemente at the 2006 All-Star Game at PNC Park. Said Guillen, a Venezuelan who once was ordered to undergo sensitivity training and who would have been eight years old the night Clemente died: "He was a Latino who opened the doors for the rest of us. A lot of people remember Roberto because of the way he died. A lot of people remember Roberto for the way he played the game. What Roberto gave to the community, day in and day out…and the way he showed up to the ballpark, that's the way people should be taking steps in life."

Against this degree of ongoing respect and admiration and influence, perhaps the original question was actually framed incorrectly. Despite all the years that have passed, perhaps it should be reframed to ask not who Roberto Clemente was, but rather who Roberto Clemente still is.

5 Power Before Pops

He was of another time, the prototypical power hitter. His was a body that measured 6'4' and 225 lbs. but seemed bigger. Big chest. Big arms. Big legs. Big, air-moving, oxygen-sucking swing. More Babe Ruth than Barry Bonds, more Harmon Killebrew than Ken Griffey Jr. Built not through weight training or diet as has become the way of the twenty-first-century hitter, but born naturally of life that once saw him work in a meat processing plant moving 50-lb. slabs of beef in a time before *Rocky*.

Everything about Willie Stargell was big, right down to the 35", 34-oz. bat he used. Of another time? When Bonds made his assault on Hank Aaron's all-time home-run record three decades after Stargell, he swung a bat that was 3" shorter and 3 oz. lighter. Bonds was about quick wrists and bat speed. Stargell certainly possessed some of both, but who broke down such things in the pre-video, pre-ESPN middle of the twentieth century? Particularly early in his career, you had power or you didn't. Stargell did.

From 1962 to 1982, he hit 475 home runs, drove in 1,540 runs, and collected 953 extra-base hits—all franchise records. He led the National League in home runs twice. Those numbers likely could have been even greater had he not played his first 7½ seasons in Forbes Field with its (ahem) right-field power alley of 436' where home runs went to die for a left-handed batter like Stargell. Still, he averaged 24 home runs in his seven full seasons at Forbes. It could even be argued that Forbes' stinginess with the home run is greater proof of Stargell's power. In the last seven full seasons the team played there before moving into Three Rivers Stadium in the middle of 1970, the Pirates hit 304 home runs at home. Of those, Stargell hit 70. Nearly one of every four. One man alone out of 25.

Said Hall of Fame pitcher Don Sutton: "He didn't just hit pitchers, he took away their dignity."

Stargell would go on to hit at least 30 home runs four times after moving into Three Rivers and twice hit more than 40. He would drive in 356 runs from 1971–73. He would earn two World Series rings, share a National League MVP, and evolve into the team's unquestioned leader and elder statesman by the late '70s even as he fought health issues—his own and those of his first wife, Dolores.

Still, no recitation of numbers captures Stargell in his prime. They do not adequately convey what he was in those years before he evolved into Pops, the warm 'n' fuzzy story America embraced of a man who fought back time to lead the Pirates to their fifth World Series championship in the fall of 1979.

Crazy as it sounds, that story may actually have diluted the memory of Stargell; made us in some ways forget the giant he was from a time when home runs were measured by wide eyes and word of mouth and not computer models.

"Nobody could hit a ball as far as Willie," said Chuck Tanner, Pirates manager from 1977–85.

At one time Stargell owned the longest home runs in half the stadiums in the National League. He owned seven of the 18 balls hit over Forbes Field's right-field roof. He was the first to homer into the upper deck at Three Rivers in 1970. He was the first to hit a ball completely out of Dodger Stadium in 1969. He hit a ball so far at old Jarry Park in Montreal in 1969 that it wound up in a municipal swimming pool. He hit three homers in a game twice in the first month of the 1971 season. Such were many of his shots that victimized opponents in Montreal's Olympic Stadium and Philadelphia's Veterans Stadium even went so far as to mark the seats in the nether reaches of their stadiums where Stargell hit balls.

Distances have been attached to most of them, most either side of 500'. But it is the story that endures, not the computation.

One-time Pirates pitching coach Joe Kerrigan was a teenager at the game the night Stargell hit the blast that would be marked at Philadelphia's Vet—one of the cavernous multi-purpose stadiums built in the 1960s and '70s. Kerrigan was in the stadium's 700 level. The ball landed in Section 601. It was a high slider off future Hall of Famer Jim Bunning.

"It's all we talked about around the playground for the next few weeks," said Kerrigan, then a teenager growing up in Philadelphia. "Two innings later, people still couldn't believe a man could hit a ball as high as we were sitting."

Said Phillies shortstop Larry Bowa: "That ball was still going up [when it hit]. As an infielder, when a guy hits one that you know is a home run you give it a casual look. When he swung, you didn't take your eyes off it because you wanted to see where it was going. It was majestic. I couldn't believe how far it went."

The day after Stargell hit his marked-seat ball in Olympic Stadium, Tanner climbed up to the seat and sat in it. "Everybody on the field looked like puppets, that's how far it traveled," he said.

Numbers in books don't tell those stories. An aging Stargell, good as he was in '79, wasn't that giant any longer. As time continues to pass since his death in 2001, that is the Stargell we've come to remember. The '79 Stargell that is the good story.

But the Stargell that came before is the truer measure of who he was, the truer memory. In his prime. At his best.

6 The First Dynasty

Barney Dreyfuss. Deacon Phillippe. Fred Clarke. Even Honus Wagner. They are names as yellowed and faded and relatively unknown in our memory as pictures of great grandparents you never met. Yet let it be known that once upon a time these Pirates were the New York Yankees before the Yankees were (literally) the Yankees. They were young and successful and made Exposition Park, itself reduced to a few marks in a twenty-first-century parking lot, the place to be in the early days of the twentieth. Ask a fan today to name the sport's most successful and storied franchise and he'd name the Yankees. Ask a fan as 1909 gave way to 1910, and he'd as likely have said the Pittsburg Pirates, a team remade out of luck and rejuvenated by the talent that good fortune brought with it in the winter of 1899–1900.

With the National League set to contract from 12 teams to eight in time for the 1900 season as the result of its ongoing war

Denis Repp stands in a parking lot at Three Rivers Stadium looking at a marker for first base in old Exposition Park. (Pittsburgh Post-Gazette)

with rival leagues, Dreyfuss, a 34-year-old owner of the soon-to-be-defunct Louisville Colonels, was a willing and wanting owner with nothing to own. About that time, the Pirates went up for sale. Cincinnati Reds owner John Brush was primed to buy the team but pulled out. Dreyfuss, who had made his money in the distillery business, stepped in and purchased half the franchise.

Lady Luck was never so kind. As part of the deal, he arranged to "trade" 14 of his Colonels to the Pirates, including outfielder/

manager Clarke and Wagner—both future Hall of Famers—as well as Phillippe, a pitcher who would win 168 games for the Pirates; Tommy Leach, a young and versatile infielder; and pitcher Rube Waddell, who would win the league ERA (2.37) in 1900. They joined a roster that already included outfielder Ginger Beaumont and pitchers Sam Leever and Jack Chesbro. Most of the key components like Wagner (26), Phillippe (28), Leach (22), and Clarke (27) were still in their twenties with their best years still ahead.

In 1899, the Pirates had finished seventh and the Colonels ninth—both more than 25 games behind National League champion Brooklyn. But together in 1900, the new Pirates finished 79–60 and 4½ games back. It was merely a warmup for the best decade in Pirates history. With Clarke—a Dreyfuss discovery who was made manager of the Colonels when he was only 24—as player/manager, the Pirates would win 945 games, including the only two 100-win seasons in franchise history, four National League championships, one World Series, and the team would play in another by the end of 1909.

Individually, they were equally as celebrated. By the end of the decade, Wagner had won seven of his eight batting titles and led the National League in stolen bases five times, RBIs four times, runs scored twice, and was hailed as the best shortstop in the game. Beaumont led the league in hits four times. Leach led the league in home runs once and runs scored once. And Chesbro, who would join Clarke, Wagner, and Dreyfuss in Cooperstown, led in wins once and shutouts twice. This was a team so strong and deep it withstood the loss of Waddell to the Cubs in 1901and Chesbro to the New York Highlanders in '03. Dreyfuss always seemed to have talent to fill any hole.

National League president John Heydler said that Dreyfuss "discovered more great players than any man in the game." One decade into the twentieth century, who would have argued?

No collection was better than the team he assembled in 1902. While the 1903 squad is remembered for playing in the first World Series and the '09 team for winning a club record 110 games and the franchise's first world title, the '02 team was considered the best of that early Dreyfuss/Clarke dynasty. At the end of the twentieth century, long after anyone who had seen it play was gone, that team still was so well thought of that it was ranked among the top five in major league history in rankings published by *Baseball Almanac* and *Baseball Prospectus*. Its numbers still amaze. It played 142 games and won a then–National League record 103, finishing an astounding 27 games—or about one full month—ahead of second-place Brooklyn. It outscored opponents by 2.41 runs per game, scoring a league-high 775 while allowing a league-low 440. It never lost more than two games in a row. Beaumont led the NL in hitting (.357) and hits (193). Wagner led in runs scored (105), runs batted in (91), and doubles (30). Leach led in triples (22) and home runs (6). Chesbro (28–6, 8 shutouts, 2.17 ERA) was the leader among three 20-game winners. There wasn't a statistical category in which that team didn't dominate.

How good was it? As ridiculous as it sounds, maybe too good. In a time when teams depended primarily upon gate receipts for solvency, the Pirates "were so good that they killed the race," one official associated with the St. Louis Cardinals said. "Pittsburg, by being in front, not being weakened, and trying all the time, cost the other National League clubs, say $250,000."

For a franchise that won more than 63 percent of its games through that decade and only twice failed to win 90, Dreyfuss' bunch probably cost them a whole lot more before their run finally ended.

7 New Year's Day 1973

"February made me shiver
With every paper I'd deliver,
Bad news on the doorstep,
I couldn't take one more step."
——"American Pie"

Don McLean's mournful tribute to the night rock-and-roll icons Buddy Holly, Ritchie Valens, and J.P. "The Big Bopper" Richardson died in an airplane crash in 1959 had been the No. 1 single on Pittsburgh radio in the just-ending year of 1972. Little did Pittsburghers realize how its words would resonate as they awoke from their New Year's Eve merriment to learn in the first moments of 1973, their eyes still sleepy, their minds not yet awake to the day, that Roberto Clemente was dead. He died in a plane crash at 9:22 PM on New Year's Eve.

He and four other men were ferrying relief supplies collected by Clemente from San Juan, Puerto Rico, to Nicaragua, which eight days before had been hit by a 6.2-magnitude earthquake. There had been reports that previous shipments had been waylaid by profiteers. Clemente would go this time in person to ensure the supplies got into the right hands. After several delays, the plane took off just after 9:00, banked left while climbing, and then fell into the Atlantic Ocean about 1½ miles from the airport. In the days before 24-hour news, ESPN, Twitter, and the Internet, word was slow to spread. It made it no less stunning or tragic when it finally made its way to Pittsburgh four hours into January 1, 1973. "When someone tells me, 'Happy New Year,'" one Pittsburgh-area politician said, "it will seem to be a hollow wish."

Thanks, Roberto

Tom Walker intended to be on the plane with Roberto Clemente the night the DC-7 carrying Clemente, three other men, and relief supplies for earthquake stricken Nicaragua crashed shortly after takeoff from San Juan Airport on December 31, 1972. Clemente instead told Walker, a teammate on his Puerto Rican winter league team, to stay behind and enjoy New Year's Eve. "He saved my life by not letting me get on that airplane," Walker told a reporter in 2010. Walker, a pitcher, went on to play six seasons in the major leagues with four teams. He also married, and he and his wife had four children, the last of whom was born September 10, 1985, or nearly 13 years after that fateful night. The last child was Neil Walker, who in 2010 would become the Pirates' starting second baseman and a mainstay in their lineup. "If not for Clemente, I wouldn't be here today," Walker said.

The news plunged Clemente's native Puerto Rico and Pittsburgh, where he had evolved into "The Great One" over the previous two decades, into first disbelief, then mourning, and finally into a melancholia that lingered through those first days and weeks of the new year like the smoke from the city's steel mills. Clemente's impact in his 38 years had been about so much more than running, catching, hitting, and throwing.

He had been an All-Star right fielder, to be sure. And he had been the player little kids in canvas P.F. Flyers and Keds and patched jeans wanted to be when choosing sides in backyard ballfields from Windber to Beaver Falls. But he had also been a man of both passion and compassion.

"He died caring," Pirates general manager Joe L. Brown said. "I'm sorry about baseball last. The big thing is losing Roberto Clemente the man."

"There were so many things he did for people that nobody knew about and he didn't want anybody to know about," teammate Dave Giusti said.

They came to learn that week. Pittsburgh Mayor Pete Flaherty proclaimed "Roberto Clemente Memorial Week" in Pittsburgh.

Puerto Rico governor-elect Rafael Colon, who was to be inaugurated the day after New Year's, canceled all inaugural festivities. President Richard Nixon issued a statement of condolence. Memorial funds were established to continue Clemente's efforts for Nicaragua and the other causes he championed. An overflowing interfaith memorial service was held in Pittsburgh's Trinity Cathedral. Another, attended en masse by Pirates officials and players, was held at San Fernando Catholic Church in Carolina, Puerto Rico.

People famous and otherwise wanted, and needed, to share in the loss—a loss that was as great as the expanse of Pirates history and as personal as the fan who paid $1.90 to sit in the nosebleed seats atop Three Rivers Stadium and imagine what it must be like to play the game with the artistry and grace with which he played. And with which he lived.

Wrote columnist Roy McHugh in the *Pittsburgh Press*: "When a symbol passes from existence, it leaves a disturbing void. It takes a piece of those who remain. It causes a sort of general melancholy."

Perhaps no act, no eulogy, no contribution of dollar bills captured the confusing mix of despair and love and denial and hope in a miracle felt by most people as the life Manny Sanguillen lived in the days after Clemente's plane went down. Some days, he strapped on a diver's oxygen tank and dove the shark-infested waters off San Juan near the crash area. Others, he simply walked the beaches, scanning the waters, looking to the horizon, believing he would impossibly see his teammate and friend emerge from the sea.

He never did.

Clemente's body was never recovered.

"And in the streets the children screamed
The lovers cried and the poets dreamed,
But not a word was spoken
The church bells all were broken…
The day the music died."

8 Who the Heck Is Francisco Cabrera?

Francisco Cabrera had just four hits in all of 1992. By the time he disappeared from the major leagues a year later, he had a grand total of 92 to show for five years' work. They are figures that only make that one damnable single he got at seven minutes before midnight on October 14, 1992, that much more galling in a collective Pirates memory. His should have been a name forgotten forever by the next morning. Instead, it has lingered for decades like a childhood bogeyman that can't be outgrown or a tattoo that remains on the aging, sagging skin as a reminder of a night of impetuous youth.

Even Cabrera was surprised when Braves manager Bobby Cox told him to get a bat in the ninth inning that night in Atlanta's Fulton County Stadium. It was, after all, Game 7 of the 1992 National League Championship Series. Cox still had a young All-Star-in-waiting on the bench by the name of Javy Lopez; Cabrera was a late-season callup with 10 at-bats. The bases were loaded, but the Pirates were ahead 2–1 and needed just one out to finally reach the World Series in what would likely be their last-best chance after losing in both the 1990 and 1991 NLCS. Even as the champagne chilled, it was already expected that stars Barry Bonds and Doug Drabek, who carried a shutout into the ninth inning that night, would be gone by Christmas. Bobby Bonilla had left the year before. The king of the NL East Division was breathing its last. Except what was believed to be days were actually just minutes.

Atlanta's Terry Pendleton had already scored from third on a sacrifice fly by Ron Gant. David Justice was on third. He had reached on a rare error by Pirates Gold Glove second baseman Chico Lind on a grounder that "wasn't a tough play. It wasn't an easy play. It was a play Lind normally makes," Paul Meyer of the *Pittsburgh Post-Gazette* wrote. Just not that night. Former Pirates first baseman Sid Bream was on second. He had walked—the last batter Drabek faced.

Reliever Stan Belinda came out of the bullpen to face Damon Berryhill. Berryhill forced a walk to load the bases. But Belinda got pinch-hitter Brian Hunter to pop out for the second out, and it suddenly became a little more possible that perhaps the Pirates would escape. Perhaps Belinda would preserve the win for Drabek, who had allowed just five hits entering the ninth inning. Perhaps Belinda would make a first-inning, run-scoring sacrifice fly by Orlando Merced and an RBI single by Andy Van Slyke in the sixth hold up.

"Probably not one other person on the planet wanted to come into that situation more than I did," said Belinda, who had 18 saves and a 3.15 ERA that season.

Cabrera, a 26-year-old first baseman/catcher from the Dominican Republic, was all that stood between the Pirates and a date with the Toronto Blue Jays to decide the champion of baseball for 1992.

"I knew that if I got that hit, I'd become a hero. But if I didn't, it would have been okay because people didn't know me anyway," Cabrera said later. "Nobody was going to remember that I was the last out in that situation."

It neared midnight—literally and figuratively for him, the Pirates, and the Braves.

Cabrera worked the count to two balls, one strike. Then Belinda threw a fastball. It was up and over the plate. Cabrera swung. He connected. The ball shot through the hole between third and short and into left field. For a second, it appeared as if shortstop Jay Bell might reach it. That was a mirage. Justice scored easily from third. Bonds charged the ball in left. Bream—a 6'4", 215-lb. first baseman with just enough speed to attempt to steal 90 bases in his career but not enough to avoid being thrown out nearly half the time—hit third and was waved home. Bonds scooped the ball and came up throwing. Bream lumbered on. Bonds' throw was to the first-base side of the plate. Bream slid. Catcher Mike LaValliere fielded the throw and in the same motion dived back toward the plate and toward what he hoped was Bream.

He just missed. How close was just? How far on the first-base side of the plate was the throw?

"Since I'm 5'8", it was probably 5'8½"," LaValliere said. "A half-inch too far."

Bream was safe.

The Braves had won 3–2 because of Francisco Cabrera. The Pirates had lost 3–2 because of Francisco Cabrera. "Unbelievable" blared the headline in Atlanta the next day. "Heartbreaker" read the one in Pittsburgh. Because of Francisco Cabrera.

"Without question, the toughest loss I've ever had," Pirates manager Jim Leyland said.

"Stunned," LaValliere said.

As for Cabrera? It was the proverbial dream come true. And for the most part the only one that ever did. But it was a big one.

"Now I'll be in all the Braves fans' memories for all time," he said.

The postulate that went unspoken in those 12 words was that he would also be in Pirates fans' memories for all time.

9 The First Legend

Few would argue that Dwight Eisenhower led a distinguished life. West Point graduate. Supreme Commander of Allied Forces Europe. Planner of D-Day. Liberator of Europe. Thirty-fourth

President of the United States. A guy could hold his own at any class reunion of the twentieth century sporting that resume. Yet Ike never got to be who he wanted to be as a boy growing up in Kansas—Honus Wagner.

Babe Ruth boasted a pretty strong list of accomplishments, too, not the least of which was his other-worldly ability to hit a baseball out of any park including, as the joke goes, Yosemite. To Eisenhower, Wagner was "perhaps the greatest right-handed hitter of all time."

Clark Griffith, the owner of the New York Highlanders in the early 1900s, once offered Wagner $20,000 to jump to the American League. "I told Griff I didn't think there was that much money in the world," said Wagner, who was making $3,000 from the Pirates and once worked for $3.50 a week in the coal mines near his native Carnegie, Pennsylvania, outside Pittsburgh. "He calmly pulled out 20 thousand-dollar bills." Although tempted, Wagner was a Pirate.

When the Hall of Fame was founded in 1936—nearly 20 years after Wagner retired—and the baseball writers of the day voted to select the first class for induction, they had pretty much any man who had ever played the game from which to choose. They cast 226 ballots; Wagner was named on 215, the same as Ruth. Only Ty Cobb (222) was named on more.

All four anecdotes speak vividly across time to the revered place Wagner occupies in Pirates history. Considering that no one is alive who ever saw him play, it also might be the most compelling way in which to convey just how big a figure he cut in early twentieth-century America. Numbers, great as they are, can age into mere figures in a book. They can reduce a career into something rote rather than blood-in-the-veins witness. Testimony from the other side of time can be a powerful thing.

At the same time, numbers are part of Wagner's greatness. To the likes of fabled Giants manager John McGraw, legendary sports-writer Grantland Rice, and even Cobb, Wagner was the greatest

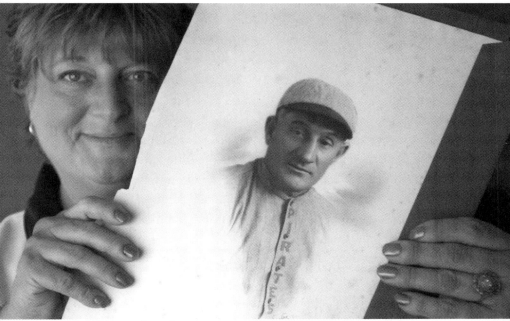

Leslie Wagner Blair of Carnegie, Pennsylvania, holds a portrait of her grandfather, Honus Wagner. Blair, the last direct descendant of the Pirates shortstop, in 2003 auctioned off some of his memorabilia (although not this photo or the 1909 pendant given to Wagner and other members of the winning Pirates team in the 1909 World Series). (Pittsburgh Post-Gazette)

ballplayer who ever lived. After several years at various baseball way stations, he came home in 1900 when Barney Dreyfuss bought the Pirates and brought along the core of his defunct Louisville franchise, with whom Wagner had played since 1897. The Pirates embarked on the greatest decade in franchise history and Wagner would be their star—a star so bright that when Major League Baseball celebrated its centennial in 1969, he would be the shortstop on its all-time team, and when it compiled its All-Century team in 1999, he would be among its 25 players.

From 1900 to 1917 the Pirates won four NL pennants, played in two World Series, and won their first world championship. Wagner hit .328, won a record eight National League batting titles, led the league in runs batted in five times, stolen bases five times, and played such a beautiful shortstop despite a stocky frame and bowed legs that it was said you could roll just about anything between them except a ground ball. His salary increased to a major league–high $10,000 a year at a time when many of the factory workers who watched him play weren't even making $600.

Yet such was the level of respect with which Pittsburghers held him, a coal miner who had become something more, that few begrudged him the money. "It was not uncommon for admirers to back Wagner up against the right-field boxes, and he'd run through the ink in four fountain pens [signing autographs].... [His wife] Bessie Wagner claimed Honus never ate a hot meal at a restaurant. By the time devotees stopped buzzing around the table, his dinner was cold."

This, too, was Honus Wagner.

The city's affection for him never waned nor his for it. By the 1950s, a move was afoot to erect a bronze statue of him near Forbes Field. A fundraising campaign was begun to raise $50,000 needed for the monument, which now sits outside PNC Park. The wealthy made donations. But so did thousands of Pittsburghers, many in amounts as small as a single dollar. All their names were written on a scroll and placed within its base when the 18', 1,800-lb. statue of him was unveiled not long after his 80th birthday. Coincidentally, that was the birthday on which he received a letter, part of which read, "I venture to say that your name and records are as well known to the boys of today as they were to me, and that, I think, must prove that you are truly one of baseball's immortal heroes."

The letter was signed, "Dwight D. Eisenhower," then President of the United States.

Unfortunately, history does not record which of the two men was more excited.

10 KDKA Goes Live

Before Ernie Harwell and Red Barber. Before Bob Prince and Vin Scully. Before "Kiss it goodbye!" and "The Giants win the pennant! The Giants win the pennant!" Before supermarket home-run innings and today's lineups brought to you by Olde Frothingslosh. Before all the elements we've come to know as baseball on radio, there was a 25-year-old electrical engineer with a "tomato can," a box seat at Forbes Field for a Friday afternoon game in August 1921, and a willingness to experiment with a medium as impossible and unexplored then as television would be in the 1940s and the Internet in the '80s.

Nine months before, Westinghouse employee Harold Arlin had been the voice behind newly minted Pittsburgh radio station KDKA's maiden broadcast of results from the 1920 presidential race between Warren Harding and James Cox. So new was radio, KDKA had only signed on as a commercial station at 8:00 PM that night. It was estimated that perhaps 1,000 people heard him declare Harding the winner. So how many could realistically have been expected to hear—or would even care to hear—his "call" of something as trivial as a Pirates home game against the Philadelphia Phillies on the afternoon of August 5, 1921? "Our guys at KDKA didn't even think baseball would last on radio," Arlin told Curt Smith in his book, *Voices of the Game*. "I did it as sort of a one-shot project."

The Pirates held a 3½-game lead in the National League standings as the day began; the Phillies were dead last, 32½ games out of first. Hal Carlson was the starting pitcher for the Pirates. Third baseman Goldie Rapp was the leadoff batter for the Phillies. And with Carlson's first pitch to Rapp and Arlin's call of the play

Following Grandpa

Nearly 50 years after Harold Arlin began radio's love affair with baseball at Forbes Field, his grandson returned to the city where he'd made history. However, Steve Arlin was not in the radio booth on May 2, 1971, but on the pitcher's mound at Three Rivers Stadium—the starting pitcher for the visiting San Diego Padres. He pitched 6⅓ innings against the eventual World Series champions that Sunday afternoon, allowing four runs on eight hits. He would make five more starts in Pittsburgh, including a two-hit, 1–0 shutout of the Pirates in June 1972. But the most poignant may have come later that season. With Arlin on the mound vs. the Pirates on August 30, 1972, Pirates radio voice Bob Prince turned the mic over to a special guest for a few innings. The special guest? Harold Arlin.

sometime after 3:00 PM, the marriage of baseball and radio was consummated. What he said or who heard what, no one knows. It wasn't recorded as it might be today. Pittsburgh's daily newspapers didn't even mention Arlin's experiment the next day. No one then could have imagined the romance that would develop between the two during the coming years.

Like all marriages, though, the beginning had its rough patches. Arlin's setup consisted of a handheld telephone that looked like "a tomato can with felt lining" connected to a transmitter in a box behind home plate. He also had no guide as to what to say or how to say it. Remember, the game's first wave of great play-by-play men were still in short pants and years from being out there to emulate. Arlin didn't know of catbird seats and Holy Cow! and a bloop and a blast. "Nobody told me I had to talk between pitches," Arlin said. "Sometimes the transmitter didn't work. Often the crowd noise would drown us out."

Among the events Arlin would have had to describe that afternoon were cleanup hitter Possum Whitted's two hits and three runs scored and first baseman Charlie Grimm's two RBIs as the Pirates rallied from 4–2 down to win 8–5 and make a winner of reliever

Jimmy Zinn. For 1 hour and 57 minutes, Arlin worked. All nine innings. Alone. With no commercial breaks. And with one mental eye on the notion that for all he knew no one was even listening. "Quite frankly, we didn't know what the reaction would be—whether we'd be talking into a total vacuum or somebody would actually hear us," Arlin said.

Was anyone out there? History long ago told us there was, and continued to tell us every time a 12-year-old hid a transistor radio under his pillow to listen to a game after bedtime, a father fell asleep listening to a game on the back porch as August twilight gave way to full-fledged night, and a soldier found one halfway around the world in Japan or Korea or Vietnam. Baseball and radio. It was quite the love affair that Arlin sparked that afternoon.

11 1960: A Love Affair

It was a Sunday. April 17. Three-thirty-six on the afternoon of October 13 was still six months off. It was Easter Sunday—apropos for a team that had finished last six times in the previous decade and had been mostly picked to finish no better than fourth or fifth in the eight-team National League as 1960 began. The Pirates had won the opener of a doubleheader against the Cincinnati Reds 5–0 on the strength of a four-hitter by Bob Friend. As Game 2 played out, it looked as if they would have to settle for a split. They trailed 5–0 entering the bottom of the ninth inning. No one, of course, recognized it at the time. But it was in those next few minutes that players and pundits alike will tell you that this team, which would shut down the city six months later, first foresaw its destiny.

31

With one out, Smoky Burgess and Bill Virdon singled. Bill Mazeroski singled to drive in Joe Christopher, who had run for Burgess. Hal Smith then pinch hit for pitcher Joe Gibbon and hit a Bill Henry offering for a three-run homer to pull the Pirates within 5–4. Reds manager Fred Hutchinson replaced Henry with Ted Wieand. He discovered that destiny doesn't care who is on the mound. After Don Hoak grounded out, Dick Groat singled. As the early spring shadows crawled across Forbes Field, Bob Skinner then "caught a pitch in his bat's sweet spot and it clanked off a pipe on top of the right-field screen" for a two-run homer and a 6–5 Pirates win. They were 3–2 and within a week would be in first place where they would sit for all but a few days the rest of the season en route to the 1960 National League pennant and a date with the New York Yankees in October.

Their Easter Sunday exploits would become their modus operandi. "I thought that was a game that triggered, 'Gosh, we really have something here,'" Friend said. The Pirates went on to win 95 games. Forty-one times they came from behind to win. Twenty-three times they won in their final at-bat and in 12 of those went down to their final out. "It was a team that never thought it was going to lose," general manager Joe L. Brown said. Shortstop Dick Groat hit .325 and was National League MVP. Vernon Law won 20 games and the Cy Young Award. Dick Stuart hit a team-high 23 home runs. Roberto Clemente hit .314 with 16 homers and 94 RBIs and could have been the MVP.

Yet numbers cannot explain this team or the relationship it carried on with its fans. Those around in the summer of 2013 thought they had to wait a proverbial lifetime before seeing another winner. History argues that their grandparents and great-grandparents knew better the definition of enduring. Consider—a child born in 1927 could have grown up, graduated from high school, fought in World War II, returned home, attended college on the G.I. Bill, gotten married, moved to the suburbs, bought one of those newfangled radios with moving pictures in it, had a couple of kids, liked Ike (twice), and still not have seen the Pirates win like this. The 33 years between being swept by the New York Yankees in the 1927 World Series—the Pirates previous postseason appearance—and clinching the pennant on September 25 that year was the longest drought in the history of the game. And unlike the children of 2013 who had Super Bowls and Stanley Cups to distract them, the Steelers were decades from being Super and the Penguins did not exist. The Pirates were all there was.

This Pirates team of Friend and Clemente and Burgess, of Elroy Face and Don Hoak and Dick Stuart, this band of players that wasn't the best team ever to wear a Pirates uniform but was the one that finally gave the fans reason to cheer, was their reward. Such was their affection that an estimated 100,000 people—more than took to the streets to celebrate V-E Day or V-J Day at the end of World War II—descended on the city to welcome them home late on a Sunday night after they had clinched the pennant in Milwaukee earlier in the day. The pennant. Not the World Series. But a league championship. After 33 years, it didn't matter. The players landed smack in the middle of a confetti-dumping, band-playing, convertible-sitting, chest-thumping, horn-honking parade. "Time stood still, money grew on trees, and Santa Claus arrived three months early," read a story in the next day's *Pittsburgh Press*.

The city cheered the team. But sociologists say it cheered itself, as well. The team was just the plucky manifestation of a second-tier city that was a decade into a self-proclaimed renaissance that would take it from the smoky, hell-with-a-lid-off city of the first half of the twentieth century toward what would become America's most livable by its end. "That 1960 Series was that symbolic civic cement," said Robert Ruck, a Pittsburgh sports historian. "Pittsburgh had shown its ability to rebuild, but it still needed something psychologically that announced to the world that we were back."

At the same time, that may be digging too deep, reaching too far for what 1960 was about at its most basic. That was love; a classic love affair between fans who had waited, endured, and dreamed, and—at long last—a team that finally loved them back.

12 Turn On the Lights

On October 13, 1971, an experiment was staged at Three Rivers Stadium, the results of which we still live with—for better or worse—decades later. On that night, because commissioner Bowie Kuhn thought the World Series would attract a larger audience during a mid-week evening than afternoon, he had convinced NBC to put on Game 4 of the 1971 World Series in prime time. The decision had been made long before the Pirates or Baltimore Orioles were the known participants, so it was pure happenstance that not only were the Pirates involved but that the game that Wednesday night would be staged in Pittsburgh. Preempted for the night were *Adam-12*, *The NBC Mystery Movie*, and *Night Gallery*. In their place was Pirates-Orioles. It was pitted against the likes of *The Carol Burnett Show*, *The Courtship of Eddie's Father*, *Bewitched*, and *Mannix* on the Nielsen meters.

It was a night befitting a first anything. The city requested of its downtown skyline tenants only the fourth non-holiday light up night in history—the better to be seen by the TV cameras. Stan Musial, a St. Louis Cardinals legend but also a local-boy-done-good, threw out the first pitch. He sat next to Hollywood legend and Pirates minority owner Bing Crosby. Nearby were Kuhn and other dignitaries. More than 51,000 fans—a record to see a game in Pittsburgh—filled the 15-month-old park from box seats to peanut heaven.

Stan Musial, flanked by his wife and Bing Crosby, throws out the first ball for the World Series' first night game on October 14, 1971. (Pittsburgh Post-Gazette, Ed Morgan)

The Orioles carried a 2–1 edge in games going into the contest. Opposing them and receiving the honor of throwing the first pitch on this historic night was Luke Walker, a left-hander who hadn't pitched in three weeks. It showed. The Orioles reached him for three runs in the top of the first, and he quickly became the answer to a second trivia question: What pitcher was the first to be pulled from the first World Series game played at night?

Fans who switched over too fast to catch that week's suburban antics of Darrin Stephens and his nose-twitching wife, however, would be disappointed that they did. For as unlikely as it seemed after those first seven Orioles batters produced a 3–0 Baltimore lead, the Pirates came back to win "the most lopsided 4–3 game ever played," as the *Pittsburgh Press'* Bill Christine wrote the next day.

Willie Stargell and Al Oliver delivered back-to-back run-scoring doubles in the bottom of the first off Pat Dobson to pull the Pirates within 3–2, then turned things over to gangly 21-year-old Bruce Kison, who had replaced Walker in the top of the inning. The Orioles got three runs on three hits off Walker but just one hit off Kison in the ensuing 6⅓ innings—enough time for the Pirates to get out of their own way and finally figure out how to win a game in which they outhit the Orioles 14–4. Kison, in the majors only since July 4 of that year, hit a World Series record three batters. But he also faced just three batters over the minimum from the second through seventh innings.

His performance allowed the Pirates to tie the game 3–3 in the third inning on an Oliver RBI single. But it could have—or, some insisted, should have—been at least 4–3. After a Richie Hebner single, Roberto Clemente lashed a slicing drive down the right-field line. To most in the stadium, it looked like a home run. To most, but not to right-field umpire John Rice. Rice signaled foul ball, eliciting arguments from Clemente, first base coach Don Leppert, and manager Danny Murtaugh. When the shouting died down, Clemente returned to the batter's box and promptly sent the next pitch from Dobson into right for a single, giving Oliver the chance to tie the game.

But would the run they didn't get cost them? Manny Sanguillen got caught off second with no outs in the fourth. The Pirates left the bases loaded in the fifth and again in the sixth. Tensions and doubts mounted. "NBC's writers couldn't have wanted a better script than what we gave them," Orioles manager Earl Weaver said.

The Pirates threatened again in the seventh and, despite Sanguillen getting caught in another base-running gaffe, were able to finally break through against Orioles reliever Eddie Watt when Milt May lined an RBI single to right field that scored Bob Robertson from third. It was all the room Dave Giusti needed. He retired the final six Orioles in order, and the Pirates went off into the rest of the night having evened the Series at 2–2.

It vindicated their belief that the Series wasn't over after they'd lost the first two games in Baltimore. And it vindicated Kuhn's vision that the World Series could be pried from its traditional afternoon start times and succeed. More than 61 million people tuned in for Game 4. By 1988, all Series games were being scheduled at night. Again…for better or worse.

13 The Whole Pie

Who was Pie Traynor? As the years have passed, the more the correct answer has been chipped away, his legend eroded by time perhaps more so than any other Pirates great. To a generation of Pittsburghers in the 1960s, he was an aging, white-haired sideman on local TV's *Studio Wrestling* and the stiff-looking pitchman for a heating and cooling company. ("Who can? Amer-i-Can.") To another, he was the voice of sports at Pittsburgh radio station KQV-AM from 1945 to 1966. In either case, his on-air skills were so sparse and lacking that any other man never would have lasted. He did because he was Pie Traynor.

In their own way, however, those two Pie Traynors offer an indication of just who—and how big—was the real Pie Traynor, the Pirates' good-hitting, slick-fielding third baseman from 1920 to 1937. [Note: He became the regular third baseman in 1922, and his last year as a regular was 1934. He missed the 1936 season and played just five games in 1937.] So real and so big and so good that not only was he selected by fans as the third baseman on the Pirates Team of the Century in 1999, he was also named the third baseman on Major League Baseball's all-time team in 1969 as part of its centennial celebration. "I've never seen anything like him," fabled New York Giants manager John McGraw said. Traynor was the first third baseman elected to the Hall of Fame in 1948 and still one of only five voted in by the Baseball Writers Association of America. And in 1999, when Major League Baseball announced its 100-player All-Century Team ballot, Traynor was one of only six third basemen on it.

Ironically, fan voting for the All-Century Team offered some of the starkest evidence of what time has done to Traynor's legacy. Thirty years after being hailed as baseball's all-time greatest third baseman, he finished sixth (out of six) in fan voting. That he fell short of Mike Schmidt and Brooks Robinson, third basemen who starred in the latter half of the twentieth century—and players who found themselves measured against Traynor early in their careers— was no surprise. They had become the gold standard for third basemen. Though not as good defensively, Schmidt hit 548 home runs; Robinson was dubbed "The Human Vacuum Cleaner." But Traynor also finished behind George Brett, Eddie Mathews, and Paul Molitor, all Hall of Famers but none of whom so stood out in their time as to prompt someone to say of them that watching him play third base was "like looking over da Vinci's shoulder," as famed columnist Red Smith wrote of Traynor.

Certainly, Traynor was not the only player whose legacy has faded with time. Of the 25 players voted to the team, only five played their entire careers prior to 1950. Even legendary fellow Pirate Honus Wagner didn't make the cut in comparison to the more modern trio of Cal Ripken Jr., Ernie Banks, and Ozzie Smith. But at least Wagner was remembered well enough to finish fourth and to draw appreciably more than the 3.5 percent of the vote Traynor received. "What hurts Pie is that there are no films of him playing," noted longtime Pittsburgh sports columnist Roy McHugh in 2000.

What fans would see is a third baseman who hit .300 10 times, including .342, .337, .356, and .366 from 1927 to 1930; who seven times drove in 100 runs including each season from 1927 to 1931; and who fielded his position like no one ever had (though his arm was often erratic) and on fields that would make a Little Leaguer shake his head. Traynor helped the Pirates win the 1925 World Series against Walter Johnson and the Washington Senators by hitting .346 with a home run and four RBIs. He helped them win another National League pennant in 1927. Among third basemen, his .320 career average ranks behind only Wade Boggs (.328) in the history of the game. On the Pirates charts, he is top-five all time in hits (2,416), triples (164), runs batted in (1,273), and extra-base hits (593). And, for the record, he also ranks sixth in wins among Pirates managers with 457, including three as player-manager.

They are indicative of why the words *legend* and *immortal* were used freely when he died in 1972. And why none other than Robinson, one of the men whose play with the Baltimore Orioles from 1955 to 1977, forced him to the fringes of history, said of Traynor, "For my money, he was the greatest third baseman of all time."

14 Kissed by the Gods

Before he stepped on the rubber to begin the bottom of the seventh inning that overcast Sunday afternoon in Baltimore, Steve Blass turned his back to home plate and looked around old Memorial Stadium. "I…just paused for a moment or two and did my best to soak it all in. I didn't know if I was ever going to be in this kind of situation again, and I wanted that entire image to stay with me the rest of my life." The image he captured would keep any man warm in old age.

The 1971 World Series belonged to Roberto Clemente, the Pirates' magnificent right fielder who finally, at age 37 and in his 17th season, earned the respect and appreciation of the entire baseball world that October by hitting .414 with two doubles, a triple, two home runs, and four RBIs against the Baltimore Orioles. In addition, he got at least one hit in each Series game for the second time in his career to tie a then–World Series record by hitting in 14 consecutive games. The afternoon of October 17, however, belonged to Blass, a 29-year-old right-handed pitcher from Falls Village, Connecticut, who had only ever dreamed one dream—to pitch in the major leagues. He had so far lived that dream. He owned a career record of 81–59 and had established himself as a cornerstone of a perennial postseason contender.

He had already pitched a three-hitter in the Pirates' 5–1 win in Game 3 that prevented the Orioles from taking a 3–0 Series lead. But this was not just any game, even by World Series standards. This was Game 7. Winner take all. A story to tell your grandkids. A story for other people to tell your grandkids. There had only been 22 others. Unable to sleep, Blass rose before dawn and walked the streets of Baltimore accompanied by his thoughts and by time that wouldn't move fast enough toward a 2:05 PM first pitch. He likely envisioned a Pirates victory—whether or not he dared allow himself to imagine staring down the biggest moment of his career as brilliantly as he would is something only he knows.

Over the course of 2 hours and 10 minutes and in front of 47,291 witnesses in Memorial Stadium and millions more watching on TV, Blass followed his complete-game three-hitter in Game 3 with a Series-clinching, complete-game four-hitter in a 2–1 win

With This World Series Ring...

It's doubtful Bruce Kison, a 21-year-old rookie on the Pirates' 1971 championship team, has ever forgotten his wedding anniversary. When Kison and fiancée Anna Marie Orlando chose Sunday, October 17, 1971, to get married, the baseball season should have been over. At least that's what teammates had told him. "I should have checked myself," said Kison, the winning pitcher in Game 4 after throwing 6⅓ mostly brilliant innings out of the bullpen. Had he checked, he would have discovered that if the Pirates reached the World Series and the World Series went to seven games, Game 7 was scheduled for October 17. They did and it did. What's more, Game 7 was in Baltimore with a first pitch scheduled for just after 2:00 PM, and Kison's wedding was scheduled for 7:30 back in Pittsburgh. Kison, with an assist from Pirates announcer Bob Prince, determined he would not miss either. And he didn't, although how he didn't had all the makings of the final madcap scenes from the 1963 comedy *It's a Mad, Mad, Mad, Mad World*.

Steve Blass took care of business on the field in a nifty 2 hours, 10 minutes. The traditional clubhouse champagne showers followed. "It seems an awful waste. I'd rather drink it," Kison told a reporter. But he knew there was other champagne to be opened that night that wouldn't be wasted. By 6:30, Kison, best man Bob Moose—still in uniform—and Moose's eight-months-pregnant wife, Alberta, were climbing in a helicopter across the street from Memorial Stadium for the ride to Baltimore's Friendship Airport, where a private jet arranged by Prince waited to take them to Pittsburgh. By 7:12, the plane was circling Pittsburgh airport. From the airport, they hailed a taxi that took them to Three Rivers Stadium, where they picked up their cars. By 7:45, Kison—with the aid of a sirens-going police escort—was speeding up Pittsburgh's Parkway East in his clattery Volkswagen toward Churchill Country Club east of the city. At 8:03, he pulled into the club's parking lot. He and Moose hurried into the men's locker room to change into their tuxedoes. By 8:30, he and Moose, along with the judge who was to perform the ceremony, emerged from the locker room. The organist sounded the wedding march—just a little more than an hour late. But all things considered, it was still a pretty fair save by the Pirates' young reliever.

in Game 7. He faced trouble only in the second and eighth innings. He got out of it in the second by inducing Mark Belanger to ground into a double play. In the eighth, Blass allowed the Orioles their only run on a ground-out to first, then he preserved a 2–1 Pirates lead by getting Davey Johnson to ground out to shortstop Jackie Hernandez with a runner on third. In the other seven innings, Blass allowed only one Orioles runner to get as far as second base.

Clemente, meanwhile, gave Blass a 1–0 lead in the fourth with his second home run in two games—a drive to left-center after Orioles starter Mike Cuellar had retired the first 11 Pirates. They scratched out their second run in the top of the eighth inning when Willie Stargell, big as he was and knees creaking as they were, scored all the way from first on a Jose Pagan double.

It was the run that gave the Pirates their fourth world championship.

Clemente was named the Series' Most Valuable Player. Orioles manager Earl Weaver sounded as if he'd have cast his vote elsewhere.

"Clemente was great," Weaver said, "but all I know is that without Blass we might not be popping corks."

"People ask me to this day, 'Don't you think you had a legitimate chance to be the World Series MVP in '71?'" Blass wrote in his 2012 book, *A Pirate for Life*.

"I say, 'Yeah, I do. But that was Roberto Clemente's World Series'.... That was his show."

Besides, Blass received something arguably of greater value on the flight back to Pittsburgh. Blass was seated with his wife. Clemente was a few rows behind. "I had the window seat," Blass wrote, "when Roberto walked up the aisle and said, 'Blass, come here. Let me embrace you.'

"I would have trampled six buffalos or walked over glass and fire to get into that aisle. Here was Clemente...we'd won it all, and he wanted to acknowledge my contribution. All Roberto did was give me a hug. Didn't say a word. Just a hug. I didn't say a word, either. All I did was hang on. The embrace spoke volumes."

The image he captured standing in the middle of an electric Memorial Stadium hours earlier then and for all time had its companion piece.

15 The Curse of Barry Bonds

When a body is weary and frustrated, and when all rational thought has been exhausted like a bullpen on a muggy night in July and logic dealt away for a couple of Class A prospects, what's left to explain two decades of losing? Irrational answer: the curse of Barry Bonds. Let history be thy guide. The owner of the Boston Red Sox, winners of three of the previous five World Series, sold 24-year-old Babe Ruth to the New York Yankees in 1920 so that an early version of *No, No, Nanette* could go on. The Red Sox didn't win another World Series for 84 years. The Pirates, winners of three consecutive division championships, let Barry Bonds walk away over money (lots of money) in December 1992 and didn't win—period—for the next 20 years. Ooooh! Spooky! The curse of Barry Bonds obviously came from the same page of spells as the curse of the Bambino. The modus operandi of the baseball gods' fiendish minions was as clear as The Gunner's hidden vigorish. "Twenty consecutive losing seasons is more than bad luck or bad baseball… more than the random indifference of the universe," wrote one open-minded columnist. "Come on, admit it. Embrace the mysticism. It's a curse."

Now, of course there was no witch huddled over a steaming cauldron. There was no Druid priest or Black Sox Merlin or

$1.99-a-minute 1-900 Psychic Friend having their way with the Pirates after Bonds took his talents—and eventual Greek tragedy—to the San Francisco Giants. Yet that doesn't mean there wasn't a curse. This curse just happened to be the economic state of Major League Baseball in 1992, a time still two years before the great baseball shutdown of 1994 and several years before any real revenue sharing became part of the sport's business model. Big market and small market. The former's ability to pay and the latter's inability. In all instances, the financially ailing Pirates walked under the latter. Feeling compelled to allow Barry Bonds to leave as a free agent after the 1992 season was only the most visible and most costly of a series of financially forced decisions that would define the team for the rest of the decade and well into the next.

They had already watched as slugger Bobby Bonilla left the previous offseason, lured by a record $29 million, five-year contract from the New York Mets. The Pirates had already traded pitcher John Smiley for two minor-league prospects six months after he won 20 games in 1991. They had already stood by helplessly as 1990 Cy Young winner Doug Drabek signed a $19.5 million, four-year free-agent contract with the Houston Astros the week before. But it was on December 8, 1992, that baseball reality dealt its starkest blow.

Barry Bonds had arrived in Pittsburgh on May 30, 1986, the son of a three-time All-Star, and the godson of a Hall of Famer, carrying the promise and expectations of a first-round draft pick, which he was in 1985. Over the next seven seasons—his well-documented failings in October and a tempestuous relationship with the fans and media notwithstanding—he lived up to them. Twice he was the National League's Most Valuable Player and runner-up for a third. In 1990, the first of his two MVP seasons, he hit .301 with 33 home runs, 114 RBIs, 52 stolen bases, and an NL-leading .565 slugging percentage. In 1992, a season in which the Pirates were expected to fall off without Bonilla and Smiley, Bonds led the league in seven offensive categories and the Pirates to a third consecutive NL East Division title.

It was also a season that began with the Pirates resigned to the fact that they would be unable to re-sign Bonds, particularly in light of Bonilla's contract. "Barry knows he's a better player than Bobby," said general manager Larry Doughty at the 1991 winter meetings and 369 days before the team ultimately lost him. "He knows if he's a better player, he should want more money.... [And] somebody out there in the baseball world is going to pay Barry Bonds more money than Bobby Bonilla is being paid." It just wouldn't/couldn't be the Pirates. "We're trying to cut our payroll, not double it," Doughty said.

And so it came to December 8, 1992, in the Galt House East Hotel in Louisville, Kentucky—site of that year's winter meetings—when the San Francisco Giants signed the best player in the game at the time and the best player ever to don a Pirates uniform, according to several Pittsburgh columnists in the years after, to a staggering $43 million for six years. Bonds' salary would climb from $4.5 million in Year 1 to nearly $9 million by Year 6. The Pirates' entire payroll in those same six years would decrease from $25 million to $15 million. Although they had been prepared to see Bonds go, the amount for which he went was stunning. Said Ted Simmons, who had succeeded Doughty as Pirates general manager on February 5, 1992, "It's somewhere beyond the black hole."

Funny. He was talking about the enormity of Bonds' contract. But he just as easily could have been talking about what lay ahead for the Pirates and their fans between 1992 and 2013. And between reality and what some would call a curse.

16 Big Poison and Little Poison

Before a game at old Busch Stadium in St. Louis in the early 1960s, a Pittsburgh newspaper writer introduced Roberto Clemente to Paul Waner, the man who at that time was the gold standard of Pirates right fielders. Afterward, Clemente caught up with the reporter and whispered as much in disbelief as in amazement, "You mean to tell me that little fellow had 3,000 hits?" At 5'8" and 153 lbs., that little fellow was one of the two Waner brothers who terrorized National League pitchers through much of the 1920s and '30s. Paul was "Big Poison" to little brother Lloyd's "Little Poison."

There have been no better—and more fitting—nicknames in franchise history, just as there have been no better hitting brothers in major league history. According to *Baseball Almanac*, just more than 350 sets of brothers have played in the majors. None amassed more hits than Paul (3,152) and Lloyd (2,459), whose 5,611 easily beat out the Alou brothers (5,094) and the DiMaggios (4,853) despite the fact there were three Alous and three DiMaggios. Cementing their status as the greatest siblings ever to play the game, the Waners are the only brothers in the Hall of Fame.

Paul arrived in Pittsburgh first, opening the 1926 season as the Pirates right fielder at age 22 just three days before turning 23. A left-handed batter who sprayed line drives to all fields, he hit .336 with a National League–leading 22 triples. Lloyd, after a recommendation from Paul to team owner Barney Dreyfuss, arrived a year later at age 21 with a rare combination of speed and an uncanny ability to make it work for him both as the team's center fielder in Forbes Field's spacious outfield and also as a left-handed slap hitter at the plate. He led the National League with 133 runs scored out of the leadoff spot. Just as ridiculously good, he hit .355 and had 223 hits—198 of them singles. Brother Paul enjoyed an even better sophomore year, hitting .380 with 131 runs batted in and 237 hits—all National League bests—en route to the league MVP. Together with Pie Traynor, Paul and Lloyd helped the Pirates win their sixth NL pennant and reach the World Series before being swept by the "Murderer's Row" New York Yankees.

As fate would have it, even though both Waners were still young and their stars on the rise, there would not be another trip to the World Series nor another MVP in their careers. Still, the brothers went on to produce similarly spectacular seasons over the next decade-plus. Paul won two more batting titles, hitting .362 in 1934 and .373 in 1936, had seven more 200-hit seasons, set a franchise single-season record for doubles with 62 in 1932, and by the time he was released on December 5, 1940, had a career average of .340 that remains the highest in Pirates history. He also ranks among the franchise's top 10 in games played (sixth, 2,154), runs scored (second, 1,493), hits (third, 2,868), doubles (first, 558), triples (second, 187), and RBIs (fifth, 1,177). Lloyd, meanwhile, added three more 200-hit seasons, two seasons in which he scored 120-plus runs and, evidence of an incredible batting eye honed while hitting corn cobs thrown

Double Shot of "Poison"

The Waner brothers were known for a great many things on a baseball field, but hitting home runs was not one of them. In 38 combined seasons, Paul (113) and Lloyd (27) hit a total of 140, or only a little more than seven a season. Yet until 2013, they were the only brothers to have accomplished a particularly special power feat. On September 15, 1938, in the fifth inning of a game at the Polo Grounds in New York, they hit back-to-back home runs off Giants pitcher Cliff Melton. Twenty-seven sets of brothers have homered in the same game in major league history, but until B.J. and Justin Upton went deep on consecutive pitches for the Atlanta Braves on April 23, 2013, the Waners had been the only bash brothers to go back-to-back.

by Paul growing up on their family farm in Oklahoma, struck out only 103 times from 1931 to 1940—the entire decade of the '30s—in 5,330 plate appearances. His .319 career average at the time he was traded to the Boston Braves six months after Paul was released still ranks ninth on the Pirates' career list. Lloyd is also sixth in hits (2,317) and seventh in runs scored (1,151).

What the record books won't reveal is the origin of their famous handles. As the story goes, they were given to them, oddly enough, in Brooklyn—home of the Dodgers and that unique Brooklyn accent. It was there that "person" can sound a lot like "poison" when uttered by a native, as in, "Every time you look up, those Waner boys are on base. It's always the little poison on thoid and the big poison on foist." Paul, an inch taller and perhaps 10 lbs. heavier, was, of course, the "big poison," although no one would ever have known it by Clemente.

17 What Couldn't He Do?

Because of time, his is a career easily forgotten at worst or too often overlooked at best. Nevertheless, Fred Clarke's position in Pirates history is as unique today as it was when he retired to his Kansas ranch at the end of the 1915 season while only 42. As they say, you can look it up. Clarke is the only person to rank in the top 10 in franchise history in both wins as a manager and hits as a player. He is No. 1 in wins (1,422) and No. 10 in hits (1,638). For the record, he also managed the Pirates to four of their nine National League pennants, took them to two World Series, won one, and as a player ranks 10th in games played (1,479) and at-bats (5,472), fifth in triples (156), and sixth in stolen bases (261).

The amazing aspect, particularly when viewed through the game's modern prism, is that he did all these concurrently. He was from 1900 to 1911 a full-time player/manager and only from 1912 to 1915 more manager than player. The major leagues haven't seen a player/manager since Cincinnati's Pete Rose in 1984–86 and only three others since the 1950s. But in Clarke's era, the practice was common, and Clarke was one of the best no matter in which combination he served—player/manager or manager/player.

"With the possible exception of [Ty] Cobb and John McGraw, baseball never knew a sturdier competitor," wrote Fred Lieb for *The Sporting News* upon Clarke's death in 1960.

Maybe that was what Dreyfuss saw in Clarke. Maybe it was something else. But it was certainly something beyond simply the talent to play the game when he made him a player/manager of the Louisville Colonels in 1897 at age 24, then ensured that he came with him to Pittsburgh—as left fielder and manager—when the Colonels folded and Dreyfuss purchased the Pirates three years later. The Colonel/Pirates merger along the three rivers became one of the first major league dynasties of the twentieth century, and Clarke was at the helm and a mainstay in the lineup along with fellow future Hall of Famer Honus Wagner. The Pirates went 79–60 that first season, then they embarked on a run of three consecutive National League pennants, set the NL record for wins in 1902 with 103, and played in—and lost—the first World Series, opposite the Boston Americans, in 1903. Clarke hit .324, .316, and .351 in those three seasons and averaged 103 runs scored.

By the time the decade ran out, the Pirates and Clarke would look back at a run that included no finish worse than fourth (once in 1904) and another NL pennant in 1909—the year they set the franchise record for wins with 110 and then defeated Ty Cobb's Detroit Tigers in the World Series. Clarke hit the only two Pirates home runs in the Series.

No Pirates team—no manager—has enjoyed a decade like it since. From 1901 to 1910, the Pirates won 945 games and lost 545—a .634 winning percentage. Clarke played in 1,251 of the 1,508 games and hit an even .300. Only the Pirates of 1970–79 would be comparable. They won six division titles and two World Series, but their winning percentage of .569 doesn't come close to the consistency and dominance of Clarke's teams.

While the Pirates were still a first-division team into the beginning of the 1910s, the team and Clarke began to show signs of age. They dropped to fourth in 1913, then they plummeted to seventh in 1914 and fifth in '15. Clarke's numbers also tailed off to the point that by 1912 he didn't play at all and then only sporadically from 1913 to 1915. Over those last years, it's possible he was being pulled in two directions. "We have become deeply attached to the Smoky City," his wife, Annette, told the *Chicago Tribune*, "but there is a big ranch in Kansas that requires Fred's attention, and according to the program, it will be the simple life for us in the future."

And so it was. His love of the ranch that he added to with each raise and bonus made in baseball, made it possible for him to walk away from the game as early as he did with 1,602 career wins between Louisville and Pittsburgh—still 18th on major league baseball's all-time list—a .312 career batting average, and enough on his resume to earn enshrinement in the Hall of Fame in 1945. Other than a brief return to the Pirates in 1925–26 as an assistant to both manager Bill McKechnie and Dreyfuss—one marked by a World Series victory in 1925 and a near player revolt against his influence in '26—Clarke did live the simple life on his ranch in Winfield, Kansas, for the last 45 years of his life. Or what passed for simple after oil was discovered on an already thriving 1,320-acre ranch. By 1917, his wealth was estimated at $1 million.

18 An Even 3,000

It was a double pretty much like any of the previous 439 he had hit in his glorious major league career. But, of course, it wasn't. It was special and different and historic and ultimately poignant. It was all those things in ways known already that last Saturday afternoon in September 1972 and in ways that would only reveal themselves three months later on a devastatingly sad January morning.

Roberto Clemente and Pirates fans everywhere had waited all season for this hit. Had it been any other Clemente season, it would have come well before late September. But injuries had limited him to 102 games and a career-low 378 at-bats. And so it came to Saturday, September 30, Game No. 152 of 155, and Clemente still needed the last of the 118 hits he needed at the beginning of the season to become the first Pirates player—and only the 11th player in major league history—to reach 3,000 hits in his career.

The game was meaningless. The Pirates had already clinched the National League East Division championship for a third consecutive season and were set to start the NL Championship Series the following Saturday against the Cincinnati Reds. Clemente would have preferred to rest his 38-year-old body for the playoffs. "I hate to play exhibition games, and these games to me are exhibitions." But he couldn't rest—literally or figuratively—until he got No. 3,000.

He believed he'd gotten it the night before when, in his first at-bat against Tom Seaver, he hit a hard bouncer over the mound. Mets second baseman Ken Boswell got to the ball, momentarily fumbled it, then threw to first. Clemente easily beat the throw. The 24,193 at Three Rivers stood and cheered, believing they'd witnessed history. Many others thought so, too. First-base umpire

51

John Kibler got the ball to Clemente. First-base coach Don Leppert patted him on the backside and congratulated him. Then the scoreboard flashed the signal for error. Clemente was incredulous. "There was no question in my mind about it being a hit," he said later that night after finishing 0-for-4 against Seaver in a 1–0 loss. "But this is nothing new. Official scorers have been robbing me of hits like this for years." How many, he was asked to guess? "How many hits? You mean how many batting titles." The pressure of the hits chase, the thwarted chance to begin resting for the playoffs, the frustration over an injury-plagued season, and his long-running battle with reporters who at the time also served as official scorers, played demolition derby with each other that Friday night.

Still, when manager Bill Virdon gave him the option to sit the next afternoon, Clemente said, "I'll play. I want to get that hit right away."

And so Clemente was in his usual third spot in the batting order, behind Rennie Stennett and in front of Willie Stargell. He struck out in the first inning. Then he led off in the fourth. The game was still scoreless. He walked to the plate. It could have been any at-bat in any game of his career. He reached down for some dirt. He rubbed it between his hands. He tapped his spikes with his bat. First his right foot, then his left. He stepped into the batter's box. He took a called strike. Then Jon Matlack threw a curveball. Clemente strode and he reached and he swung in that way that could make an observer wonder how he ever hit a ball. And in the way he always seemed to show them, he lashed a drive into left-center field between Mets outfielders John Milner and Dave Schneck. The ball bounced once and struck the wall. Milner fielded it and threw it back to the infield. By then Clemente was standing on second base with No. 3,000, a double.

The 13,117 in attendance cheered, seeing the history that the crowd twice its size the night before had been denied. Before their applause died, Clemente assumed the pose that would be captured in the defining picture of the moment. Facing toward the infield, his left foot on the bag, his right foot just off, he looked toward the first-base side of Three Rivers and regally raised his cap. He didn't just tip it or big-time it. He raised it, proud and upright and strong, much as he had always played.

Who knew it would also be the image that would come to serve as his goodbye to the city, to the fans, and to the game? After coming around to score in that fourth inning, he returned to right field in the top of the fifth but was then pinch hit for in the bottom of the inning. While there were still the playoffs, he would never again bat or get a hit or throw out a runner at the plate from deep right field in another regular season game. He got his much wanted rest over the final three regular-season games. And when the 1973 season opened the next April, someone else—however incongruous it seemed—would be starting in right field.

Ninety-two days after recording his 3,000[th] hit, Roberto Clemente died in a plane crash.

19 He Had Us All the Way

It was ironic that the Pirates would hold a moment of silence for Bob Prince before their game against the St. Louis Cardinals that night at Three Rivers Stadium. It is certainly the custom when a legend dies, as Prince did the afternoon of June 10, 1985, but it was ironic nonetheless. It may have been the only time that Prince and silence were ever found in the same place in time. Prince, the voice of the Pirates from 1955 to 1975 and a sidekick to Rosey Rowswell for eight years before that, had lived loud, dressed loud, and most certainly broadcast Pirates games in a style that was loud. Too loud for some as he discovered in the years after he was removed from his "life's work" in '75, but just right for several generations of fans of whom Prince was unashamedly one.

He would root along with them from the booth, exhorting Willie Stargell to spread some chicken on the hill, pleading for a bug on the rug from Manny Sanguillen, or begging for a Hoover when that night's opponent (how dare they!) threatened to score. For the uninformed, he was, in order, asking for a home run from Willie Stargell, a hot shot into one of the gaps or down the lines on the artificial turf at Three Rivers Stadium, and a double play from the Pirates infield. He also, at one time or another, bestowed magical powers on The Green Weenie, your grandma's babushka, and taught fans the meaning of hidden vigorish.

The Green Weenie, a plastic hot dog that became as much a part of the 1966 season as Roberto Clemente winning the National League Most Valuable Player Award and Matty Alou the NL batting title, came to hold particular sway with Pirates faithful and decades later is still spoken of with reverence. Its powers, if directed at an opposing player, could bring even the game's biggest stars kneeling before its might. One particular night "we waved the Green Weenie at Don Drysdale," one of the dominant pitchers of the 1960s with the Los Angeles Dodgers, "and we chased him out of the ballgame," Prince said. "Bases were loaded, and Drysdale turned to umpire Eddie Vargo and said, 'How can you concentrate with that silly idiot up there in the booth getting everybody to wave those weenies at me?' Vargo said, 'I don't know, you'd better pitch.' And Clemente tripled."

Believe. Don't believe. Like. Dislike. Prince made the games fun, even when his anecdotes often trampled the play-by-play. The latter offended traditionalists (or most any out-of-towner), but the former endeared him to fans. His voice was one of gravel passed through a twisted nasal passage, but it was Pittsburgh and he was theirs. "He was the voice under the pillow," wrote a fan in a letter

One Last Blast

Logic would insist that Bob Prince had nothing to do with the Pirates' 16–2 romp over the Los Angeles Dodgers on May 3, 1985. But those who were at Three Rivers Stadium and those who were listening to the game on the radio might say otherwise. For the first time since he had been fired in 1975, Prince, then 68 and just three weeks after cancer surgery, made his return to the radio booth after being hired to rejoin the broadcast team on a limited basis. He was scheduled to do the middle three innings. The Pirates led 3–2 when he took the microphone in the top of the fourth. By the time the inning was over, the Pirates—a team that would lose 104 games that summer—led 12–2 en route to a 16–2 win. Eleven consecutive Pirates reached base. All nine runs had scored with two outs. "When the inning ended," wrote Ron Weiskind of the *Pittsburgh Post-Gazette*, "the crowd faced the broadcast booth behind home plate chanting 'Gun-ner, Gun-ner" and gave him a standing ovation." An inning later, Prince asked for a home run from slugger Jason Thompson. "Just park one into the seats and we'll have had a little of everything," Prince said. Thompson obliged. Prince was too weak to work the sixth. He would work a few more home games, but by early June he was back in the hospital and died on June 10—barely a month after that magical Friday night. "A night to remember," fellow Pirates broadcaster Jim Rooker said.

to author Jim O'Brien for a book he did on Prince. Their affection for him was only helped by all that he shared with them. He was not only the guy with the colorful sports coats who once dived off the balcony of a hotel in St. Louis into a swimming pool several stories below to win a $20 bet from Dick Stuart. He was also the guy with whom they celebrated world championships in 1960 and '71, watched the careers of their heroes Clemente and Stargell and Mazeroski, and voiced their frustrations on those nights when the bloop and a blast never came. His is the voice that they hear providing the play-by-play of their memories.

"Rosey taught me an important lesson," Prince said. "If you're losing 14–2 in the second inning, you've got to keep the people interested with funny stories, names, and reminiscences. You can't be worried about who batted .280 in 1943. You got to be concerned with the Hill District, Wheeling, and Johnstown."

It was why those fans returned that concern after he and longtime partner Nellie King were fired in 1975. Fans—hundreds of them—rallied in protest and paraded through downtown Pittsburgh demanding the two be reinstated. They weren't, and Prince subsequently worked for the Houston Astros and ABC's *Monday Night Baseball.* Neither job lasted more than a year. His style was, he discovered, out of place everywhere but Pittsburgh. Yet in 1986, the year after his death, Prince was named that year's Ford C. Frick winner, as awarded by the Baseball Hall of Fame.

20 Mecca

Speaking to the magic of that day, many of the men and women who gather each October 13 have gone gray, but not the memory that draws them to that spot of green and brick and history. That sort of moment—once in a lifetime if it comes at all—rarely reveals a wrinkle. It is still as new as first love and as timeless as the hope of each new season. A few more show up each year just as a few more say goodbye. The celebration that began with one man's personal reminiscence of the home run Bill Mazeroski drove over that stack of bricks at 3:36 PM on October 13, 1960, has grown into, as longtime Pittsburgh sports author Jim O'Brien noted, "one of the most unique expressions of a love of the game to be found in a major league city."

Mazeroski beat the New York Yankees 10–9 that afternoon in Forbes Field with the only home run to end a Game 7 in World

Still Home

The Mazeroski Wall is not all that remains of Forbes Field. Its home plate can also still be found by the diehard Pirates fan, though unlike the wall, it requires some keener sleuthing. When Forbes Field came down in 1971 to make way for the expansion of the University of Pittsburgh's campus, Wesley W. Posvar Hall went up. Originally known as the Pitt Quadrangle, it is the largest academic-use building on the sprawling campus. It is home to administrative offices, classrooms, lecture halls, a food court, and computer labs. And in the tile floor of the main lobby, encased in Plexiglas and just feet from its original spot in history, from where Bill Mazeroski hit his famous home run and where Babe Ruth hit his last, is Forbes Field's home plate.

Series history. Some argue it was the greatest home run in baseball history. Whether it was or was not does not matter. It touched the heart and soul of a city that had gone 35 years since its last championship. It touched old men who had given up hope of seeing another and young ones who had grown up only on second- and third-hand stories of Pie Traynor and Paul Waner and the murky wonder of what must've been. That day was their day. The connection to it and the celebration that swept the city are what prompted a man named Saul Finkelstein to walk to that spot near the corner of what is now Roberto Clemente Drive and Schenley Drive on the University of Pittsburgh campus, near the one piece of surviving wall of old Forbes amid the sprawling Pitt campus, and sit down with his lunch on the 25th anniversary of the home run and listen to—in its entirety—an old audio tape of the original NBC broadcast.

It was a tradition he maintained mostly alone until the early 1990s, when O'Brien wrote of it: one man's relationship to the home run and the man that moved a city. Other media picked up on the story. A handful of pilgrims became a hundred. Each year they came. Finkelstein died in 2004, but Herb Soltman, a youngster who was among the 36,683 who were there on that original October 13 and had worked his way down into the box seats by the time Mazeroski stepped in against Ralph Terry—"in case something happens"—took up the torch along with a group that has come to be known as the Game 7 Gang. And each year they continue to come, including old-timers and Pirates fans who weren't even born but seek an understanding. Newcomers are always welcome.

The tape recording is now on compact disc. The sound system covers more ground. A tent houses October 13 artifacts. A plaque marking the site and its importance to Pittsburgh history has been installed. There is a pre-broadcast ceremony, and often there are special guests. Most years, at least a few hundred gather. In 2010, on the home run's 50th anniversary, more than 1,000 people crowded near the wall. Among them were 10 of the surviving 1960 Pirates, including Maz himself.

What has not changed is the broadcast, which that day was handled by broadcasters Chuck Thompson and Jack Quinlan. It begins each year at 1:00 PM—just as it did that day, the day after Soviet leader Nikita Khrushchev pounded his shoe on the table at the United Nations as the Cold War was settling into a deep freeze and just hours before the third Kennedy-Nixon presidential debate. The devoted bring coolers and lawn chairs. They eat ballpark food and sing "Take Me Out to the Ballgame" during the seventh-inning stretch. And at 3:36 PM, as Maz sends a 1–0 Terry slider arcing yet again into transcendental orbit, they clap and cheer and lose themselves as if it were the first time. And for so many, it always will be.

21 T-206

Even though he won a record eight National League batting titles, and even though Babe Ruth regarded him as the game's greatest right-handed hitter, and even though he was an inaugural member of the Baseball Hall of Fame, it's possible that fans nearly a century after he retired know Honus Wagner more for a 1¼" x 2½" piece of cardboard that has turned over time not to dust but to gold. On that piece of cardboard that bears the face of Wagner in his prime, the game's nostalgia has come to intersect with another of America's pastimes—making money.

It is a Wagner baseball card, produced by the American Tobacco Company beginning in 1909 and pulled from the set after Wagner refused to give permission for his picture to be used. By then, as many as 200 of the cards had been distributed. No more than 60 are believed to still exist. Thus the demand. Thus its reverential place atop the baseball memorabilia world. Often referred to as the Holy Grail, it is the Honus Wagner T-206.

Two theories exist for why he balked. One held that he didn't want to be a bad influence on children by making them have to buy a pack of cigarettes to acquire the cards; the other theory is that he wanted to be paid more. Most adhere to the former.

No matter the reason, the fact that it was pulled gave the card a life of its own. The most famous of the Wagner cards—a near-mint version of which there is only one—that could have been had for a few pennies in 1909 sold in 2007 for $2.8 million to Ken Kendrick, owner of the Arizona Diamondbacks. It was only the most recent in a string of stops for the card that at one time belonged to hockey great Wayne Gretzky. Gretzky and then–Los Angeles Kings owner

Bruce McNall purchased it at auction for $451,000 in 1991, then the card continued on its journey through memorabilia history for $500,000 in 1995. A jumbo version—a card with slightly larger borders due to an incorrect factory cut—sold for $2.1 million in 2013.

"There are other cards that are more scarce but far less valuable," said Mike Heffner, president of Lelands auction house. "The legend of the Honus Wagner card has been built up over time like no other, and for this reason it is the most recognizable and valuable single baseball card on the planet."

Even lesser conditioned versions have sold for between $100,000 and $500,000. Said Brian Seigel, at one time the owner of the near-mint version, "These others you could stick in the middle of the street and let cars drive over it through the day, take it in your hand and crumple it up, and it still would be a $100,000 card."

One such card surfaced in 2010. The brother of a nun left all his possessions to her order, the Baltimore-based School Sisters of Notre Dame, when he died. In one of the boxes was a T-206 on which three of the sides had been trimmed. It came with a note: "Although damaged, the value of this card should increase exponentially throughout the twenty-first century!" A godsend? Expected to command between $150,000 and $200,000 at auction, it sold for $262,000. The sisters distributed the proceeds to their ministries around the world. With them went the tale of the Holy Grail and, by the way, the story of a little shortstop from Pittsburgh, too.

22 The Best Ballpark in America

One of the few balms during the Pirates' run of losing to open the twenty-first century was the place it called home. Practically from the weekend PNC Park opened in 2001, two things were a given: The Pirates played bad baseball, but they played it in a place so grand that the losing almost didn't matter. As one stunned Philadelphia writer wrote when she saw it after spending so many years in completely enclosed Three Rivers Stadium: "There was a skyline right next door? Who knew?" From 1991 to 2012, 22 of the 30 teams in Major League Baseball built new stadiums. None were able to meld the retro feel and look of the 1940s and '50s with the amenities of the 2000s and then seemingly drop it with care into just the right spot that captured the sense of place and time and make it seem as if it was all one as the Pirates accomplished.

It doesn't have monuments or a green monster. It doesn't have ivy on its outfield walls nor a swimming pool beyond. Not a single all-time great, legend, or Hall of Famer has called it home (yet). It has never been home to a world champion and never had a game of consequence until October 2013. And the banners that flutter above its outfield grandstands and adorn the façade in front of the press box were all won in other times and other places. Yet a game in PNC Park, an intimate 38,000-seat park—not a stadium—will touch a fan's soul. PNC Park is not about the memory but the sensory.

It has become a must-do for fans in Chicago and Boston, New York and Detroit, Cincinnati and Philadelphia. It is about walking across the Clemente Bridge, which feeds into the stadium. It is about walking past the larger-than-life statues of the franchise's larger-than-life heroes at its gates, perhaps snapping a picture, perhaps remembering that this wasn't always a losing franchise. It is about taking your seat. Lower bowl, perhaps. But upper tier is better. It is about settling in and realizing that no seat is ever too bad. It is about taking in the field and the scoreboard and the North Side Notch and the Clemente Wall (a perfect 21' high in homage to the greatest right fielder in franchise history), and it is about looking out and looking up. It is seeing the city skyline fan out like a magician flourishes his deck of cards—seamless and one. As if built along with the stadium and not over time and a river away. It is having your breath taken away, for the first time or for the 100th.

It is, as Jim Caple of ESPN.com wrote in rating PNC Park the best ballpark in America, "as if The House That Ruth Built had first been designed by Frank Lloyd Wright and then run past Ray Kinsella for final approval." That was 2003—in just its third year. Although San Francisco's AT&T Park, built along China Basin—part of San Francisco Bay and opened the year before PNC Park—has its fans, PNC has stood the early test of time. In 2011, a writer for *The New York Times* went to the website Yelp.com, home to dozens—if not hundreds—of fan reviews about each stadium on a scale of 1 to 5, added them up for each park and averaged them. "The winner by a country mile is Pittsburgh's PNC Park," he concluded. And a decade after ESPN established it as the gold standard and long after its wrapper was balled up and discarded, ABC News and the CBS Morning News in 2013 joined the choir in proclaiming it the best ballpark in America.

Still.

It's a destination for out-of-towners. And as for Pirates fans who suffered through a North American professional sports record of 20 years of losing, as they waited for their next winner, it's a place that long ago was determined to "make the wait easier."

23 The First Championship

As the 1909 World Series began, all eyes were on the teams' two stars—shortstop Honus Wagner for the Pirates and outfielder Ty Cobb for the Detroit Tigers. Wagner, 35 by then but showing no signs of age, hit .339 that season en route to his seventh National League batting championship. He also led the NL with 100 runs batted in for a Pirates team that set the franchise record with 110 wins and was finally back in the Series after losing the first six years before. Cobb's resume was even better. Just 22, he won the Triple Crown in the American League, hitting .377 with 9 home runs and 107 RBIs. It was big then, but one can only wonder how the 24-hour news cycle of the twenty-first century would have fed on such a matchup.

Yet for all the Wagner vs. Cobb drama, it was a decision that Pirates player/manager Fred Clarke made before Game 1 at Forbes Field that likely made the difference. Some say it was a manager's hunch. Others credit it to a scouting report fed him by NL president John Heydler. To start the series, Clarke had at his disposal a veteran trio of pitchers in Howie Camnitz, Vic Willis, and Lefty Leifield who were a combined 66–25 with a 2.05 ERA. Instead, Clarke tapped a 27-year-old rookie right-hander who had split time between the rotation and bullpen that season by the name of Charles "Babe" Adams. "I'll never forget the look on Adams' face when I told him I wanted him to pitch the opener," Clarke said.

If there were any nerves, they were quickly shaken off as Adams' numbers that afternoon attest. With 29,264 fans looking on at Forbes Field—the Pirates state-of-the-future concrete-and-steel palace that had opened that June—Adams allowed a run in the first inning and then nothing more. Clarke tied the score 1–1 in the fourth with a home run off George Mullin, and the Pirates took the lead with a two-run fifth. They added another in the sixth for a 4–1 lead, more than enough for Adams, who went the distance while allowing just six hits that included hanging a collar on Cobb in four trips to the plate.

Finding out early what he had in Adams proved even more fortuitous for Clarke and the Pirates. Given their chances in Games 2, 4, and 6—all Pirates losses—Camnitz, Willis, and Leifield combined to go 0–3 with a 7.58 ERA.

Tied at two games apiece, Clarke turned back to Adams in Game 5 at Forbes Field. Adams again delivered, pitching another complete-game six-hitter in an 8–4 victory. After Willis and Camnitz were unable to protect an early 3–0 lead in a 5–4 loss in Game 6, Clarke went back to the well and started Adams on two days rest in Game 7 at Detroit's Bennett Park. He was even better. On short rest, he pitched his third six-hitter of the series and this time shut out Cobb and the Tigers 8–0. Dots Miller gave him a lead in the fourth with a two-run single, and Wagner broke open the game with a bases-loaded triple in the sixth. Adams allowed the Tigers just two hits from that point on, and when he induced Detroit's Tom Jones to fly out to Clarke in left field for the final out in the ninth, the Pirates—on October 16, 1909—owned their first World Series championship.

Wagner won the showdown with Cobb, hitting .333 (8-for-24) with six RBIs and six stolen bases, while Cobb batted .231 with five RBIs, including just 1-for-11 vs. Adams. Clarke drove in seven runs, scored seven times, and hit two of the four home runs of the series. Tommy Leach also scored eight runs while batting .360. But it was Adams who stole the series for the Pirates and the city.

So elated were the city's fans—many of whom had followed Game 7 thanks to a man outside the offices of the *Pittsburgh Press* with a megaphone and access to the play-by-play as it moved over the telegraph—that they passed the hat and presented Adams with a cash gift of $1,243 when the team returned. That was in addition to the World Series winner's share of $1,825 that each player received in a ceremony at Forbes Field that attracted an estimated 20,000. The ceremony was held only after a parade from downtown to the Oakland section of the city where the stadium stood.

Adams would continue to pitch for the Pirates into the mid-1920s and win 194 games—second on the franchise's all-time wins list. But nothing would compare. In fact, after witnessing the reception the team received upon its return, NL boss Heydler said, "There is nothing in the annals of baseball to compare with it."

24 The One-Man Show

Of all the great players who have worn a Pirates uniform, none—not Honus Wagner nor Barry Bonds, not Willie Stargell nor Roberto Clemente—did what Ralph Kiner did. He brought fans out to the ballpark in the late 1940s and early '50s just because he was Ralph Kiner; just because he was young and strong and charismatic and could hit a ball like no one since Babe Ruth. "Pittsburgh had never known an athlete like Kiner," wrote longtime Pittsburgh sportswriter Bob Smizik years later.

Since moving into Forbes Field in 1909, the Pirates had experienced three World Series seasons and had never drawn more than 869,720 fans in any of them. In Kiner's heyday from 1947 to 1952—mostly bad seasons in which the Pirates finished a combined 165 games under .500 even as Kiner was leading the National League in home runs each year—the Pirates four times drew more than 1 million with a high of 1,517,021 in 1948. To put that figure in further perspective, the Pirates won six division titles and two World Series in the 1970s and never topped that number despite playing in much larger Three Rivers Stadium. In fact, for the next 40 years, only the championship season of 1960 exceeded the attendance for 1948.

"He was a drawing card unparalleled in the history of Pittsburgh sports," Smizik wrote in 1998.

Kiner, a 6'2", 195-lb. right-handed hitting outfielder and veteran of World War II, broke in with the Pirates in 1946 at age 23 and immediately set about re-writing record books. He hit 23 home runs, a relatively modest figure, yet one that tied the club record, led the NL, and set him off on a home-run tear through 1952 that would go unrivaled in baseball until Mark McGwire came along in the late 1990s. In 1947, under the tutelage of an aging Hank Greenberg—a home run hitter in his own right for whom the Pirates created a contrived left-field fence also known as "Greenberg Gardens" that reduced the distance for hitting a home run by 30', a move that ultimately benefited Kiner—he more than doubled his total to 51. For a time he even challenged Ruth's single-season record of 60. The Pirates were on their way to a 62–92 finish, but fans took note of this basher the likes of which they'd never seen. Not in a Pirates uniform, anyway.

Kiner followed with home-run seasons of 40, 54, 47, 42, and 37. He led or tied for the National League home-run crown for seven consecutive seasons, a feat no player in either league had done before and no player has done since. He homered a major league record eight times in a four-game span from September 10–12, 1947, and in the third of those games became the first Pirate to hit three in one game. He blew past Paul Waner's franchise record of 109 homers in only his third season and in that same 1948 season became the first in NL history with two 50-homer seasons on his resume.

Fans came out to be amazed. "His home runs…were fan-friendly," Reds pitcher Joe Nuxhall said, "because you watched

Ralph Kiner throws out the first pitch prior to the Pirates-Brewers game on April 8, 2003. The Pittsburgh Pirates honored Kiner before the game.
(*Pittsburgh Post-Gazette*, Peter Diana)

Go Figure

Despite the fact that he led the National League in home runs for a record seven consecutive seasons, was No. 6 on the all-time home-run list when back problems forced him to retire at age 32 in 1955, and was among the greatest single draws in the game for a decade, Ralph Kiner nearly didn't make the Hall of Fame. Only in his 15th and final year of eligibility in 1975 did he receive the necessary 75 percent of the vote. And even then he narrowly made it, appearing on 273 of the 362 ballots cast (75.4 percent) by the Baseball Writers Association of America.

them go for a l-o-n-g time." The mounting losses didn't seem to matter; they were so inconsequential, it seemed, that teammate Joe Garagiola joked, "People would get up to leave after Ralph's last at-bat and walk across the field while we were still on it."

Like his home runs, Kiner's salary soared. By 1950 he was the highest-paid player in the National League at $65,000. His off-field image sizzled, too. He escorted actress Elizabeth Taylor to a Hollywood premiere, dated actress Janet Leigh, and married well-known U.S. tennis star Nancy Chaffee. "He was a superstar when we didn't even have that term," teammate Bob Friend said.

Yet he and general manager Branch Rickey never meshed. Whether the $90,000 Kiner was making by 1952 offended Rickey's penurious sensibilities or Rickey saw Kiner as a way to infuse his otherwise woebegone roster with new blood at multiple positions, it became evident that Rickey—who had inherited Kiner when he was hired before the '51 season—wanted to trade him. Rickey cut (yes, cut) Kiner's salary to $75,000 in 1953, arguing that his home-run total had dropped—all the way from 42 to 37. During this tense period between the two, Rickey reportedly uttered his famous line: "We finished last with you, we can finish last without you." Rickey's desires finally came to a head June 4, 1953, when he traded Kiner to the Chicago Cubs in a 10-player trade.

The *Post-Gazette* treated the deal with a front-page headline in type befitting the end of the world. In some ways it was. The

Pirates again finished last in 1953, '54, and '55, but without Kiner they didn't draw even 500,000 fans in '54 or '55. As things turned out, it was also the beginning of the end for Kiner. While he hit 68 more home runs over the next two-plus seasons with the Cubs and then Cleveland Indians, a back injury forced him to retire after the '55 season at age 32. He finished with 369 home runs—one every 14.11 at-bats, a figure that at the time was better than any player but Ruth in the history of the game and nearly 60 years after his retirement was still sixth all time.

"He had the kind of natural power that comes along once in a lifetime," Friend said. Power that is remembered with a distinctive sculpture inside PNC Park of hands and bat at the ready. Power that still makes his 301 home runs hit as a Pirate good enough for second on the franchise's career list behind only Stargell's 475. Power that once made Kiner—alone—worth the price of admission.

25 No. 712, No. 713, and No. 714

Baseball's all-time home-run mantle has since been passed on, first to Hank Aaron and then to Barry Bonds. First to 755 and then, now, 762. Yet those numbers have hardly captured the little kid imagination quite the way that the number 714 did for years. Maybe 762 one day will. But not yet. Not now. For nearly four decades, 714 stood in the clouds of our mythology, tethered through time to the man who may not have written the home run into baseball's rule book but who certainly came to symbolize it in American culture.

Babe Ruth.

As evening approached on May 25, 1935, no one yet knew that it would be The Number. But it had, in fact, been chiseled into marble monument earlier that day against the Pirates at Forbes Field. Set in a way befitting Ruth—big, long, loud, and bold. For that one day, against first Pirates pitcher Red Lucas and then Guy Bush, he was Babe Ruth again. Not a 40-year-old man hitting .153 playing out his days not in Yankee pinstripes, but in Boston Braves greys.

Until that afternoon, he had just three homers and five RBIs in 1935 for a team that would go 38–115. Playing in the National League after 21 seasons in the American League, he was more side-show attraction than Sultan of Swat. Yet, only about 10,000 people showed up that Saturday afternoon.

The third batter up in the top of the first, Ruth lofted a tower-ing home run to right off Lucas that dropped into the lower section of seats.

In the third inning, he did the same against Bush, only this time he deposited the ball in the second tier.

In the seventh, fans, as the story goes, challenged him to go farther. Since the right-field stands had been added in 1925, no player had cleared the roof that stood 86' above the playing field. Ruth, still the showman if no longer the show, heard them. He pointed to right with his bat. The count went to 3–1. Bush offered a breaking ball. Ruth swung and the 10,000 in the stands sounded like 10 times that.

No one doubted its count as it carried long and high toward the roof. Wrote *Pittsburgh Press* baseball writer Volney Walsh, "Pirate players stood in their tracks to watch the flight of the ball." Bush later told Robert Creamer in *Babe: The Legend Comes To Life* that, "I never saw a ball hit so hard before or since. He was fat and old, but he still had that great swing."

Even Ruth was impressed. Was it the sheer distance of the home run itself, estimated at well over 500'? Or was it—to borrow from legendary voice Vin Scully in describing fictional Billy Chapel in *For Love of the Game* 64 years later—the notion that for one game he had been able to push the sun back into the sky and give us one more day of summer?

In those days, both teams had to go through the Pirates dugout to reach their clubhouse. Although it was only the end of the seventh inning and the Braves trailed 10–7 in a game they would lose 11–7, Ruth's day was done. Upon circling the bases and touching home, he doffed his cap and headed for the showers. But, as if perhaps wanting to enjoy the feel of that which he might never feel again, to hear sounds he might never hear again, he paused in the Pirates dugout and sat down next to pitcher Mace Brown.

"He said, 'Boy, that last one felt good,'" Brown told a reporter from the Associated Press years later.

It was home run No. 714, destined to sit up there by itself, alone and unreachable, for nearly 40 years.

Ruth would go to the plate just 13 more times before, on June 1, he announced his retirement.

The Magnificent 7

As 24-year-old Rennie Stennett stepped into the batter's box at Chicago's Wrigley Field the afternoon of September 16, 1975, he already owned 628 major league hits. As he left the ballpark that evening, another 604 awaited him in his baseball future. However, it was the seven he collected in the nine innings in between that forever changed how his 11-year career would be remembered.

Beginning with that first at-bat against Cubs starter Rick Reuschel, Stennett went to the plate seven times over the next 2 hours and 35 minutes, and seven times, he got a hit. Although the Pirates won by a record 22–0 that afternoon—a win that helped their journey to a fifth National League East Division championship in six seasons—Stennett's feat out of the leadoff spot in the batting order is what made the game. He got two hits that first inning as the Pirates scored nine runs, got one in the third, two more in the fifth, one in the seventh, and one in the eighth.

His line in the box score: 7 AB, 5 R, 7 H, 2 RBIs.

No player since 1900, or since the beginning of baseball's modern era, had ever gone 7-for-7 in a nine-inning game. And only one other player in baseball history had done so—Baltimore's Wilbert Robinson in 1892.

Stennett, playing second base that day, said later he was getting a running commentary of his progress from an unlikely source—second-base umpire Dutch Rennert. After the two hits in the first inning, Rennert opined to Stennett that he had a chance for a four-hit game. After the two in the fifth, hey, a six-hit game was even possible.

But seven? That had never been done.

Until Stennett. And without even having to bat in the ninth.

He doubled off Reuschel, touched up Tom Dettore for two singles and a double, singled off Oscar Zamora, and singled off Buddy Schultz to make him 6-for-6 through seven innings. At-bat No. 7 came in the eighth against Paul Reuschel, brother of starter Rick. Stennett drove the ball to right, toward Cubs outfielder Champ Summers.

"I thought the ball was a hit, then it started to rise and I wasn't sure," Stennett said. His doubts proved unfounded. The ball dropped, then it skipped past Summers. Stennett wound up on third with a triple and a piece of immortality. At least until someone can find a way to go 8-for-8.

As a postscript, Stennett singled his first two times up the next night in Philadelphia, giving him nine consecutive hits. He added a third in the seventh to give him yet another line in the record books as the first player of the modern era to total 10 hits in two consecutive games.

27 The First All-Black Lineup

The lineup Pirates manager Danny Murtaugh made out for the September 1, 1971, night game against the Philadelphia Phillies at Three Rivers Stadium was—and still is—remembered as more trivia answer than cultural statement. Perhaps in that, though, some sort of statement was made about the Pirates if not the progress baseball had made over two-plus decades. Twenty-four seasons after Jackie Robinson famously broke baseball's color barrier, every player Murtaugh penciled in to start against Philadelphia's Woodie Fryman that night was black. And few noticed. At first, anyway. Along about the third or fourth inning, first baseman Al Oliver recalls third baseman Dave Cash stopping him and, in some cross between amazement and pride, exclaiming, "Hey, Scoop, we got all brothers out here."

The Lineup:
Rennie Stennett 2B
Gene Clines CF
Roberto Clemente RF
Willie Stargell LF
Manny Sanguillen C
Dave Cash 3B
Al Oliver 1B
Jackie Hernandez SS
Dock Ellis P

Five African Americans, two Panamanians, one Puerto Rican, and one Cuban. Or, as Murtaugh would reply later, "The nine best athletes.... The best nine I put out there tonight happened to be black. No big deal. Next question." Third baseman Richie Hebner and shortstop Gene Alley—both white—might normally have been in the lineup, but both players were injured. The move that swung the lineup historically—and created the most speculation over the years—was Murtaugh's decision to start Oliver at first rather than Bob Robertson. Robertson was the regular first baseman that season, playing 126 games there. Oliver was primarily a center fielder with some first-base experience, but mostly earlier in his career. Murtaugh never strayed from his earlier comments, and no player ever believed otherwise, either.

If anything, it said more about how the organization embraced and cultivated the Latin American talent pool as well as the black, in the process giving Murtaugh the option of fielding the lineup he did that night. His 25-man roster at the time was comprised of 14 whites, six African Americans and seven Latinos. They meshed well together, an early incarnation even of "The Family" that would win a championship eight years later. "It didn't make a difference if you were black, yellow, green, purple, whatever," Robertson said. "We enjoyed each other's company. We got along fine." So well, in fact, that Hebner recalls that "some of the guys joked around the club-house saying, 'Hey, you white guys, you can take a rest tonight.' Back then, Ellis and Stargell would get on us [white players], and we'd get on them. You could do that."

Yet the milestone night went mostly overlooked the next day and has met a similar fate over time. In part it can be attributed to the fact that Pittsburgh's two daily newspapers were on strike from May 15 to September 19 of that year. But even in a twenty-first century sports world that has grown accustomed to microanalysis of all things present and past, the game against the Phillies that night—a game the Pirates won 10–7—has gone mostly forgotten

The Pittsburgh Post-Gazette*'s 1971 Dapper Dan Sportsman of the Year co-winners were Willie Stargell (left), Danny Murtaugh (right), and Roberto Clemente.* (Pittsburgh Post-Gazette)

other than being the basis for the occasional trivia question. In an interview 40 years after the fact, Oliver was baffled. This wasn't just Jackie Robinson; it was a whole lineup of Jackie Robinsons.

"In the '30s, it would have been totally impossible in most people's minds to believe what happened in 1971. If you were living in the '40s, you wouldn't have believed it," Oliver said.

Yet just 24 years after Robinson, whether by fate or design, it was so. Remembered or not.

28 Astro-Naught

The 1997 season had already confounded expectation. A team with an Opening Day payroll of just more than $9 million and 100-loss potential penciled in on every lineup card manager Gene Lamont wrote out was somehow 43–45 and just a game out of first place in the National League's Central Division as it arrived at Three Rivers Stadium on July 12. It was a Saturday night, the Houston Astros—the team just above the Pirates in the standings—were in town, and a sellout crowd was expected, albeit a crowd enticed as much by postgame fireworks as the thought of seeing a battle for first place in what was an obviously mediocre division. No matter. To their good fortune, they were there. "They came to see fireworks. They saw history," wrote Bob Smizik in the next morning's *Pittsburgh Post-Gazette*.

History? The Pirates were tied for first place by night's end, and the fact wouldn't merit a mention. When Pirates starting pitcher Francisco Cordova, a 25-year-old right-hander who had spent more of his career pitching in Mexico than the major leagues, induced Houston leadoff batter Craig Biggio to ground out to second baseman Tony Womack for the first out, it set Cordova, the Pirates, and 44,119 fans off on one of the most memorable one-night journeys in club history. For nine innings and 121 pitches, Cordova baffled an Astros lineup that included Biggio (a future Hall of Famer), Jeff Bagwell, and Luis Gonzalez. Only four balls left the infield against Cordova. He struck out 10. "It was like we were swinging at butterflies," Houston manager Larry Dierker said. At some point in one of the middle innings, Pirates radio analyst Steve Blass scribbled a short blurb on his scorecard: "possible no-hitter."

But, as Blass made his notation, lying just beneath the surface tension was one inexorable fact: For as good as Cordova had been, the score was still 0–0. Fifth inning. Sixth. Seventh. Houston rookie Chris Holt had been nearly as effective, allowing just five hits and a walk in 7⅔ innings. The ghost of Harvey Haddix's night in Milwaukee 38 years before began to creep in at the edges of the evening like the thick fog in one of Bill Cardille's *Chiller Theater* B-movie late shows. Shortstop Lou Collier, making only his seventh major league start, thought to himself: "I don't want to be the guy that gives it up." He was not alone.

When Cordova went out for the ninth, it was still 0–0. The crowd was on its feet. Lamont couldn't allow Cordova to go much further. His pitch count was already more than 100. Due up for the Astros were pinch hitter Ricky Gutierrez, Biggio, and Chuck Carr. Gutierrez came closer than anyone to wrecking Cordova's gem. He lashed a drive down the third-base line. Third baseman Dale Sveum couldn't reach it. "For an instant it appeared as if the no-hitter was history," Smizik wrote. "But the ball was foul by inches." Reprieved, Cordova got Gutierrez to hit that way again. That ball Sveum fielded and threw out Gutierrez. One out. Biggio grounded back to the mound. Two down. Cordova then hit Carr with a pitch but regrouped, got ahead of Bagwell 0–2, and ultimately got him to fly out to Jose Guillen in right. Three outs. Nine innings. No hits. The crowd roared. Yet, oddly, there was no celebration. Cordova was done, but the score was still 0–0. And it was 0–0 still after Astros closer Billy Wagner struck out Jermaine Allensworth, Al Martin, and Kevin Young in the bottom of the inning to send the game—and the no-hitter—to extra innings. Cordova would not even qualify for the win should the Pirates score first. "You couldn't help but feel the injustice," wrote Ron Cook of the *Pittsburgh Post-Gazette*.

Yet, like Haddix that night in Milwaukee, there was also a sense that the history in progress would stand more profoundly against the measure of time and memory than whether Cordova won or lost. Lamont called on left-hander Ricardo Rincon. Talk about unfair. "One minute, he's watching the game like you or me," pitching coach Pete Vuckovich said. "The next minute it's all on his shoulders." The weight did not prove too great. Rincon got Gonzalez to ground out and, after walking Derek Bell, retired Bill Spiers and Brad Ausmus. The crowd rose again. So, too,—impossibly—did the night's levels of disbelief and improbability as the top of the 10th gave way to the bottom.

In the Pirates' 10th, Jason Kendall and Turner Ward reached on walks by Astros reliever John Hudek, walks scattered between a strikeout by Sveum and a flyout by Guillen. Two on. Two out. Rincon was due up. Mark Smith, a 27-year-old right-handed hitting outfielder who had been with the team only since May and with just 59 at-bats in a Pirates uniform, reached for a bat. Most everyone not from Houston would have settled for a single, particularly in light of the fact that not only had the Pirates not scored in nine innings that night, they had also not scored in the 18 before them, either. Twenty-seven scoreless innings. By rights, a single should have been all anyone had any right to wish for at the moment. Pretty much anything on the ground in the outfield would have been enough to get Kendall in from second. Who wants to be greedy? Who had the right?

Yet gold is what Smith struck. Looking for a fastball, he got one. Second pitch. He swung with the force of thunder in his

Francisco Cordova pitches against the Blue Jays on March 11, 2001.
(*Pittsburgh Post-Gazette*, Peter Diana)

bat. "I can still hear the sound," Young said. "It was explosive." Funny, but Smith only heard silence. "You don't hear anything," he said. "You're kind of in your own little world" even as that world rocked. Replays show owner Kevin McClatchy jumping from his seat behind home plate as quickly as the ball flew off Smith's bat; it was a ball that arced high toward left field and onto any list of most memorable home runs in franchise history. "It was something out of a movie," McClatchy said.

Except, as they say, even Hollywood would have rejected this script as being, well, too Hollywood. Too preposterous. Too much junior high English comp, too little true grit. But it was true. As true as the fact that 44,119 chose to come out on that particular night of all nights when for 20 years the Pirates had not had such a crowd other than on Opening Day. Cordova and Rincon had thrown the first combined extra-innings no-hitter in major league history. And Smith had ended it with a walk-off, three-run home run.

Said Kendall afterward: "I guess they'll be talking about this for a while, won't they?"

Train Derailment

In October 1925, the Pirates had already done what no other team in World Series history had. They had rallied from a 3–1 deficit to force a deciding Game 7 against the Washington Senators. But to actually come all the way back and win the championship might have been asking a lot, even for a team that had three future Hall of Famers in its lineup in third baseman Pie Traynor and outfielders Max Carey and Kiki Cuyler. Why? Pitching for the Senators that afternoon was Walter Johnson, himself destined to be an inaugural member of the Hall of Fame 11 years later. Even though he was 37, he had won 20 games for the 12th time that summer and had shut down the Pirates in Games 1 and 4. He was not the hard-throwing "Big Train" any longer, having struck out a mere 108 in 229 innings that season, but he was still good enough to have gone the distance in both games against the Pirates, giving up just one run and 11 hits. He had even flashed his old fireballing self by striking out 10 in Game 1.

The skies were gray and rain was steady as the gates opened at Forbes Field on October 15, 1925. Senators outfielder Goose Goslin said later that conditions were so poor he couldn't see the infield during the last three innings. The game probably should have been postponed, but Pirates owner Barney Dreyfuss—aided by temporary outfield seats put in for the Series—was expecting his fourth crowd of 40,000-plus and didn't want to give that up. Before the game was a half-inning old, he might have been wishing he'd reconsidered. The Senators scored four times in the top of the first inning and knocked Pirates starter Vic Aldridge from the game—and Johnson hadn't yet thrown a pitch. When he did, he added two more shutout innings to his total and had still not been scored on since the fifth inning of Game 1. The weather, the game's feel, the mood of the 42,856 all had a funereal air.

It was a mood broken by, of all people, a pitcher named Johnny Morrison, who had replaced Aldridge in the first. He led off the bottom of the third with a single. Maybe Johnson was not some unbeatable legend. Leadoff hitter Eddie Moore followed with a double that scored Morrison. Carey followed with a run-scoring single. Cleanup hitter Clyde Barnhart later plated Carey. The Pirates had pulled within 4–3 after three innings. The rain continued, but the sound of the dirges ceased.

Momentum swung back and forth through the middle innings. The Senators pushed the lead back to 6–3 in the fourth on a two-run double by Joe Harris. The Pirates got one back in the fifth and then tied it in the seventh on an RBI double by Carey and an RBI triple by Traynor. The outcome that seemed destined in the first inning had devolved into random possibility. The only sure thing seemed to be Johnson; sure not of an infallibility that most living legends play with, but sure that he was 37 and didn't have all the answers anymore. Time and again he asked for sawdust to be spread about the muddy mound, stalling for time and looking for the pitcher he'd been in Games 1 and 4. He never found him.

Even when his teammates gave him the lead again in the top of the eighth, Johnson could do nothing with it despite getting out the first two Pirates. Catcher Earl Smith doubled. Emil Yde ran for Smith. Carson Bigbee batted for pitcher Ray Kremer. Bigbee lashed a double. Yde scored to tie the game 7–7. Johnson then walked Moore, bringing up Carey. Carey bounced softly to shortstop

Roger Peckinpaugh, who had already committed seven errors in the Series. He made it eight when he threw high to first. The bases were loaded for Cuyler, who had hit .357 with 102 RBIs that season. Cuyler made sure Peckinpaugh would be the goat of this series for all time. He smashed a Johnson pitch to deep right-center field that went for a ground-rule double and a 9–7 lead. Red Oldham then pitched a 1-2-3 ninth that included strikeouts of Hall of Famers Sam Rice and Goslin.

The game was over. The Pirates had become the first team in World Series history to overcome a 3–1 deficit to win the title. Carey had gone 4-for-5 with two RBIs and three runs scored in one of the best World Series performances in franchise history. And for one of only two times in the history of the four major pro sports, a Pittsburgh team celebrated a world championship on home soil. To accomplish it all, they had beaten Johnson. He would finish his career with 417 wins, a 2.17 ERA, and 110 shutouts. But on that dreary afternoon, the Pirates reached him for nine runs and 15 hits.

30 8 for 8

The Ed Sullivan Show was must-see TV in the 1950s and '60s. It brought Elvis, the Beatles and the Rolling Stones into America's living rooms. In 1956, only *I Love Lucy* sat above it in the ratings. And on the Sunday before Memorial Day of that year, it wanted a late-arriving, left-handed hitting first baseman from the Pittsburgh Pirates by the name of Dale Long. For those last two weeks in May, Long was that big.

Beginning on May 19 against Chicago Cubs knuckleballer Jim Davis and continuing until Dodgers ace Don Newcombe induced him to pop out to second baseman Jim Gilliam in the eighth inning May 29 at Forbes Field, Long jazzed the city and the baseball world by hitting home runs in an unprecedented eight consecutive games. Until Long, no player in major league history—not Babe Ruth, not Hank Greenberg, not Jimmie Foxx—had homered in more than six.

The fact that his binge coincided with an unexpected early challenge to the Braves, Dodgers, and Giants atop the National League standings energized a drought-ridden city that hadn't seen the Pirates win more than 64 games in a season since the late 1940s and had three times seen it lose more than 100.

Fans and media began to pay attention in earnest to Long's every at-bat after home run No. 5, but not so much for the streak as for the prodigiousness of the shot that extended it. Facing Lindy McDaniel in the bottom of the seventh inning May 23 vs. the Cardinals at Forbes Field, the left-handed hitting Long hit a ball that cleared an exit gate—a quirk of the old stadium—at the 436' mark. None of the old-timers in the press box nor either dugout could recall a ball leaving the stadium at just that spot in the 47 years Forbes had been open.

An off day that followed as the Pirates traveled to Philadelphia for a weekend series at Connie Mack Stadium allowed the buzz to percolate. It reached the boiling point when Long tied the record in the fifth inning of a Friday night game against Phillies pitcher Curt Simmons. It boiled over the following day, a Saturday, when he went homerless into his final at-bat before connecting against Philadelphia's Ben Flowers in the top of the eighth to set the record.

It was at that point that reality gave way to the fairy tale. Philadelphia fans who would one day throw snowballs at Santa Claus stood and applauded. *The Ed Sullivan Show* wanted him. Future Hall of Famer Robin Roberts came over from the Phillies clubhouse to congratulate him. A picture of him kissing his bat dominated the front page of the next day's *Pittsburgh Press*. Reporters asked Joe DiMaggio what he thought of Dale Long. Even Jackie Robinson would seek him out. All fairly heady stuff for a player who scuffled through the minor leagues for most of his 20s, who during one spring training helped the equipment men move trunks to earn an extra $5, and who was 29 before he earned a full-time major league job.

But perhaps, nearly two decades before players earned free agency and teams had all the power, nothing was more time out of mind than what general manager Joe L. Brown did that weekend. He tore up Long's contract and gave him a $2,500 raise.

Long's thank you? Back at Forbes Field against the Dodgers and in front of 32,221 fans—a stark bump from the 6,863 who were there to witness HR No. 1—Long drove a Carl Erskine curveball out to right in the fourth inning to make it eight homers in eight games. What followed has become common. But until that night, no one had seen it in Pittsburgh. The fans wouldn't stop cheering until Long emerged from the dugout for the first curtain call in the history of Pirates baseball.

The streak ended the next afternoon against Newcombe. Long hit a long fly ball in the third inning, but to center field—the deepest part of Forbes Field. A home run in most other parks, wrote one writer. Not in Forbes. Dodgers center fielder Duke Snider ran it down. It would prove to be Long's last best chance. He popped out in the sixth and then to Gilliam in the eighth. The streak was over.

He hit .500 (15-for-30) during its run and was hitting a National League–leading .411 when it ended. He was never quite the same after the streak, though. He hit just 13 more home runs in 1956 while batting .214 the rest of the way. And in a homage to how fleeting is fame, on May 1, 1957—just 338 days after his homer binge began—Brown traded Long to the Chicago Cubs as part of a four-player deal. A story in the next day's *Pittsburgh*

Post-Gazette referred to Long as having become "a strikeout patsy for southpaw pitchers." No surprise, but *The Ed Sullivan Show* had no interest in a man of those base talents.

31 Good Morning and Good-Bye

There had been storms overnight in Pittsburgh. Loud, house-rattling storms whose thunderous blasts could have passed for the mighty bats of angels playing a pickup game in heaven overhead. Yet by mid-morning, the sun was out and the skies were blue for Opening Day on April 9, 2001; the first day for the Pirates' new ballpark along the Allegheny River. The promise of PNC Park already assured it would be like few Opening Days before. Then the stunning news that franchise legend Willie Stargell had died of a stroke just past midnight—not 48 hours after his statue was dedicated outside the ballpark's left-field entrance—ensured that it would not be forgotten in ways no one envisioned.

Stargell's last public appearance in Pittsburgh had been the previous October for the final game at Three Rivers Stadium. In postgame ceremonies, he threw the last pitch in the stadium where for years he had been its strongest man, basher of 475 home runs, first-ballot Hall of Famer, and patriarch of its '79 Family. On that night he could only produce "a depressingly feeble ceremonial pitch, its bounces telegraphing his growing weakness." Stargell, just 61, had been fighting a variety of ailments since contracting kidney disease four years before, and the pitch was jarring to those who saw it. Many people wouldn't have found it difficult to imagine Stargell's demise that night, but who could have imagined it on this morning?

Willie Stargell tips his hat to the crowd after he threw out the first ball of the game at Three Rivers Stadium on Opening Day April 11, 1997, when the Pirates hosted the L.A. Dodgers. (Pittsburgh Post-Gazette)

"This was supposed to be one of the greatest days in Pirates history," wrote Ron Cook of the *Pittsburgh Post-Gazette*. "It doesn't seem quite fair that it will also be remembered as one of the saddest."

There was a definite emotional dichotomy that day as the Pirates prepared to play the Cincinnati Reds. What to do? Cheer or cry? Stand or kneel? Outside voice or inside voice? Look ahead or look back? Said Steve Blass, a teammate of Stargell's, an analyst on the Pirates' broadcast team and part of the organization for more than 50 years, "When we heard about [Roberto] Clemente's death at 4 o'clock in the morning, I went to Willie's house. I'm not sure where to go this morning."

Fans filled the area around Stargell's newly unveiled 12' statue with flowers, signs, balloons, and candles and pictures—the knick-knacks of the heart that seemed to find their way into impromptu sidewalk memorials in the late twentieth and early twenty-first centuries. Mementoes piled and scattered in a manifestation of what people do when they don't know what to do but need to do something. He, of course, didn't get to see this love. Sadly, he also never got to see the statue, only a model.

There was a roar when Pirates pitcher Todd Ritchie delivered the first pitch in the new stadium just after 1:35 PM. And there was a bit of a skirmish for the ball in the outfield stands when Reds first baseman Sean Casey hit the ballpark's first home run as the Reds won that inaugural game. Yet what was the final score? Most people would probably need to look it up. But no one has forgotten the impact "Pops" had on the day, probably because no one could forget the impact he'd had in the two decades he played in a Pirates uniform. The Pirates showed a four-minute video tribute on their new electronic scoreboard. No. 8. Jokester. Leader. Giant. Hero. "Chins quaked from foul pole to foul pole," wrote Gene Collier of the *Pittsburgh Post-Gazette*.

It's hardly a stretch to think that of the hundreds of games played inside PNC Park since, none have ever been like its first. The return of baseball after 9/11 came close on an emotional scale. But at the same time, it was not quite so personal.

As Collier wrote a decade later in recalling that day, "Not since Bob Prince died on a June night that was too cold and too mean in 1985 had I felt so much hurt for the city."

It had come to say hello. And it was forced to say goodbye.

The Original Pirate

Fans won't find his number retired along the façade at PNC Park. They won't find his bust in Cooperstown. They won't even find a bobblehead of him tucked away in the team vaults. Yet Lou Bierbauer changed the course of franchise history like no one else. Where's the poetry in "Beat 'em Alleghenies?" It lacks a certain ring. But because of Bierbauer, fans for generations have been able to say "Beat 'em Bucs" or "Let's go Bucs!" Lou Bierbauer, a 5'8", 140-lb. second baseman from Erie, Pennsylvania, is the reason the Pirates are the Pirates and not the Alleghenies as they were for most of their early years. "In a way, you could consider Bierbauer the father of the Pirates," wrote David Finoli and Bill Ranier in *The Pittsburgh Pirates Encyclopedia*.

When the short-lived Players League folded after the 1890 season, players who had jumped from the National League and the American Association were expected to revert back to their former teams. Bierbauer had jumped to Brooklyn from the Philadelphia Athletics of the American Association. However, in filing the paperwork to reacquire its players, Philadelphia management failed to include the names of Bierbauer and Harry Stovey.

As a story written by *The Sporting News* founder Alfred Spink goes, it was the middle of winter when Pittsburgh manager Ned Hanlon realized Bierbauer had gone unprotected—a rare free agent in the early days of major league servitude. Undeterred by the weather and lack of good roads, Hanlon went to see Bierbauer, who lived on Presque Isle—a peninsula that reaches out into Lake Erie. As Spink wrote it, Hanlon crossed an iced-over harbor in a snowstorm to find Bierbauer. He doesn't say whether it was uphill both ways. It was a foolhardy mission, nonetheless. Yet Bierbauer signed to be the Alleghenies' second baseman for the 1891 season.

There was one problem. The A's still believed Bierbauer and Stovey were theirs. The American Association thought so, too. Hanlon and the Alleghenies wouldn't back down. A board was formed to hear arguments from both sides. It found in favor of the Alleghenies. It was at this moment, so the story goes, that one Philadelphia official shouted out that Pittsburgh had "pirated" Bierbauer. American Association bosses said the same. Fans, too. It caught on. The funny thing is, Pittsburgh officials liked it, too. A term meant to be an insult became their calling card for all time, or at least the next 123 years and counting.

Pirates.

Bierbauer didn't disappoint. He played six seasons at second base, hit .260, knocked in 109 runs in 1894, was a perennial leader in assists, and became one of the early kings of National League second baseman, according to Spink. The Pirates sold Bierbauer to the St. Louis Browns in 1897, but Bierbauer remained a Pirate at heart and rooted for them—his team—until he died in 1926.

33 Pops' Night

As Willie Stargell circled the bases in Baltimore's Memorial Stadium that October night in 1979, just as he'd done 467 times before in his major league career, he likely wasn't thinking about 1971. Nor was he likely thinking about how sports often find a way of paying back those who love the game. He didn't have to. A nation's media would do it for him over the next few days and, really, for as long as the game is played.

The Pirates trailed 1–0 when he came to bat against Orioles starter Scott McGregor in the sixth inning. It was Game 7 of the World Series, and it was getting late. "Pops, you've got to do it for us," manager Chuck Tanner was heard to tell Stargell as he walked to the plate following a single by Bill Robinson. "I didn't hear anything," Stargell said. "I was concentrating on McGregor."

Stargell stepped in. He windmilled his big bat as was his trademark. Once. Then 1-2-3 times. McGregor threw a breaking ball on the first pitch. Stargell swung. "I was out in front of it, but I got the bat speed I wanted," said Stargell, who had already hit two home runs in the series. "At first I didn't think it would travel that far." Orioles right fielder Ken Singleton ran back to the fence. "I don't know how many people realize how close Singleton came to catching it," said Pirates pitcher Jim Rooker, who was in the Pirates' bullpen beyond the right-field wall. But Singleton didn't.

Stargell's blast gave the Pirates a 2–1 lead. By the time Kent Tekulve induced Pat Kelly to fly out to Omar Moreno to end the ninth, the score was 4–1 and the Pirates had their fifth world championship—only the fourth team to come back from a 3–1 deficit in games—and Stargell had his World Series moment. Make that His World Series. He had already singled in the second and doubled in the fourth. He added a double in the eighth and finished the night 4-for-5 with two doubles, the home run, two RBIs, and a locker-room meeting with President Jimmy Carter. It is the best World Series box score line in franchise history and topped in Pirates post-season history only by Bob Robertson's three-homer performance in Game 2 of the 1971 National League Championship Series. He'd hit .400 in the seven games (12-for-30). He'd tied a series record with 25 total bases. And he'd tied Reggie Jackson for most extra-base hits in a World Series (7).

"Willie Stargell played like a 25-year-old," Tanner gushed.

This was nothing like his first World Series experience eight years before. In 1971—also against the Orioles—the Pirates had won, but they'd done so because of Roberto Clemente's bat and Steve Blass' right arm and, in some ways, in spite of Stargell. After hitting .295 and leading the National League with 48 home runs in the regular season, his bat turned cold in October—0-for-14 cold in the league championship series, an only slightly thawed 5-for-24 with nine strikeouts, and just a single run batted in during the World Series. He scored the winning run in Game 7, but otherwise he'd been invisible, a bit player diminished by expectations of a career to that point filled with big hits and bigger home runs.

In some ways, though, his individual failures of 1971 made what he did over those eight days in 1979 that much more grati-fying and memorable. Underlying its made-for-TV storyline was the fact that Stargell was 39 and Father Time should've denied him that chance. His home run and RBI totals had showed steady decline from 1974 to 1977 because of age and health issues—his own and his wife's—and bottomed out at 13 and 35 in '77. He rebounded in 1978 with 28 homers, a .295 average and 97 RBIs. But who had seen '79 coming? The golf world refers to the PGA championship as glory's last shot, coming on the downside of the calendar, a player's last chance to do something big before the leaves turn and winter makes a man feel his age. That season,

We Are Family

Disco was not dead, but by the summer of 1979 the undertaker had been called. The Bee Gees were on the tired side of *Saturday Night Fever*, and Disco Demolition Night at Chicago's Comiskey Park had set a match to the funeral pyre. That didn't matter to Willie Stargell. A song on the PA system in Busch Stadium early that season spoke to him.

Ev'ryone can see we're together
As we walk on by
and we fly just like birds of a feather
I won't tell no lie
all of the people around us they say
Can they be that close
Just let me state for the record
We're giving love in a family dose.

The song: "We Are Family." The group: four sisters from Philadelphia by the name of Sister Sledge.

"We Are Family" became the anthem of the '79 Pirates; a Three Rivers Stadium mainstay. "The Family" was stenciled on the roof of the dugout. T-shirts were made. And when the Pirates took off, so did the song in ways that transcended its time at No. 1 on Billboard's disco charts in June. It was the song Pirates wives danced to atop the dugout the day the team clinched the East Division title. It was the soundtrack that a city celebrated to when the team brought the World Series trophy home that October.

In just a few months, "We Are Family" went from being just another No. 1 hit to a song synonymous for all time with that championship team. "We thought the song had made as much noise as it ever would," said Kathie Sledge, who sang lead. "Then the Pirates came along. God can act in mysterious ways."

baseball borrowed it with Stargell in mind. He hit .281 with 32 homers, 82 RBIs, shared the National League's Most Valuable Player Award with Keith Hernandez of the St. Louis Cardinals, was named National League Championship Series MVP, and on that night in Memorial Stadium was named World Series MVP. It capped an unprecedented sweep of the three MVPs.

92

Glory's last shot? Over the next three seasons—his forgettable final three—he would hit just 14 more home runs and drive in 64 runs as the Pirates began a slow, dark decline into baseball wasteland. When Stargell jumped into the mass of celebrating black-and-gold on the infield grass that night, he would never jump so high again. It didn't matter. Going on two decades in the game, the man who had lifted his game and lifted teammates and lifted spirits and lifted others through off-field work raising money to fight sickle cell anemia finally had that moment that seemed impossible as the distance between him and 1971 grew. All of baseball had that moment. His moment.

As Stargell told a writer from *Sports Illustrated*, which that year named him its co-Sportsman of the Year with Steelers quarterback Terry Bradshaw, "If you respect this game and do what you're supposed to, it's very rewarding. But if you take it for granted, it will embarrass you."

Stargell never took it for granted. And that season, that month, that night, Stargell earned his reward.

34 How Long Was It?

Would anyone have been surprised had an autopsy on the longest streak of losing in the history of North American professional sports revealed the entire inventory of Area 51, an egg laid by the Loch Ness Monster, and the original blueprints for Stonehenge (a pagan timeshare stopped after only a few stones had been laid when financing fell through)? The seasons endured by the Pirates from the beginning of 1993 through the end of 2012—the run of years in which the franchise earned the ignominious sports mantle—are almost as absurd. In those 20 years, they had three principal owners, seven managers, were outscored by 1,986 runs, lost 422 games more than they won (1,374–1,796) and finished a cumulative 462 games—or nearly three full seasons—out of first place. Said manager Clint Hurdle, who like so many of his players was around only for the last three or four years of the losing, on the night the Pirates won their 82nd game of 2013 to officially end the streak: "We don't really understand what the fans have been through." Really? He might have added, "Nor do we really understand how long 20 years is in the human lifetime, or more specifically, the life of a fan."

Consider how long those two decades were:

Jason Kendall and Brian Giles, two of the franchise's few bright spots during the skid, played their entire major league careers— Kendall from 1996 to 2010 and Giles from 1995 to 2009—within that 20-year run.

In 1992, Mario Lemieux was at the height of his legendary playing career with the crosstown Penguins of the NHL. By 2013, he had retired, bought the team, made a five-season comeback, and retired again.

The average salary in Major League Baseball increased 325 percent—from $1.12 million in 1992 to $3.65 million at the beginning of 2013.

The Florida/Miami Marlins were an expansion team in 1993, yet they had won two World Series by the end of 2012.

The United States military engaged in the longest (Afghanistan) and third-longest (Iraq) wars in the history of the nation.

A total of 213 pitchers appeared in a Pirates uniform; 164 of them lost at least once.

In 1992, Barack Obama was a relatively unknown member of the faculty at the University of Chicago Law School. By 2013, he was well into his second term as the 44th president of the United States.

Sid Bream went from the guy who scored the run that kept the Pirates from going to the 1992 World Series to being three years into AARP card eligibility.

The runs of *Friends* (1994–2004) and *The Sopranos* (1998–2007)—two of the most popular series in television history—and J.K. Rowling's entire *Harry Potter* series of books (1997–2007) and their accompanying movies (2002–11) fit comfortably into all that Pirates losing.

So, too, did the impeachment of a president, a NASA mission to Mars, and the entire life and ascent to stardom of teen sensations Miley Cyrus and Justin Bieber, who weren't even alive the night Francisco Cabrera spray-painted graffiti on the psyches of an entire generation of Pirates fans.

In 1992, Amazon was a large rain forest in South America. By 2013, it was the largest online retailer not just in South America but the world. Similarly, the Internet as a whole grew from a relative handful of users to more than 2.3 billion, and mobile phones in service went from a few million to more than 6 billion. Can you hear me now?

And if you still need an idea how long 20 years is and how long Pirates fans had to wait to celebrate a winning team, consider the starting lineup Hurdle penciled in September 9, 2013—the night the Pirates defeated the Texas Rangers 1–0 for their 82nd win of the 2013 season and the win that ensured the streak of losing would not reach 21. Second baseman Neil Walker would have been 7 the night the Pirates had finished their previous winning season, star center fielder Andrew McCutchen would have just turned six, third baseman Pedro Alvarez would have been five, and starting pitcher Gerrit Cole two.

In life's grand scheme, it may be true that time flies. But just never use the expression on a suffering fan. That's one truth that will never change, no matter how much time may pass.

35 One Sweet Night

The odds against what occurred the night of August 9, 1976, stagger the mathematics-challenged mind. But one thing's for certain—if the prescient guy in the Pirates' marketing department who thought it would be a good idea for the team to pass out free candy bars to the first 10,000 fans through the gates didn't play the daily number that day, he probably cost himself a bundle.

Consider this. Of the 15 other major league franchises that had been around since 1900, none owned fewer no-hitters than the Pirates' four as the lights came on at Three Rivers Stadium. And of those four, only one had been pitched in Pittsburgh, and that had been 69 years and two ballparks before. So to think that marketing wiz picked that night of all nights to pass out candy bars to honor that evening's young pitching star—John "The Candy Man" Candelaria—blew right past serendipitous and into the zip code of happily ever after.

Candelaria, a 6'7", 22-year-old left-hander with the back of a 62-year-old, didn't have his best fastball that night against the Los Angeles Dodgers, but what he lacked in velocity he made up for with wicked movement and spot-on control. When he induced Davey Lopes to fly out to center fielder Al Oliver to open the game, he set off on a journey not traveled by a Pirates pitcher in front of a home Pirates crowd since Nick Maddox on September 20, 1907, against, ironically, the Dodgers' Brooklyn ancestors—the Superbas. But even then, Maddox allowed a run in a 2–1 Pirates victory at Exposition Park.

No Dodger would cross home plate against Candelaria. Although how they didn't in the third inning can only be credited to the same lucky star that the aforementioned marketing guy lived

John Candelaria and Duffy Dyer celebrate after Candelaria's no-hitter on August 9, 1976, at Three Rivers Stadium. (*Pittsburgh Post-Gazette*, Ed Morgan)

A Left-Handed Connection

John Candelaria won 124 games, pitched a no-hitter, won Game 6 of the 1979 World Series, and was the second-best Pirates left-hander of the twentieth century as determined in a *Pittsburgh Post-Gazette* fan vote in 1999. Yet Candelaria also holds another unique and not necessarily glorious distinction in club history. After being traded to the California Angels in 1985, he began a major league odyssey that would see him also pitch for the Mets, Yankees, Expos, Twins, Blue Jays, and Dodgers over the next eight years. Ultimately, it brought him back to Pittsburgh for the final 24 games of his career. The season he returned was 1993—the first of the club's 20 consecutive losing seasons. It makes him the only player to have won a World Series ring in a Pirates uniform and also been part of the worst two decades in franchise history.

under that day. The Pirates committed two errors in the inning, and Candelaria also walked Steve Yeager. Yet none of the three crossed home plate. He erased Yeager on a force out at second and, with the bases loaded and two outs, got Dodgers shortstop Bill Russell to ground out to shortstop Frank Taveras. Otherwise, he was perfect, retiring the final 19 Dodgers in order. Bill Robinson, meanwhile, provided the only runs he needed—and the only runs of the night—two innings later when he doubled to left off Doug Rau to score Richie Zisk and Dave Parker.

In fact, against an All-Star lineup that included Steve Garvey, Dusty Baker, and Ron Cey, "So much was Candelaria in control that there were no spectacular defensive plays necessary," as there often are in the anatomy of a no-hitter, wrote Bob Smizik of the *Pittsburgh Press* the next day, but "only a handful of good ones."

He needed one of those good ones for history, though. With two outs in the top of the ninth, Russell lofted a short fly behind second base. Or, as Smizik wrote in keeping with the storybook feel, not too deep, not too shallow. Candelaria only saw the big bad wolf. *Geez, what a way to lose it*, he thought. But the ball stayed up, allowing Oliver to race in and make the catch just before brushing against the shoulder of shortstop Frank Taveras, who had been charging into the outfield just as aggressively. "Lucky we didn't collide, or someone might have been killed," Oliver said.

Only the second Pirates no-hitter in Pittsburgh—and still one of just three in the franchise's 127-year history—was in the books. He threw 101 pitches, 70 for strikes. He had seven strikeouts. And, in his 39th major league start, he had done what no Pirates pitcher had done in 69 years. Just how long was that? Consider that Forbes Field opened in 1909—less than two seasons after Maddox's gem—closed in 1970 and not only was never home to a no-hitter by a Pirates pitcher, but never home to one by a Pirates opponent, either. St. Louis' Bob Gibson ended the drought for opposing pitchers on August 14, 1971, at Three Rivers Stadium, which also factored into the strange-but-true quality of the night. Candelaria's no-hitter was broadcast regionally as part of ABC's *Monday Night Baseball* package. In the booth were Al Michaels, Norm Cash...and Gibson, who had retired from the Cardinals after the 1975 season.

Again, what were the odds?

36 Twenty-One Years in the Making

As evening settled over PNC Park that night, that was unlike any other in more than two decades—and, to listen to those who were there, unlike any other night ever—one truth became apparent. Reality, in this instance, surpassed the dream. Black outpolled blue as the most popular color in the Crayola box. And Auntie Em's Kansas farm outshined Oz. No question, there was no place like home for the Pirates on October 1, 2013—the night postseason baseball came back to Pittsburgh for the first time since Sid Bream, Francisco Cabrera and, well, any Pirates fan knows the rest of that story. It was only a National League wild-card game, a one-game set-to against the Cincinnati Reds for the right to move on to play a full series of such games in the 2013 postseason, but "that's not how it tasted. And that's definitely not how it sounded," wrote one visiting reporter.

Practically from the afternoon the park opened in 2001, fan and player alike had imagined what a game in October would be like there on Pittsburgh's North Shore. If, they reasoned, it was the best ballpark in America when home to a perennial loser as the Pirates were from 1993 to 2012, how much better it would be when a winner finally played there. This summer of 2013, they got their winner—a team that won 94, lost 68, finished second in the National League Central Division and earned the higher of two wild-card spots. That latter distinction channeled everyone and everything into that Tuesday night: the game, the franchise, the history, the pain, the jokes, the losses, the ridicule, the national TV cameras, the promises, the frustrations, the anger, the wasted days, the fans who had stayed, and the fans who had strayed. All converged into that one point in space and time. What spilled forth was like nothing even long-time baseball watchers had seen.

More than 40,000 people squeezed into a stadium with a listed capacity of 38,362. At the request of players, they came dressed in black, the color of sadness and mourning, but on this night it was the color of strength and of the steely survivor. Those who couldn't score a ticket lined the Clemente Bridge beyond the left-center field stands, three and four and five deep. "It was pure energy from pitch one to the last out," said Neil Walker, not only the Pirates' starting second baseman but also one of them—a native Pittsburgher who, because of that, understood better than any of the players how long the wait for that night had been and how often was the creeping wonder if it would ever be. "I've been to AFC playoffs, AFC championship games," he said. "There were only 40,000 in the stands, but I'm pretty sure this was the loudest. This was absolutely incredible."

When the players were introduced, the black towel–waving mass cheered. When Marlon Byrd homered to lead off the second inning, it rocked. And when Reds starting pitcher Johnny Cueto—a Pirates nemesis since he'd entered the league in 2008—attempted to collect himself and navigate the rest of the inning, it chanted in sing-song fashion: "Quay-to, Quay-to, Quay-to." Out of nowhere and all together. Cueto, alone in the middle of this decades-long buildup that had finally found its release, dropped the ball. It plopped into the mound's scuffed-up clay and trickled down into the infield grass. He would insist later that the crowd did not affect him. The 40,487 who were there will forever disagree. Two facts will be on their side—the ball dropping from his hands as he stood in a set position, and the pitch he delivered next—a 2–1 fastball, fat and belt high, that Pirates catcher Russell Martin turned on and drove into the stands in left field for the Pirates second home run in the span of three batters. The Pirates would go on to score four more times, including a second Martin home run, over the next seven innings and win 6–2 to advance to an NL Division Series meeting with the St. Louis Cardinals. But most will say the game was over as soon as Martin's bat met ball.

"B-E-D-L-A-M is too mild a word to describe the ambiance of a ballpark that had waited a generation for a moment like this," wrote Jayson Stark, a national baseball writer who had covered 30 years of postseasons but never a scene like the one that played out that night. Loud, also, is not in the ballpark. Deafening is closer but lacks subtext for the emotional venting that coursed through the stands like the wave. Locomotives, jet engines, AC/DC concerts, and memories of Stanley Cup runs at old, close, cramped Mellon Arena where the NHL's Pittsburgh Penguins once played were ready fallback comparisons. But no words ever quite captured the sensory overload that touched PNC Park that night. That was a night where you really did have to be there; a night when a sea of black somehow lit up the dark, and home never meant so much.

37 Who the Heck Uses the Word *Gloamin'*?

By definition, gloamin'—or more properly, gloaming—is a twelfth-century Scottish word for twilight or dusk. It is the low light that is seen in the evening as the sun sets.

Until the late afternoon of September 28, 1938, it was most commonly known as the atmospheric backdrop of a popular love song written a quarter century before. Penned by Sir Harry Lauder, "Roamin' In The Gloamin'" sung of young lovers who find the time "when the sun has gone to rest, that's the time we love the best. O, it's lovely to be roamin' in the gloamin'."

Then 37-year-old Gabby Hartnett stepped to the plate for the Cubs in the fading light of a Wednesday afternoon at Chicago's Wrigley Field, and the gloamin' became the place forevermore where Pirates hopes for the 1938 pennant disappeared and died.

Tied 5–5 in the bottom of the ninth inning, the Pirates had been a half-game up on the Cubs in the National League pennant race when Hartnett stepped into the batter's box. A half-game up when pitcher Mace Brown—the Pirates' best pitcher that season—got ahead of him no balls and two strikes. And then, just like that, a half-game down one pitch later after Hartnett, also the team's manager in addition to its aging star, sent a Brown curveball hurtling into history, which that evening masqueraded as Wrigley's left-field bleachers.

"No baseball fiction ever outrivaled the situation which saw the Cubs win 6 to 5 to take first place from the Pirates," wrote Havey Boyle in the next morning's *Pittsburgh Post-Gazette.*

It was The Homer In The Gloamin', a term credited to Chicago's Associated Press writer at the time, Earl Hilligan.

The Pirates of the Waner brothers and manager Pie Traynor had been in first place since July 18. Twenty-seven games over .500 and 6½ games up as late as mid-August. But they had staggered in September as the Cubs got hot. And so, at 3:00 PM—a routine mid-afternoon start time for Cubs games in those years, even late in the season as days grew short—they met with first place in the balance. There were five more games to be played after that one, but the race effectively ended that day. Or more specifically, in the late-summer, late-day light on a ball hit at 5:37 PM, an hour before official sunset in Chicago.

Umpires had previously determined that the ninth inning would be the last played that day. If the game remained tied, it would have been replayed in its entirety per National League rules of the day and the Pirates still would have been in first place until another day whose destiny might have been written differently.

But it never had a chance, wrote Boyle, the sports editor of the *Post-Gazette.*

"It must have been written ages ago by the baseball gods that come September 28, in the year 1938, the Pirates at all costs were not to win the ball game," Boyle wrote. "When the sun was first hung out to light the earth, it must have been timed so that at a certain second the earth's revolving would bring on the mantle of approaching dusk to doom the Pirates."

A year later, Hartnett recounted that afternoon in detail to Hal Totten, a Chicago broadcaster.

"In our half Phil Cavarretta hit one a country mile to center, but Lloyd Waner pulled it down. Carl Reynolds grounded out. And it was my turn.

"Well, I swung once—and missed; I swung again and got a piece of it, but that was all. A foul and strike two. I had one more chance. Mace Brown wound up and let fly; I swung with everything I had, and then I got that feeling...the kind of feeling you get when the blood rushes out of your head and you get dizzy.

"A lot of people have told me they didn't know the ball was in the bleachers. Well, I did—maybe I was the only one in the park who did. I knew it the minute I hit it."

Hartnett wasn't entirely correct. Brown, too, had known it was gone.

"At the precise split second Hartnett's bat hit the ball, Brown's gloved hand and his right hand shot to his face," Boyle wrote. "His head came down to meet the hands. It was the perfect picture of a man suddenly shocked into abject horror."

It was the gloamin'. For Brown. For the Pirates.

Hartnett 18 years later would be inducted into the Hall of Fame and, until Johnny Bench came along, would be regarded as the best catcher in National League history—a .297 hitter with 236 home runs. Brown would go on to pitch six more seasons in the majors, but he lived the first line of his obituary that day.

The Homer In The Gloamin' was named the 47th greatest home run in major league history when ESPN.com put together its top 100 in 2003. It was the home run that left no one in Pittsburgh feeling much like singing that night.

38 The Old Irishman

He was so laid back some wondered whether he dozed off on the bench during games. He had a rocking chair in his office and the occasional glass of milk in his hand. He had a sense of humor reporters loved, yet never said look at me. He came across as a benevolent Irish grandfather or at the very least an easy-going father; a hard shell outside with a soft chewy center like some 1960s TV dad, albeit one who spit tobacco with the best of 'em. Yet no one should have been fooled: Danny Murtaugh was a winner; a winner not in spite of who he was but because of it.

He served four separate stints as Pirates manager from 1957 through 1976—a modern record until Billy Martin and George Steinbrenner turned their New York melodrama into a Miller Lite beer commercial—and had a winning record during each. Were it not for health issues, most notably ulcers, that forced him to step down after the 1964, '67, '72, and '76 seasons and cost him about six full seasons, he likely would have had a Walter Alston–like career and long ago have made it into the Hall of Fame. As it is, he won 1,115 games—second only to Fred Clarke in franchise history—and guided two very different teams 11 years and two "retirements" apart to World Series championships.

Bill Mazeroski credits Murtaugh with giving him the chance to develop into the player who became one of the game's premier second basemen after Murtaugh replaced Bobby Bragan in his first go-round as manager in 1957. "I suddenly felt as if an elephant had just climbed down off my shoulders," Mazeroski said.

Within four years, Murtaugh guided the 1960 Pirates—a major league punch line as recently as six years before when they lost 100 games in three consecutive seasons—to their first World Series in 33 years and their first world championship in 35. Thanks to Mazeroski's time-stopping home run in Game 7, they stunned the New York Yankees in a seven-game series that is as ingrained in the fabric of life along the three rivers as steel, Andrew Carnegie, pierogies, and Kennywood Park. "He knows how to handle men," said Dick Groat, Pirates shortstop from 1952 to 1962 and league MVP that season. Ten years later, at the other end of the turbulent

Danny Murtaugh congratulates Bill Mazeroski (left) after the 1960 World Series victory. (Pittsburgh Post-Gazette)

'60s, he took over a Pirates roster of Roberto Clemente and Willie Stargell, of Steve Blass and Manny Sanguillen, and by the end of the second season helped it, too, win a world championship. Even those who wouldn't have been considered Murtaugh disciples could appreciate him. Dock Ellis, a pitcher born and raised in inner city Los Angeles, pitched for the Pirates from 1968 to 1975. He did not always see eye to eye with management or with the world. Yet of his manager, Ellis told *Sport Magazine*, "Murtaugh's a beautiful dude. Beautiful. Winning. That's all he cares about. Nothing else. Screw up, you hear about it. Black or white."

But if you heard about it, you probably heard about it in private. Or at the very least, one on one and face to face. And often sprinkled with droll humor. "I was pitching in spring training and was wild as could be," Blass said. "Danny came to the mound and asked me what was the matter. I told him I just couldn't seem to find the plate. 'Rather remarkable,' he said. 'It's been in the same damned place for 78 years.'"

There was a sense that Murtaugh had been on the Pirates' bench almost as long when he retired for the final time after the 1976 season at the end of his fourth run that produced 285 more wins and two division titles in three-plus seasons. In fact, he was only 59. Time and years battling his health only made him appear older to those watching from the stands or on TV. This time, he would not return. He managed his final two games on October 3—a pair of 1–0 wins against the St. Louis Cardinals in a season-ending doubleheader at Three Rivers Stadium. He died two months later. His final record was 1,115–950 with four division championships, two National League pennants, two world championships and, in 1999, manager on the franchise's Team of the Century. All of these accomplishments validate the assurance he gave general manager Joe L. Brown when Brown gave him the chance to succeed Bragan all those years before. "Don't worry, Joe," Murtaugh told him, "I'm a better manager than you think."

39 Under Cy-zed

From 1956—the year commissioner Ford Frick established the Cy Young Award—through the end of the 2013 season, the Pirates had exactly five pitchers win 20 games with no pitcher accomplishing it more than once. To put that in some sort of perspective, the Los Angeles Dodgers had 13 different pitchers win 20 games a total of 17 times in that same span, and the Baltimore Orioles had 11 do it 24 times. Incredibly, the Orioles even had four 20-game winners in a single season in 1971. Over that same 58-year period, 23 pitchers who went on to be enshrined in the Hall of Fame pitched the bulk of their careers. While three wore a Pirates uniform at some point—Jim Bunning, Rich "Goose" Gossage, and Bert Blyleven—they did so only for a combined 5½ seasons out of the 61 they played in the major leagues.

That history lesson serves two purposes. It reinforces the notion that if the Pirates were ever perceived as a pitching powerhouse, that notion died about the time old-timers Deacon Phillippe and Vic Willis retired. And it makes two singularly brilliant seasons three decades apart in the second half of the twentieth century stand out that much more in Pirates history.

In 1960, Vernon Law, a 30-year-old right-hander from Meridian, Idaho, went 20–9 with a 3.08 earned run average and 18 complete games, then added two more wins in the World Series. His numbers helped the Pirates win a world championship. They also helped him win the Cy Young Award, a feat enhanced by the fact that only one award was presented for both leagues from 1956 to 1966. Thirty years later, Doug Drabek, a 27-year-old right-hander from Victoria, Texas, went 22–6 with a 2.76 ERA. His numbers helped the 1990 Pirates win their first National League East Division title in 11 years. They also helped him win the National League Cy Young Award in near-unanimous fashion. As 2013 ended, Law and Drabek remained the only Cy Young winners in franchise history, and the Pirates remained ahead of only the Cincinnati Reds (0) in number of Cy Young Awards won among the original eight National League franchises.

Law was never better than from the middle of July through the end of August in his Cy Young season. As the Pirates battled Milwaukee and St. Louis, Law ran off a string of nine starts from July 21 through August 29 in which he went 8–0, pitched six complete games—including 10 innings against Hall of Famer Juan Marichal and the San Francisco Giants on August 6—and posted a 2.97 ERA. "Practically everything good that can happen to a person has happened to me this year," Law said the day he won the award. Although he would go 17–9 with a 2.15 ERA in 1965, arm problems prevented him from approaching the pitcher he was in that magical summer of 1960.

Like Law, Drabek never again found the dominant stuff he exhibited in 1990. He turned his Cy Young season into a $3.35 million arbitration win before the 1991 season—the largest award for a player at the time—and then into a $19.5 million, four-year contract from the Houston Astros as a free agent after the 1992 season. He went 15–14 and 15–11 in his last two seasons with the Pirates, but he was never again 1990 good, the season he "threw the slider from hell," raved friend and former teammate Brian Fisher. "He threw the kind of slider that, as a pitcher, you dream of throwing." In his final 17 starts, Drabek went 14–2 with a 2.31 ERA. He was 12–3 after a Pirates loss. He pitched 8⅔ no-hit innings against the Philadelphia Phillies August 3. He threw a 2–0, three-hit shutout against the St. Louis Cardinals to clinch the division championship September 30. "He was there for us whenever we needed him," manager Jim Leyland said.

The fact that neither pitcher repeated his brilliance should never diminish what they did. That they were the historic exception, the anomaly like a liberal Republican and a Halley's Comet sighting, should only enhance their value, particularly in a Pirates narrative that is filled with batting titles and home-run crowns but so few summers when it could be written that no pitcher had a better season than that of a Pittsburgh Pirate.

September 1985: The Drug Trials

Pirate Parrot—middle man in a web of rampant cocaine use? The mental image might have been *Saturday Night Live* funny in the summer of 1985—"Psst! Hey buddy! Ever seen such pure bird seed?"—had it not been so *Nightline* serious. How serious? The Pirates lost 104 games and finished 43½ games out of first place, yet that wasn't the worst part of an embarrassing season. Maybe not even top 10.

For months, even as the Pirates lost game after game just six years removed from a world championship and fans—the few that there were in a season in which the Pirates averaged just 9,000 a game— endured Joggin' George Hendrick and Jose DeLeon, a far sadder story had been building toward a seedy head in Pittsburgh's federal courthouse. It was there that seven drug dealers had been indicted in May. Front and center in the government's case was the testimony of about a dozen major league players who had been among their customers. For many, the Pirate Parrot also known as Kevin Koch, had been the go-between. The list included current and former Pirates Dave Parker, Dale Berra, Rod Scurry, Lee Lacy, Lee Mazzilli, and John Milner, and National League stars Keith Hernandez, Tim

Raines, Lonnie Smith, Enos Cabell, and Jeffrey Leonard. All testified before the grand jury and/or in court under a grant of immunity. "That black era," team president Carl Barger lamented.

History will show that cocaine was not just a problem endemic to Pittsburgh in 1985, but that it was America's recreational drug du jour for the yuppie generation of the 1980s. It will also show that the FBI's investigation encompassed all of baseball. Yet it was only in Pittsburgh and Three Rivers Stadium and on Pirates players that all paths converged in 1984–85. "Because it was in Pittsburgh and called the Pittsburgh drug trials, the association was more with the club than it should have been," said Steve Greenberg, then the Pirates' marketing director.

What should have been, however, could never erase what was.

On September 5, Curtis Strong went on trial in the courtroom of U.S. Judge Gustave Diamond. Tom Balzer and Kevin Connolly had already pleaded guilty. Dale Shiffman would be sentenced a month later, the day a verdict was returned against Strong. Robert McCue would be convicted September 26 at the conclusion of a separate trial. Shelby Greer would plead guilty on September 30. Jeff Mosco would also plead guilty. But who were they, and why did anyone care? For the record, no one would have. They were, in fact, bit players to every television network and major print publication that set up shop on Grant Street near the courthouse that September. The stars were the witnesses.

"Baseball was not on trial in that courtroom," J. Alan Johnson, then U.S. attorney for Western Pennsylvania, told the *Pittsburgh Press* six years later, "but baseball was certainly on trial in the public's mind after the revelations started coming out."

The details were unbelievable, even 15 years after Jim Bouton's *Ball Four* had gone where no book had dared—the inner sanctum that was the major league clubhouse. Milner bought 2 grams of cocaine in a clubhouse bathroom stall during a game. Scurry once disappeared from the bullpen in search of a score. Hernandez estimated 40 percent of all players were users. Berra was seen under FBI surveillance making two buys at the door of his home in the same day. Even the names of Willie Stargell and Willie Mays were dragged into the trial when Parker and Milner testified they received liquid amphetamine from the two future Hall of Famers. (Both Stargell and Mays were later exonerated by Commissioner Peter Ueberroth.)

"You knew it couldn't last forever," Greenberg said. "It only seemed that way."

The seven dealers received a combined 54 years in sentences; they served a little more than 13. As for the players, although all suffered damage to their reputations, none spent a day in jail. What real punishment they received was meted out by Ueberroth. Just after spring training opened in 1986, Ueberroth suspended 11 of the players, seven for the full season. But he offered an out. They could play if they agreed to donate 10 percent of their base salaries to drug prevention centers, submit to random drug tests, and perform 100 hours of community service. The seven included Parker, Smith, and Hernandez. The other four were suspended for 60 days, a suspension that would be lifted if they donated 5 percent of their salaries and did 50 hours of community service. That none of the players were Pirates by that point did not matter. Those days in late summer of 1985 were and always will be remembered not as the Baseball Drug Trials but as the Pittsburgh Drug Trials—"a sad chapter for the game of baseball, a sad chapter for the city of Pittsburgh and the Pittsburgh organization," Barger said.

41 High and Right

One hundred thirty no-hitters had been pitched in the major league modern era when Dock Ellis somehow found the mound at San Diego Stadium in the early evening of June 12, 1970. It's safe to say none were like the one he would author against the San Diego Padres over 2 hours, 13 minutes in a mix of Southern California mist—or was it myth?—that evening. Just as it's pretty safe to write that none have been like it since.

The record books report no hits for the Padres. But Ellis did allow one that day, one that wouldn't be learned of for more than a decade—a hit of LSD he took about six hours before in a hotel room 90 miles up the coast in Los Angeles when he not only wasn't aware that he was pitching, but that the Pirates even had a game. For the record, they had two that night, and the first—the one in which Ellis was scheduled to pitch—was to begin at 6:05 PM.

"I took the LSD at noon," Ellis told Bob Smizik of the *Pittsburgh Press* in April 1984 in the first of what would be many—and sometimes varied—recountings of the story behind the no-hitter over the last 25 years of his life. "At 1:00, the girl (I was with) looked at the paper and said, 'Dock, you're pitching today.'"

Ellis panicked. He walked circles around the room, a panic captured in a later story that appeared in the magazine *High Times*.

"It's okay, Dock," the girl told him. "You can make it. The first game doesn't start for five hours. You can catch the next flight to San Diego."

"I can't pitch. I just dropped acid," Ellis replied.

"Just throw a few pitches, and they'll take you out," the girl said reassuringly.

Ellis did make it, arriving at the park about 4:30 PM. Despite having to ask teammate Dave Cash where his locker was even though he was standing in front of it, and despite looking into a mirror before going to the dugout and seeing his reflection "pulsating and alive with color," Dock Ellis never did get taken out that night.

For nine innings, he worked himself in and out of trouble, mostly unaware of how he did, either. His fingers tingled. His first pitch bounced 2' in front of the plate. Several others wound up going past catcher Jerry May to the backstop. His breaking ball was nowhere to be found. But that was okay. His fastball, he said, emitted comet-like tails out of his hand and at times, seemed and felt like one. He knew a no-hitter was in progress; he just didn't always seem to know it was his. He walked eight Padres, he hit another. But he never allowed a hit. And he never did get taken out, right up to the moment he flung a called third strike past San Diego's Ed Spiezio for the 27th and final out.

Pirates 2, Padres 0, the runs scoring on solo homers by Willie Stargell in the second and seventh innings. They were sidebars to just the fourth no-hitter in Pirates history.

In one telling, "I was zeroed in on the glove, but I didn't hit the glove too much." In another, "I saw the catcher, sometimes I didn't." And in still another—in a story told in *The New York Times* two years after he died in 2009—he imagined at one point he was pitching against late rock guitarist Jimi Hendrix and that then–President Richard Nixon was calling balls and strikes.

For as much as the stories and interviews with Ellis might have had some details while lacking others over the last 25 years of his life, while it's been difficult sorting through what Ellis did see from what he didn't, the one storyline that never changed was that Ellis performed one of the singularly great feats in any pitcher's career while on lysergic acid diethylamide (LSD). That, and that few skeptics, particularly teammates, ever stepped up to challenge it.

Pirates pitcher Dock Ellis on the mound in April 1971. (*Pittsburgh Post-Gazette*, Ed Morgan)

42 Wild Heartbreak

Sometimes, most times, you lose and that's it. But sometimes that loss arrives with such a twist that it breaks your heart. A loss so stunning and unexpected that tears of joy turn to sadness before they can reach the bottom of your cheek. A defeat so sudden and final that summer skips autumn and turns immediately to winter. So turned the fortunes of the Pirates in the late, overcast Cincinnati afternoon of October 11, 1972. Were it not for a kid named Francisco Cabrera 20 years later, Game 5 of the '72 National League Championship Series against the arch-rival Reds would be the one that most sits in the franchise's collective stomach like the ghost of a double burrito at 4:00 in the morning.

The Pirates led 3–2 and needed just three outs to return to defend the World Series championship won the year before in Baltimore. After Ramon Hernandez snuffed out a Reds threat in the eighth, veteran closer Dave Giusti was sent out in the bottom of the ninth to get those final three outs. Giusti saved 22 games that year, third-most in the NL, and had led the league in saves the previous season with 30. "I thought when we'd got out of the eighth, we'd made it," Pirates manager Bill Virdon admitted later. "But we didn't."

Due up for the Reds: Johnny Bench, Tony Perez, and Denis Menke. Bench, who'd hit 40 home runs to lead the NL for the second time in three seasons, fell behind 1–2. Then Giusti hung his signature palmball. Bench didn't miss. "It was right over the plate," Bench said. "I don't go to right field too often, but as soon as I hit it I knew it was good." Home run. Just like that, tie game.

If only that would have been the end of it. Instead, it was only the beginning. Perez and Menke followed with singles. Reds manager Sparky Anderson replaced Perez with pinch runner George Foster, a small move that would grow in significance in the next telling moments, as would the decision Virdon made about the same time. He removed Giusti for 25-year-old right-hander Bob Moose. Moose had been primarily a starter in '72 but had split time between the rotation and bullpen in his first four seasons in the major leagues. As Virdon explained later, the home run to Bench had "upset" Giusti. "Then he tried to rush and he was a little wild. I had to get a strike thrower in there."

Moose's first batter was Cesar Geronimo. Geronimo, who had homered earlier in the game to pull the Reds within 3–2, failed in two attempts to sacrifice the runners over. But he still accomplished the job when, on a two-strike pitch, he flied out to Roberto Clemente in right field—deep enough that Foster could tag up and go to third. With one out, just about anything hit into the outfield would score the winning run. But Reds No. 8 hitter Darrel Chaney couldn't get it done. He popped out to shortstop Gene Alley.

The ways for plating Foster diminished. Could Moose wriggle the Pirates free and get them to extra innings? The Reds had already used their best relievers—Pedro Borbon and Clay Carroll. All that stood between Moose and a tenth inning was pinch hitter Hal McRae.

Moose's first pitch to the right-hand hitting McRae was a swing and a miss, the second a ball. And the third, well, the third became a pitch that decades later is still bouncing past Manny Sanguillen and through the realm of what might have been. It was a slider into the dirt and so far outside that even a lunging Sanguillen couldn't get a glove on it. The ball skidded and hopped by his attempt to backhand it.

"It looked like it hit something, I don't know what," Sanguillen said.

"I didn't want to throw him a strike. It just took a bounce and bounced over his head," Moose said.

Pirates pitcher Dave Giusti on the mound on October 13, 1971.
(*Pittsburgh Post-Gazette*, Kent Badger)

No matter what happened with the pitch or how, the result was Foster scampering home with the run that gave the Reds a 4–3 victory and sent them to the World Series against the Oakland Athletics and the Pirates into a future that they couldn't begin to fathom. That pitch did not just close the door on a chance to go back to the World Series and add to the talk of a budding dynasty, but it was also the final time in uniform for two Hall of Famers. Bill Mazeroski retired after the season. That was expected. The other loss, however, not only made that offseason colder and harder, it erased thoughts that that '72 team that came within three outs of going back to the Series would come back bigger and better in 1973. Eighty-one days later—New Year's Eve 1972—Clemente was lost in a plane crash.

43 The Forgotten Pioneer

Two days shy of seven years after Jackie Robinson made history in Brooklyn, Curt Roberts ran out to second base at Forbes Field for the Pirates' 1954 season opener against the Philadelphia Phillies. He made history, too. It just doesn't happen to be remembered to the same degree. On the timeline of major league franchises that followed the Brooklyn Dodgers' decision to break baseball's color barrier with Robinson, the Pirates were the ninth—sandwiched between the day late in the 1953 season that the Chicago Cubs sent Ernie Banks out to play shortstop and a game that started after the Pirates-Phillies opener that afternoon of April 13, 1954, when the St. Louis Cardinals began their season against the Chicago Cubs with a first baseman by the name of Tom Alston batting sixth. The Cincinnati Reds and Washington Senators would also have the first black players on their rosters that year.

Like Robinson, Roberts had been picked and prepared by Branch Rickey, who had moved from the Dodgers to the Pirates as general manager in 1950. "He used Jackie as an example," said Roberts' wife, Christine. "He told him to keep an even temper. He said, 'The reason I chose you is because you play good ball and you seem to have an even temper. When you hear things, you ignore them.'" And he did hear things. "Sometimes you want to forget it," Christine Roberts said of the racist taunts. Someone even threw watermelon onto Forbes Field.

Unlike Robinson, who was nearly 6', 200 lbs., had lettered in four sports at UCLA, and could spray line drives all over Ebbets

*The Phillies' Granny Hamner barges into Curtis Roberts at second base on April 15, 1955. (*Sun Telegraph, *Morris Berman/*Pittsburgh Post-Gazette*)*

Field, the 24-year-old Roberts was not quite 5'8", 165 lbs., and depended mostly on speed and soft hands at second. "A guy who ran like hell and played hard," said Nellie King, a Pirates pitcher from 1954 to 1957.

Neither Pittsburgh newspaper wrote of the fans' reaction to Roberts' debut that afternoon nor made any mention of his place in team history. The box score reports several successes, though, not the least of which was his first major league at-bat. Batting second in the bottom of the first inning, Roberts stepped in against future Hall of Famer Robin Roberts—a pitcher who had beaten the Pirates 15 consecutive times. Unfazed, Curt Roberts laced a ball to right field. By the time the buzz died down, Roberts stood on third with a triple. His debut was already better than Robinson's, who had gone 0-for-3 seven years earlier against Johnny Sain and the Boston Braves.

It would be the only time that Roberts outperformed Robinson. Roberts played 134 games for a Pirates team that lost 101 in 1954 and, while he hit six more triples, he hit just .232 overall with 47 runs scored, 36 RBIs, and six stolen bases. Even his defense was lacking. He committed 24 errors, second most by a second baseman in the National League. He played parts of 1955 and '56 with the Pirates—just 37 more games in all—but his chances of a long big-league career ended in that '54 season. If he contributed anything in the two years afterward, it was his role in helping another minority player by the name of Roberto Clemente get acclimated to the Pirates and Pittsburgh. By 1956, the Pirates were already looking at Bill Mazeroski as their second baseman and in the middle of that year traded Roberts to the Kansas City Athletics. He never again played in the major leagues, fulfilling a destiny that is now more trivia question than golden memory.

"Quite a few [black men] had come into the major leagues, and Curt was an average ballplayer," said Bill Nunn, then the sports editor of the *Pittsburgh Courier*, the most widely circulated newspaper among blacks at the time. "Under the circumstances, he really didn't get the [attention] some of the other guys did."

History never corrected that. At age 40, he was struck and killed by a drunk driver while changing a tire on the side of an Oakland, California, freeway in November 1969. It would be another 20 years until many of his teammates even learned of it.

44 Hall of Tears

"Words are just words. Words aren't always real. But tears never lie."
—Jayson Stark

If those words are true, then on the podium at the doors of Cooperstown and nearly 30 years of waiting after he retired, Bill Mazeroski said his thanks, praised his heroes, greeted his teammates, summed up his career, listed his triumphs, loved his wife, hugged his kids, and defined his life with the most beautiful truths ever uttered in the shadow of the game's most hallowed walls. On Hall of Fame Induction Sunday 2001, William Stanley Mazeroski stood at a place in time he'd wanted more than perhaps even he knew and he cried. Not simple tears falling softly upon an old man's cheek, but all-consuming, chest-swelling sobs big enough to swallow most of his 65 years whole. Certainly the sobs were big enough to claim him, a simple man who years before had been swept up into a destiny and role bigger than he ever saw for himself.

Mazeroski, the Pirates' brilliant second baseman who defined second base play through most of the 1950s and '60s and who struck the game's most historic home run to end the 1960 World Series, had written 12 pages of notes leading up to the Sunday afternoon of August 5, 2001. Cooperstown would open its doors to him, Dave Winfield, Kirby Puckett, and writer Hilton Smith. As part of the ceremony, living inductees are expected to give speeches. As someone spurned by the Baseball Writers Association of America for the 15 years he was eligible to be on their ballot and then for another five by the Veterans Committee, Mazeroski had lived and waited longer than most.

Winfield went first, and for 23 minutes he spoke. For 2½ minutes, Mazeroski then tried. It's difficult to remember what Winfield said before him, and what Puckett said after him. But Maz's time at the microphone that went off the rails pretty much from line one spoke to the best meaning of what it is to be a Hall of Famer because it came from who he was.

In the hours after he hit the home run that beat the New York Yankees in Game 7 of the 1960 World Series—the only home run to end a World Series Game 7—Mazeroski could not be found among the revelers that overtook Pittsburgh. He could not be found in some restaurant or club, fielding backslaps and well wishes and drinking their free drinks. Rather, he found joy in the quiet of a park bench near Forbes Field. "Sitting on that bench was easier than this," he said. "There wasn't a soul around—just a squirrel or two. That was so relaxing. But this…. From the day I was elected to the Hall of Fame, I was worried about this day. I knew this was gonna happen."

He cried.

After several aborted starts, he finally gave in. "You can flush these 12 pages down the drain…. I want to thank all of my family and friends for making their long trek up here to hear this crap. Thanks everybody…. That's it. That's enough." He sat down.

He cried.

And more than a few others, including several of the 40 living Hall of Famers on hand, did as well. "I'm not ashamed to admit it," Puckett said.

Bill Mazeroski smiles while holding his plaque during his induction at the Baseball Hall of Fame in Cooperstown on August 5, 2001. (*Pittsburgh Post-Gazette*, Peter Diana)

Steve Blass was one of 13 former Pirates teammates who made the trip. The emotional Mazeroski he saw on stage was not a surprise. "For all the things he achieved, the greatest compliment you can give him is to say he never changed," Blass said.

He cried.

"It was maybe one of the shortest speeches," master of ceremonies George Grande said. "But it was one of the most wonderful moments."

Because it was not about the words. It was Bill Mazeroski, who nine years later would be faced with the same challenges of balancing the player the world knew with the man he was when the Pirates unveiled a statue of him outside PNC Park—only the fourth player so honored in franchise history.

"Geez, how could anyone ever dream of something like this?" Mazeroski began. "All I dreamed of was being a major league player. I didn't need all of this."

He spoke—or tried to—for three minutes this time. But his emotions got the best of him again.

He cried.

True, as always, to his words.

45 Move Over, Babe

In 68 years of October baseball, only one player had managed to hit three home runs in a single postseason game. Fittingly, that player was Babe Ruth. The game's most legendary home-run hitter accomplished the feat twice—against the St. Louis Cardinals in Game 4 of the 1926 World Series and again against the Cardinals in Game 4 in '28. Then, for 43 autumns, he stood alone; alone, until the afternoon of October 3, 1971, when Ruth received some unlikely company. On a Candlestick Park field in San Francisco that included future Hall of Famers Roberto Clemente, Willie Stargell, Willie Mays, and Willie McCovey, it was a stocky 25-year-old first baseman from Frostburg, Maryland, by the name of Bob Robertson who became just the second player in major league history to homer three times in one postseason game.

It was Game 2 of the 1971 National League Championship Series, a game the Pirates had to win to avoid going down 2–0 in the best-of-five series. Recent history wasn't in their favor. The Giants had beaten the Pirates six straight times at Candlestick and 11 times in the previous 14 meetings there. Robertson went 2-for-4 in the Game 1 loss but had given no indication in that game or for most of the previous two months that he had one home run in his bat, let alone three. Although he hit 26 in the regular season, he hadn't hit one since August 25 while batting .253 with only three extra-base hits. By the end of the day, all those numbers would be little more than dust in the famed Candlestick jet stream and Robertson would admit to reporters, "I was proud of myself."

Most people would be.

Down 2–1 in the top of the fourth inning, he hit a high drive to right field off starter John Cumberland that 6'6" Giants right fielder Dave Kingman leaped for against the fence, got his glove on, but ultimately couldn't bring back. It was as close as the Giants got to slowing Robertson's home-run barrage. With two runners on in the seventh inning, he hit a long drive into the left-field seats off Ron Bryant to extend the Pirates' lead to 8–2. He then made it 9–2 leading off the ninth with a homer to a third different field—a long drive to center off Steve Hamilton.

His box score line read better than his line for the entire month of September: 4-for-5, 1 double, 3 home runs, 4 runs scored, 5 RBIs. "That fellow at first base was nasty," exclaimed Giants manager Charlie Fox.

Nasty and historic.

"Days like this just don't happen every day," Robertson said.

Few quibbled with his statement of the obvious. The Pirates won 9–4 and evened the series at a game apiece. More importantly, riding the momentum of Robertson's monster day that helped them win a game in a park where a jinx storyline had begun to percolate in the corners of the clubhouse and press box, they would return to Three Rivers Stadium and close out the series with wins in Games 3 and 4—wins that righted their course toward October 17, which would lead to the franchise's fourth World Series title.

As for Robertson, he homered again his first time at bat in Game 3 off Juan Marichal, giving him home runs in three successive plate appearances and four of five. Although he would remain with the Pirates through 1976, he would never again enjoy the type of overall success he had in 1970–71 when he averaged .278, 26 home runs, and 77 RBIs. After hitting 53 home runs in those two seasons, he would hit just 50 in the next five and be out of the game by age 32. Nothing he ever did, though, can diminish the importance of that afternoon in Candlestick Park nor the line he occupies just below Babe Ruth's in the postseason record books. Six other players have since homered three times in a postseason game, but only Robertson can claim that, for a time, it was just him and The Babe.

Jim Who?

Three days after the Pirates hired Jim Leyland as the franchise's 33rd manager on November 20, 1985, a headline in the *Pittsburgh Press* asked, "Can Leyland succeed in a job built for failure?" The

Pirates had just finished last in the National League East Division for a second consecutive year, the team had drawn barely 9,000 fans a game to cavernous Three Rivers Stadium, a cloud of uncertainty hung over the team's future in Pittsburgh, a pungent stink still lingered from baseball's Pittsburgh Drug Trials of two months before, one of the most popular managers in team history had been fired, and general manager Syd Thrift had just hired Jim who?

Nearly 11 years later, so much was as it had been then. The Pirates staggered toward a second consecutive fifth-place finish in the National League's East Division, the team was last in the National League in attendance, the franchise's financial future was again in doubt despite the presence of a new owner, bitterness and resentment remained from a 1994 labor dispute that killed the World Series and threatened to do the same to small-market franchises like the Pirates, and their beloved manager announced late in the year that he would be gone after the season. Yet the morning after Leyland managed his final home game on September 25, 1996, the headline in the paper read: "Pirates' fans to Leyland: Thanks for the memories."

Such was the measure of the impact Jim who? had on Pittsburgh and Pittsburgh had on him. He went on to manage the Marlins, Rockies, and Tigers. He would win a World Series in 1997, manage in two others, and place himself on the threshold of writing his name among the 10 winningest managers in baseball history by the end of 2013. Yet for all his travels, he never left Pittsburgh and the Pirates never left him. What's that they say about never forgetting your first? The Pirates were Leyland's "when he was just another hard-working nobody." And had it not been for a confluence of events in 1996 that included a sport that threatened its small markets, a new owner whose eyes were bigger than his wallet, the gutting of his roster, and the prospects of a never-ending rebuilding process, Leyland could have seen them being his last, too. "I don't pretend to think I can make 23 years like Chuck Noll," Leyland said not long after the legendary Steelers coach retired in 1991, "but the highlight of my career would be announcing my retirement as manager of the Pirates."

That, of course, never happened.

Between those bare days of November 1985 and the lengthening shadows of September 1996, Leyland—along with the arrivals of Barry Bonds, Andy Van Slyke, and Bobby Bonilla—helped return promise and prominence to the franchise. And he did it in such a way that Pittsburghers could relate to him. "People in Pittsburgh are appreciative of hard work. I don't think it's me. I think they just appreciate somebody who works hard," he said.

He wasn't always by the book, but he was always honest. In his second season, the Pirates flirted with .500, in his third they finished second, and by the start of 1990 were about to embark on a run of three consecutive division championships. Leyland cried after each. And he cried with every fan when they came up stunningly short of the World Series in each of those years, not the least of which was the 1992 disappointment in which they were one out from an NL pennant—an out they never got because Francisco Cabrera and Sid Bream had other destinies. Along the way, he was known to smoke a lot of cigarettes—many on the job—and to speak with a voice that was poured out of a gravel pit and then knicked up at the edges with rough sandpaper. He managed 1,716 games and won 851. He got married to a woman he met in the Pirates' offices. They had two children and another who was stillborn. He was twice named manager of the year. And he grew and aged from the unfamiliar dark-haired 40-year-old third-base coach plucked off Tony La Russa's Chicago White Sox staff to the oh-so-familiar more-salt-than-pepper 51-year-old who would have made his father proud. In all those wins and losses, triumphs and tragedies, tears and cigarettes, there was the feeling Leyland was doing it all right along with every fan "because we got to know him better than any sports figure in the history of this city."

Perhaps that is why when that day came in '96 that he knew he had to go, those who would have claimed he "should be the poster boy for what makes Pittsburghers angry about sports figures," who would have said he was jumping ship and questioned his loyalty, were few. Instead, when he managed his final home game—an 8–7 loss to old friend La Russa and the St. Louis Cardinals—he received not boos but long, from-the-heart standing ovations each time he ventured from the dugout and then again in several curtain calls afterward.

He wouldn't be remembered for bringing a World Series to Pittsburgh, but as one Pittsburgh columnist wrote, he would be remembered "as a man who has touched the heart of Pittsburgh like few sports figures before him." As a message on the Three Rivers scoreboard that night read, "Dear Jim, you'll always be a Pittsburgh guy. Thanks for the memories. Thanks for the pride."

Fairly heady stuff for a man who was introduced to the city just 11 years before simply as Jim Who? And as he was wont to do, it made him cry.

47 The Other Game

During the time of the Waner brothers and the Great Depression, of Pie Traynor and World War II, there was another game in town. Some might argue, particularly in Pittsburgh, a better game. Sadly, no one ever had the chance to find out on the field. There was Major League Baseball. There was Negro League Baseball. And never—officially, anyway—were the two to meet because of the decades-old "gentlemen's agreement" among major league owners that kept minorities out of the majors. It was an agreement that wouldn't be broken until Jackie Robinson stepped across the line at Brooklyn's Ebbets Field on April 15, 1947. Yet the Negro Leagues were as much a part of Pittsburgh in the 1930s and '40s as the Pirates, and arguably more successful. While the Pirates were settling into the longest postseason drought in franchise history—33 years from 1927 to 1960—the city's Negro League franchises, the Homestead Grays and Pittsburgh Crawfords, were winning championships, wowing fans—black and white—and on many days drawing bigger crowds.

As far back as the late 1980s, the Pirates embraced this parallel history. It isn't Pirates history, but it is Pittsburgh baseball history. And they have done so in a way unlike any other major league franchise. Since 2006, fans who enter PNC Park's left-field entrance are met not only by ticket takers and program vendors, but by Satchel Paige, Josh Gibson, Cool Papa Bell, Oscar Charleston, Buck Leonard, Judy Johnson, and Smokey Joe Williams—all Crawfords/Grays stars. Their statues with attendant interactive kiosks that explain their importance to Pittsburgh and to baseball, fill Legacy Square, an area dedicated to the city's rich black baseball heritage. To walk through that gate is to walk through Pittsburgh past.

In no other major league stadium will a visiting fan find a display of this magnitude dedicated to the Negro Leagues. But then, no other major league city had teams like Cumberland Posey's Grays and Gus Greenlee's Crawfords. Pittsburgh was the center of black baseball in the East. Five of the first six Negro League players enshrined in Cooperstown played for the Crawfords and/or the Grays. Officially, the two teams combined to win 15 league titles from 1930 to 1948 and three Negro World Series championships. The Grays won every Negro National League title from 1937 to 1945. Yet it wasn't necessarily playing each other where players like Paige and Gibson made their names, but in barnstorming tours and All-Star games against major leaguers and away from the influence of big league owners. It was in those games that feat became story and story became lore.

A player like Paige, colorful and talkative and a speedballing pitcher who would eventually play five seasons in the majors long after his prime because he was Satchel Paige, was a favorite and often a headliner. Bell, it is written, was so fast he scored all the way from first base on a bunt against the Bob Lemon All-Stars in 1948. Williams boasted a 21–7 record against white teams, including wins against Walter Johnson, Grover Cleveland Alexander, Chief Bender, and Rube Marquard.

But it was Gibson, a quiet catcher raised in Pittsburgh with "the strength of two men," who was arguably the greatest of them all. The inconsistent annals of the Negro Leagues can't agree on how big a man Gibson was or how many home runs he actually struck. However, his accomplishments and the testimonials of those who saw him play before he died in 1947 might give fans 80 years later some idea of both. He is credited with hitting 84 home runs for the 1936 Crawfords (in a 170-game season) and more than 800 in his career.

"If Josh Gibson had been in the big leagues in his prime, Babe Ruth and Hank Aaron would still be chasing him for the home-run record," Johnson said in the late 1990s. He is the only man to hit a ball out of old Yankee Stadium.

"The most imposing hitter ever," said Hall of Famer Monte Irvin. In 1946, just months before he died and already noticeably ailing, he still led the Negro National League in batting.

"One of the best natural hitters I've ever seen," said Honus Wagner.

It was—and still is—a shame that not everyone had that chance. Rooted in that regret is the foundation of Legacy Square—a reminder of what was, but also what could have been.

48 Der Bingle

John Galbreath owned two Kentucky Derby winners—Chateaugay in 1963 and Proud Clarion in 1967. Barney Dreyfuss built the Pirates into the first dynasty of the twentieth century and rated a plaque in Cooperstown. Even Kevin McClatchy bore the name of one of the last great newspaper families of the twentieth century. Yet no Pirates owner held the stature or fame of one minority shareholder in the Galbreath group that purchased the Pirates from the Dreyfuss family on August 8, 1946, for $25 million. His name: Harry L. Crosby. Fans—scratch that, the world—knew him by something more familiar: Bing Crosby. For the time, he was Jay-Z buying into the NBA's New Jersey Nets or Jennifer Lopez into the NFL's Miami Dolphins. Only bigger. Much bigger.

In Crosby, Galbreath brought to the organization a persona matched by few men in the history of pop culture. He was at his height of popularity at the time he joined the Pirates' family. From 1944 to 1948, Crosby was the No. 1 Hollywood box-office draw each year, was twice nominated for the Academy Award for best actor (he won in 1944 for his role as Father O'Malley in *Going My Way*), and also hit the radio and record charts with 60 singles, 11 of which hit No. 1. "Just imagine something five times stronger than the popularity of Elvis Presley and the Beatles put together," said Tony Bennett of Crosby's heyday. It was said at the time that "the voice of Bing Crosby has been heard by more people than the voice of any other human being who ever lived."

Incredibly, the song that he is best known for didn't even fall in this five-year window. In the 1942 film *Holiday Inn*, Crosby introduced Irving Berlin's "White Christmas." It hit No. 1 on the record charts at the end of October, stayed there for 11 weeks, and ultimately earned him a spot in America's homes at Christmas ever since. According to the *Guinness Book of Records*, the record has sold more than 100 million copies around the world.

Yet Crosby was not an owner in name only. He was a sportsman and a fan. He thrived on competition. When his schedule allowed, he was a visible face around the team. There are numerous pictures of him at Forbes Field with Ralph Kiner, Honus Wagner, Branch Rickey, and other team members. He appeared as himself in the 1951 film, *Angels In The Outfield* that featured the Pirates, and he was known to make reference to the team when kibitzing with comedian and actor Bob Hope, himself a minority owner with the Cleveland Indians. Hope and Crosby gave birth to the "buddy movie" with a series of "Road to ..." movies from 1940 to 1962 (i.e. *Road to Singapore, Road to Morocco,* etc.) in which the discerning moviegoer can also find inside references to the team. Video of Crosby in a Pirates uniform and Hope in an Indians uniform can also be found on YouTube ("Baseball's Bustin' Out All Over") discussing their teams' prospects in 1947.

Reports of Crosby's ownership stake varied from as little as 7 percent to as much as 25 percent during his association with the team that ended only with his death in 1977. Perhaps his greatest contribution as an owner, though, came 33 years afterward with the discovery of video no one—not even the originating network—believed existed. In September 2010, a producer going through old kinescopes of Crosby shows and recordings in a Crosby wine cellar happened upon one Crosby had requested of Game 7 of the 1960 World Series—the game that ended on Bill Mazeroski's dramatic home run. Crosby, too nervous to watch it live, had made a point of being out of the country when it was played. But, in case they won, he wanted to be able to watch it upon returning. They did. And he did. And then, until it was televised in an MLB Network special in December 2010, was not seen from first pitch to last by anyone for 50 years after NBC showed the game on the afternoon of October 13, 1960.

49 The Rickey Dinks

By the time he was named general manager of the Pirates after the 1950 season, Branch Rickey was 69 and had already cemented his place in history. With the St. Louis Cardinals from 1919 to 1942, he developed the model for the modern farm system while steering the Cardinals to six National League pennants and four World Series championships. More famously with the Brooklyn Dodgers from 1943 to 1950, he helped break the game's color barrier by signing and then orchestrating the promotion of Jackie Robinson to the major leagues. Yet if there was a belief that he was some sort of baseball swami, that notion came to be soundly dispelled during his time with the Pirates from 1951 to 1955. It was the time of the Rickey Dinks.

The moniker, a play on the term rinky-dink (meaning amateurish or of generally inferior quality) and the name of the man who ran the club, was at once derisive and yet playfully—almost affectionately—comical. The Pirates that Rickey inherited were already a losing ballclub, having lost 83 and then 96 games in 1949 and 1950. However, where the great Rickey took them, no one would have imagined. He took them to depths beyond Bad and into the realm of So Bad They Were Good in the way *Plan 9 From Outer Space* and *Roadhouse* make movie fans stop when they stumble over them on cable.

So bad…

Manager Billy Meyer told his 1952 team, "You clowns can go on *What's My Line* in full uniform and stump the panel."

So bad…

A sometimes-hitting catcher named Joe Garagiola turned parts of three seasons with them into enough material to form the basis for a successful broadcasting career with NBC in the 1970s and '80s. "Opposing pitchers would get into fistfights over who was going to start against us." Ba-dum-bum!

So bad…

Even with the National League home-run leader Ralph Kiner in the lineup for Rickey's first two years (1951–52), the Pirates still finished a combined 87 games out of first place.

So bad…

Out-of-town sportswriters were reduced to taking pity on them. Said one scribe in a futile search for something nice to say: "Of all the clubs in the league, your team hit the hardest foul balls."

Rickey had arrived with a five-year plan. It didn't include veteran holdovers like Wally Westlake and eventually Kiner. It did include a roster full of kids with names like Dino Restelli and teenagers Tony Bartirome and Bobby DelGreco, and the O'Brien twins, Eddie and Johnny—young players all that Rickey believed would benefit from major league trial-by-fire but who came to be remembered mostly as being overwhelmed poster children for some of the most inept baseball in franchise history.

From 1952 to 1954—the heart of the Rickey years, the height of the Rickey Dinks—the Pirates lost more than 100 games each season while going a combined 145–317. Of the three squads, none was worse than Meyer's '52 team that went 42–112. It not only finished 54½ games behind NL champion Brooklyn, but 22½ behind seventh-place Boston. In the entire twentieth century, only four major league teams lost more games in one season. "In an eight-team league, we should've finished ninth," Garagiola said. Despite the fact Kiner was still with the Pirates, that team scored the fewest runs of any in the majors (515) while allowing the most (793), committed the most errors (182), hit 22 points below the NL average of .253, and never went more than two games without losing.

"We've got everything but ballplayers," Meyer said.

While funny, that wasn't entirely true. Aside from Kiner, who would be traded early in the '53 season, the shortstop on that '52 team was a recent graduate of Duke by the name of Dick Groat. The rotation included Bob Friend. By the middle of the decade they would be joined by Roberto Clemente, Vernon Law, and Elroy Face. Still, it would be several years before that group coalesced into the team that would become one of the most revered in club history; several years after Rickey was gone, if not the memories—and the jokes—about the teams that bore his name.

50 Angels in the Forbes Field Outfield

Long before the Walt Disney Co. got hold of it in 1994 and re-shaped it to create synergy between the box office and the California Angels, the major league team in which it had a minority stake at the time, the movie *Angels In The Outfield* was all Pittsburgh, all Pirates. The original film was released in 1951 and starred Paul Douglas, Janet Leigh, and—important for older Pirates fans who dream of re-visiting the ballpark of their youth and young Pirates fans who never had the chance to take in a game there—Forbes Field.

The opening sequences alone are worth searching out the movie. Other than home plate and a piece of the wall, Forbes Field long ago was wrecking-balled into memory. The first minute or two of *Angels* gives fans the chance to visit what is no longer there. It opens with a

As the last game ended at Forbes Field on June 28, 1970, fans poured out of the stands to gather souvenirs, overrunning a scheduled ceremony. The scoreboard was picked apart number by number. (Pittsburgh Post-Gazette, Ed Morgan)

long, slow panoramic scan of the Pirates' home from 1909 to 1970, giving a sense of the stadium that is impossible to capture in old game clips. Like some long-lost postcard found in an old trunk, the right-field roof over which Babe Ruth hit his last home run is seen, as is the scoreboard and clock toward which Yogi Berra would run in vain nine years later in an attempt to run down Maz's homer. Also there is the temporary "Kiner's Korner" fence in left field, the batting cage that was stored in deep center field because no one would ever hit a ball that far, and the University of Pittsburgh's Cathedral of Learning that towered over the park in left.

The Odd Cameo

Movie goers in 1968 probably didn't make much, if any, note of it. But Bill Mazeroski earned a page in the IMDB movie database for his "role" in that year's popular buddy comedy *The Odd Couple* that starred Walter Matthau and Jack Lemmon. Sportswriter Oscar Madison (played by Matthau) is in the press box at Shea Stadium, covering a Mets-Pirates game, when he's taken away by a phone call from neurotic roommate Felix (played by Lemmon). It causes him to miss Mazeroski hitting into a triple play that saves the day for the Mets and leads to no small source of comedic aggravation for Oscar. Mazeroski's "hit" had actually been filmed before an actual Mets-Pirates game in 1967. Producers gave him 10 minutes to get it done. "I knew I had to hit a liner to the third baseman," Mazeroski said. "The first pitch, I hit a line drive that went just foul. The second one, I hit a one-hopper right to third. He caught it, stepped on third, threw to second, threw to first, a triple play. Now that took talent."

It's the least director Clarence Brown could give us. After all, Pirates general manager Branch Rickey gave him use of the stadium at no charge. The only stipulation was that the film's world premiere be held in Pittsburgh. It was—at the Loew's Penn Theater, now Heinz Hall, the home of the Pittsburgh Symphony Orchestra.

As for the movie itself, Douglas plays Guffy McGovern, the gruff, foul-tempered, fists-first manager of the bumbling last-place Pirates. Unbeknownst to him, an eight-year-old orphan girl prays to St. Gabriel to help him and the Pirates. The angel agrees, but only if McGovern will change his ways. If only life could have imitated art. The real Pirates lost 90 games in 1951, finished seventh in the eight-team National League, and would look back at '51 as high times in comparison to the standings nightmare into which they were about to descend. From 1952 to 1954, they lost 112, 104, and 101 games, respectively, and were often referred to as "The Rickey Dinks" in derisive honor of their general manager. Surely, not only orphans prayed for divine intervention in those lost years.

The movie made $1.4 million at the box office. For comparison's sake, that year's Academy Award winner for best picture—*An American in Paris*—took in $4.5 million. More than a half-century after its release, it still rates three stars out of four from noted reviewer Leonard Maltin. Douglas continued to act in movies and on TV until his death in 1959. Rod Serling, creator of the TV classic *The Twilight Zone*, even wrote an episode specifically for Douglas—"The Mighty Casey"—based on his *Angels* character. Douglas died the day after filming ended, and the episode was later re-shot with Jack Warden in Douglas' role. Leigh would also continue to act through the 1950s and '60s, appearing in such films as *Houdini* and *The Manchurian Candidate*, but she would be best remembered for making Americans think twice before taking a shower as the object of Norman Bates' affections in Alfred Hitchcock's *Psycho*.

51 I'll Walk Home

In an odd and indirect sort of way, Pirates broadcaster Jim Rooker could have blamed light-hitting Philadelphia second baseman Steve Jeltz, who chose that night of nights to hit two of his five career home runs. Or he could have blamed Pirates pitcher Bob Walk, who somehow found a 10–0 lead a tad much to work with. Or how about Jeff Robinson, who wild-pitched in the tying run in the eighth inning so that fellow reliever Roger Samuels could come in and ensure he'd never pitch in a Pirates uniform again by facing just four batters to let in four more runs?

Rooker knew better, though. It wasn't just one of them that did him in the night he taunted the baseball gods at Philadelphia's

Pittsburgh Pirates announcer and former pitcher Jim Rooker hugs his grandchildren, Brett and Tyler (right) Scruggs as he returns to Three Rivers Stadium in Pittsburgh. Rooker walked from Philadelphia to Pittsburgh as a result of saying that he would walk to Pittsburgh if the Pirates lost the June 8 game against the Phillies in which they took a 10–0 lead in the first inning. The Pirates lost. (Pittsburgh Post-Gazette, Darrell Sapp)

Veterans Stadium. It was all of them. And, most of all, it was the foot he stuck in his mouth about the time the Pirates were finishing up a 28-minute top of the first inning in which they'd scored 10 runs against Phillies pitchers Larry McWilliams and then Steve Ontiveros. Working on the Pirates TV broadcast, Rooker told play-by-play man John Sanders, "If we lose this game, I'll walk home."

Well, of course, anyone who knows anything about history and declarations knows what happened next. The Titanic sank. Apollo Creed lost. New Coke didn't sell. *Ishtar* bombed. And the Pirates coughed up a 10–0 lead the night of June 8, 1989, and lost to the Philadelphia Phillies 15–11. "By the sixth inning, I had a feeling," Rooker said. Then Jeltz, who went to the plate more than 2,000 other times in his career and managed only three other home runs, hit his second of the night. "You're going, 'This is not good.' It got to the point where you knew the Pirates weren't going to win."

Still, Rooker thought a few jokes at his expense from the Philadelphia media after the game would be the end of it. But apparently, the size of the blown lead coupled with the size of his guarantee had fans calling in to the team's radio station the next morning, wondering how Rooker's walk home was going. They were almost offended to find out he'd flown home with the team.

"There were a ton of people calling," Rooker said. He was trapped. What was he to do? Then inspiration hit. He would make the marathon walk to raise money for charity, provided sponsors could be lined up. "Too many people came forward…unfortunately," he joked to a reporter from MLB.com some years later.

Rooker and a friend went into training. Rooker had pitched for the Pirates from 1973 to 1980 and won 82 games, but nothing he'd done in the major leagues prepared him for, ahem, the road ahead: a 320-mile walk from Veterans Stadium to Three Rivers Stadium. He and friend Carl Dozzi—and a support group in an RV—set off from Philadelphia on October 5, and for 12 days they walked. And walked.

By the third day, "I really started to question this thing," Rooker said. But they walked some more. And by 11:00 AM on October 17, they could see the Pittsburgh skyline. By mid-afternoon, they were entering Three Rivers through the center-field gate. They raised more than $81,000 for charity, and Rooker—three pairs of shoes and countless blisters later—came away with a better appreciation for how lucky he'd been that he said what he did where he did.

"I could have said it in Los Angeles."

52 The Baron of the Bullpen

For an idea how important Elroy Face and his trademark forkball were to the Pirates during his 15 years in uniform and in what high regard he was held, you need only look to the day general manager Joe L. Brown sold him out of town. It was August 31, 1968. Face was 40, and the Pirates were headed for a sixth-place finish in the National League. Brown had decided to sell Face—one of the great relief pitchers that history has largely forgotten—to the Detroit Tigers. The Tigers at the time were trying to fend off the Baltimore Orioles for first place in the American League. Before the Pirates took the field at Forbes Field that afternoon to face the Atlanta Braves, the Tigers had agreed to pay the Pirates a reported $100,000 for Face.

The Pirates were not about to let Face simply leave town, though. This was not just another name on the transactions wire. This was a man who had appeared in 801 games in a Pirates uniform dating to 1953, set a major league record in 1959 by going 18–1 (his .947 winning percentage is still a record), and who insisted he was better in 1960 when he had 10 wins, 24 saves, and a 2.90 ERA in 68 games and then saved a record three games against the New York Yankees in the World Series. This was a man who Stan Musial called "the best relief pitcher around" and of whom Yogi Berra said, "I'm just glad I'm in the other league." For this kind of man, a handshake wouldn't do.

Manager Larry Shepard plotted something more fitting. After starting pitcher Steve Blass retired Braves leadoff hitter Felipe Alou in the first inning, Shepard went to the mound. He sent Blass to left field to replace Carl Taylor and called in Face, who by then knew something was in the works. "An usher told me, and then another, and I began to wonder," he said. Face took the mound for the 802nd time. He threw just one pitch. Felix Millan grounded out to shortstop Freddie Patek. Shepard then returned to the mound, brought Blass back to the mound, and wished Face well. In the process, Face not only got one last hurrah, but by appearing in his 802nd game with the Pirates, he tied Hall of Famer Walter Johnson of the Washington Senators for the most games pitched with one team—a record that stood until San Diego's Trevor Hoffman broke it in 2007.

Face had earned that day long before. In the 1950s, the bullpen was more often the place where those too young and untested or too old and ineffective were stashed. Rookie manager Danny Murtaugh envisioned something greater when he replaced Bobby Bragan in 1957. He asked Face, then 29, to buck history and become his ace out of the pen. The modern closer was born and so, too, was "The Baron of the Bullpen"—a nickname given Face by *Pittsburgh Post-Gazette* sportswriter Jack Hernon. Despite Face being just 5'8" tall and weighing only 155 lbs.—hardly the fire-breather we've come to expect of the role—it would be a name well-earned over the next decade, and no more so than in that historic season of 1959.

"The only word you could use to describe it was amazing," said teammate Harvey Haddix, who had 12 perfect innings in Milwaukee that same season. "He was always a good pitcher…but that season he was beyond good."

Pittsburgh Pirates great Elroy Face shows his famous split-finger pitch.
(*Pittsburgh Post-Gazette*)

In his fourth appearance of '59, he pitched two innings against Cincinnati on April 22 at Forbes Field. The Pirates scored twice in the bottom of the ninth to win 9–8. The comeback gave Face the first of what would be 17 consecutive victories and 22 in a row dating to his last five decisions of 1958. He wouldn't lose until the first game of a doubleheader on September 11 in Los Angeles when, protecting a 4–3 lead, he gave up an RBI triple to Junior Gilliam and a game-winning single to Charlie Neal. Incredibly, it was his 98th appearance since his previous loss on May 30, 1958. Unlike his descendants, many were multiple-inning outings. He finished the season 18–1—a record for wins by a relief pitcher in addition to being the highest winning percentage in history—with 10 saves and a 2.70 ERA. "It was one of those years when nothing went wrong," Face said.

Ironically, you won't find the father of the modern closer on the team's career saves list. While he is acknowledged to have saved

188 games in a Pirates uniform, 30 more than recognized leader Kent Tekulve, Major League Baseball did not officially recognize the save until 1969—the season Face appeared in his final major league game.

53 Save of the Century

It was the mid-1990s, and for the second time in a decade it looked as if the franchise that had called Pittsburgh home for more than a century, that had won five World Series and had given the game some of its greatest moments and players, was about to fail. Attendance was down to just 905,517 in 1995. Losses—on the field and at the bank—mounted, including about $18 million in '95 alone when the team went 58–86 in only the third of what would become 20 consecutive losing seasons. Its stadium was cold and outdated. The region still reeled from the shuttering of the steel industry in the late '70s and early '80s. The stars of the team's brief resurgence in the early '90s, Barry Bonds, Bobby Bonilla, and Doug Drabek, had all left town for teams that could afford them. The group of civic and corporate leaders that had saved the team for Pittsburgh in 1985 wanted out. Could a buyer be found who not only wanted to buy a distressed franchise in a baseball economic climate still scarred from a disastrous labor battle in 1994 but a buyer who wanted to keep it in a small market upon which that economic climate offered little but rain and gray skies?

After several starts and stops, the city and owners found one in a 33-year-old golden boy by the name of Kevin McClatchy, part of a distinguished California newspaper family. He was a suitor owners had earlier rejected. But with the city's and team's first

Pittsburgh Pirates manager Jim Leyland (left) holds up a Pirates jersey with "McClatchy" stitched on the back with No. 1 for new owner Kevin McClatchy (right). (Pittsburgh Post-Gazette, Peter Diana)

choice found to be wanting—wanting of cash, to be specific—and deadlines approaching to find a buyer who would sign on to keep the team in Pittsburgh, he was the suitor who ultimately won the team's hand. On February 13, 1996, he purchased the Pirates, their debts, and their humbled image for $90 million—a sum cobbled together through a list of investors so long that it filled nearly a typewritten page. Prominent on the list was $5 million from G. Ogden Nutting. That name would loom larger over time. McClatchy's personal stake was about $8 million to $12 million. That would prove to be troublesome even before his first season as managing general partner was over.

But on that day in early 1996, Kevin McClatchy was the savior of the franchise. "I guarantee you we will make this a baseball town," he promised. "I look forward to that challenge." How his hand played out over the next decade shouldn't obscure that fact. The list of prospective buyers after him as 1995 gave way to '96 who were willing to commit to Pittsburgh was neither long nor viable. McClatchy had passion. He had commitment. He had ego that made him believe he could succeed. He had a tireless work ethic that made him believe that would be enough. He had a seat right behind home plate that made him visible. And perhaps most importantly, he had it written into an agreement with the city as part of the sale that if a new stadium was not built for the team within five years, if financing was not in place within three years, he could sell and/or move the team. That was 1996. PNC Park opened in 2001.

What McClatchy didn't have was money. Money to buy the team, yes. Money to run the team, no. "I do not have the wealth that Disney or Ted Turner or George Steinbrenner or a lot of these folks have," McClatchy said of fellow major league owners. If he had, he wouldn't have needed to come up with so many investors during the purchase process. It was a sign of the future that no one seemed to read. It was a sign that ultimately went up in neon when, despite increased attendance and TV ratings that first year, payroll was slashed, what few established players the team had were traded away, the budget for player development and the farm system was gutted, and manager Jim Leyland was allowed to walk. "This is baseball by the seat-of-your-pants management," one Pittsburgh columnist wrote.

It never got better for McClatchy. PNC Park got built, a new labor contract gained revenue sharing for small-market franchises, and Major League Baseball even threw Pittsburgh a bone when it returned the All-Star Game to the city in 2006 just 12 years after it had previously been there. But the losing continued. Players on the outside didn't want to play for the Pirates. Players on the inside didn't want to stay. It even reached the point where on a Tuesday night in 2003, veteran Kenny Lofton and promising young third baseman Aramis Ramirez had to be traded to the Chicago Cubs for basically nothing just to purge salary from the books. From 1996 to 2006, the Pirates record was 783–996—a combined 213 games under .500.

By 2006, McClatchy's sway internally was all but gone. With so little of his own money in the team, he had to establish and then deal with a five-man board of directors—a board that over time had come to be controlled by Bob Nutting, son of the investor in McClatchy's initial purchase group and whose family now had the most money in the team after buying out other minority investors. In early 2007, Nutting replaced McClatchy as principal owner, and by mid-year he was out as chief executive officer, too.

McClatchy would never again occupy his regular seat behind home plate. He had not made them winners in five years as he had promised in 1996. He had not only not ended the cycle of losing that took root in 1993 but had made it worse. But the fact that, at the end, there was an empty seat to take note of at all in a stadium built for a team that had remained in Pittsburgh, that was because of him, too.

54 Flat-Out the Best

Ask a fan of a certain age which Pirates pitcher turned in the best single performance of the 1971 World Series, and without hesitation they'll reply, "Steve Blass." A good answer. And it would be wrong. True enough, Blass turned in the biggest performance on the biggest day in the biggest game that October when he threw a complete-game four-hitter to beat the Baltimore Orioles 4–1 in

Nelson Briles in October 1971. (Pittsburgh Post-Gazette)

Game 7 and give the franchise its fourth world championship. It was brilliant. It was memorable. And it was still not the best.

That distinction belongs to another right-hander who was as comfortable with a microphone on stage in nightclubs during the offseason as he was in a major league stadium, who occasionally fell flat on his stomach during his follow through and who wasn't even a regular in the starting rotation until September after coming over from the St. Louis Cardinals in an offseason trade that had sent center fielder Matty Alou to the Cardinals.

Nelson "Nellie" Briles, at 28 and already in his seventh major league season, was at once the most logical and illogical of choices to get the ball from manager Danny Murtaugh in Game 5 with the Series tied at two games apiece. In 1967 while with the Cardinals, he had gone 14–5 and started—and won—Game 3 of the 1967 World Series against the Boston Red Sox. A year later, he went 19–11 and started World Series Games 2 and 5 against the Detroit Tigers. He also, for a variety of reasons, had experienced a dropoff "on a bright career which seemed ready to be blighted during the 1970 season," Jimmy Jordan of the *Pittsburgh Post-Gazette* wrote. When he joined the Pirates, was he a reliever or a starter? Not until September did Murtaugh seem to settle on the latter. Briles responded by going 3–1 with a 1.74 ERA down the stretch, then Murtaugh did not use him at all in the National League Championship Series against the San Francisco Giants.

Because of that, Briles hadn't pitched in nearly two weeks when he took the mound in front of 51,377 at Three Rivers Stadium that Thursday afternoon. No one had any reason to expect what he delivered. By the time he walked off that same mound nine innings and 2 hours and 16 minutes later, Briles had allowed just two hits—a single by Brooks Robinson in the second inning and one by Boog Powell in the seventh—while pitching the Pirates to a 4–0 shutout and a 3–2 series lead.

Afterward, Briles was a mixed bag of emotions and feelings, of relief and vindication, of elation and fulfillment. "It's been a long two years," Briles said, alluding to his falloff in St. Louis and then his season of fitting in with the Pirates. "This game today meant the most to me of any game I've ever pitched."

He didn't overpower batters. He just got them out like few pitchers—Pirates or otherwise—in postseason history ever had. He faced just two batters over the minimum. He struck out two. He walked two. No Oriole ever got as far as second base. Even when he fell over at the end of his delivery and wound up flat on his belly, as he did several times that afternoon, the pitch still somehow found its mark.

The evidence suggests that this wasn't just the best game by a Pirates pitcher in the 1971 Series; this was the best postseason pitching performance in franchise history. Statistically, only Babe Adams' six-hit, 8–0 shutout of the Detroit Tigers in Game 7 of the 1909 World Series rivals it in terms of result and runs allowed. "Flat out, Briles pitched the best game of his life," wrote William Leggett, who covered the Series for *Sports Illustrated*. How good was Briles? Consider that when he was finished with his day's work, there were only five pitchers in the history of the World Series who had allowed fewer hits in a game. And of those five, only three had pitched complete-game shutouts as Briles had.

55 Hit Masters

The Pirates' signature through baseball's generations has been their ability to hit. Until 2013, no team produced more batting championships in the game's modern era. Beginning with Honus

Wagner's run of eight National League titles in 12 seasons from 1900 to 1911 and extending through Freddy Sanchez's championship in 2006, Pirates managers penciled 25 batting champions into their everyday lineups—a number unsurpassed until Miguel Cabrera earned No. 26 for the Detroit Tigers in 2013.

The batting titles have been won by Hall of Famers (Wagner, Paul Waner, Arky Vaughan, and Roberto Clemente). They have been won by MVPs (Dave Parker and Dick Groat). They have been won in every decade but two since 1900, coming up empty only in the 1950s and '90s. They have been earned with averages as high as Wagner's .381 in 1900 and as low as Bill Madlock's .323 in 1983. They have been won against each other, as in 1977 when Parker hit .338 to teammate Rennie Stennett's .336. And they have even been won brother against brother, as in 1966 when Matty Alou hit .342 to beat out brother Felipe of the Atlanta Braves (.327).

But it's unlikely any were won under stranger circumstances than that won by 33-year-old outfielder/third baseman Debs Garms in 1940. For much of the season, fans weren't even aware he was in the race. With no uniform criteria and no central statistical source, it was often left to publications such as *The Sporting News* and the nation's major daily newspapers to be arbiter of who was in and who was out when they published league leaders.

In that light, Garms' .345 average at the end of July wasn't even considered—or published—among the NL batting leaders. The reason was that Garms at-bats and games played had been limited through May and June by a knee injury. But in August, he got hot while the acknowledged leaders faded. By the end of an August in which he hit .390 (48-for-123), his average was up to .369, which was 40 points better than published leader Bama Rowell of the Boston Bees. By mid-September, the margin stood at 60.

Some writers began to raise the embarrassment factor that the NL batting champion might hit as low as .320 (or worse), a champion's number not seen in 20 years. Meanwhile, Garms had shown himself to be the league's best hitter over the previous six weeks. Support for his "candidacy" cropped up from such disparate sources as former pitching great Dizzy Dean and *The New York Times.*

On the other side, noted *Washington Post* writer Shirley Povich argued, "Both big leagues two years ago passed a rule at the behest of the Baseball Writers Association demanding that a player must go to bat 400 times in a season before he can win the league batting championship..." Except both leagues had not signed off. The American League had, the National League had not, said NL president Ford Frick.

Frick subsequently determined—with two weeks left in the season—that if a player appeared in 100 games it "would be sufficient prerequisite for the championship." In its timing, it foreshadowed the ruling he would make as commissioner 21 years later that Roger Maris would have to break Babe Ruth's single-season home run record in 154 games, otherwise an asterisk would be placed next to No. 61 if hit in any game thereafter.

As of the announcement on September 19, Garms had played in 93 games. The Pirates had 11 remaining. The name of Debs Garms suddenly materialized atop the NL batting leaders of 1940 in papers from New York to San Francisco. To emphasize the confusion, a visit to the daily leaders on the baseball historical website retrosheet.org from September 19, 1940, to the end of the season on September 29, 1940, will not show Garms as the NL leader on any day, but instead Chicago's Stan Hack. Only on the site's final leaders for 1940 will an asterisk appear that declares Garms the NL batting champion.

Had Garms not been so far ahead of Hack, Frick's ruling and the war of words could have turned ugly. In 36 at-bats after Frick's statement, Garms managed just five hits. His average dropped from .375 to its final .355. Still, it was 38 points better than Hack, and it was achieved in 358 at-bats and 103 games. Hack had 603 at-bats and played in 149 games.

Freddy Sanchez became the Buccos' 25th National League batting champion by going 2-for-4 on October 1, 2006, in the season-ending 1–0 shutout of the Cincinnati Reds at PNC Park. (*Pittsburgh Post-Gazette*, Peter Diana)

Garms played just one more season with the Pirates and hit .264 in 1941. Four years later, a criterion was adopted—for both leagues—that a player must average 2.6 at-bats per team game to qualify for a batting title. In 1957, it was revised to 3.1 plate appearances. And somewhere in the conversation, the name of Debs Garms was brought up—the 14th of the Pirates batting champions, and certainly the oddest.

56 Murdered

Several times in their long history, the Pirates have been able to stake their claim as the best team in baseball. For a season. Sometimes two. Yet even the most skilled barroom debater would find it difficult to compare any of those squads to the team that traveled to Pittsburgh to open the World Series against the Pirates at Forbes Field in October 1927. Many historians don't merely consider that team the best of '27, but the best of all time. The team was the New York Yankees, also known as "Murderer's Row."

Babe Ruth was its transcendent star, making $70,000 a year at a time when the average annual income for the American worker was about $1,000, and he was coming off a regular season in which he'd done the impossible and broken his own unbreakable major league record of 59 home runs by hitting 60—a record that would stand for 34 years and a number that exceeded the entire rosters of 12 of the other 15 major league teams, including the Pirates. But these Yankees could not have gone 110–44, won the American League by 19 games, and outscored opponents by 376 runs with Ruth alone. Their roster featured six future Hall of Famers; spots three through six in their lineup would all one day be in Cooperstown. Four players drove in at least 100 runs, including 175 by cleanup hitter Lou Gehrig and 164 by Ruth, who batted third. Waite Hoyt led the American League with 22 wins, and Wilcy Moore (2.28), Hoyt (2.63), and Urban Shocker (2.84) finished 1-2-3 in earned run average.

The Pirates of 1927 had Pie Traynor and the Waner brothers—Lloyd and Paul. Paul led the National League in batting (.380) and Lloyd in runs scored (133). But the odds were against them. They had outlasted the St. Louis Cardinals and New York

Giants to win the National League pennant in a thrilling race, but neither the Cardinals nor Giants had Ruth, Gehrig, Bob Meusel, and Tony Lazzeri in the middle of their batting order. The Pirates needed to play a near-perfect series. They would not.

The Pirates committed four errors in the first two games and lost by scores of 5–4 and 6–2. Both were played at Forbes Field and attracted more than 41,000 fans each day. Such was the Yankees' mystique by the late 1920s, and specifically that of Ruth, that Pittsburgh fans' disappointment in defeat was paradoxically surpassed only by the failure of Ruth to hit a home run in either game. While the home fans pulled for a Pirates win, they also came hoping to see a Ruth clout the likes of which they'd only read about in those days before television and interleague play. Until October 5–6, 1927, Ruth had played only an exhibition game in Pittsburgh. "Local fans were loath to have the Bambino spoil their team's chances," wrote *Pittsburgh Press* sports editor Ralph S. Davis, "and yet it was only natural for many of them to pull for him to spring some of his sensational stunts." While Ruth did not homer in Games 1 or 2, he did go 3-for-7 with a run batted in—his final games in Pittsburgh until he returned for a memorable last hurrah eight years later in the greys of the Boston Braves.

Such was the Yankees' momentum that when the series left Pittsburgh after Game 2, it wasn't to return that October. And, as it turned out, not for 33 Octobers. Going for the jugular and a 3–0 series lead, Yankees starter Herb Pennock retired the first 22 Pirates in Game 3 before Traynor broke up his perfect-game bid with a one-out single to left field in the eighth inning. Pennock finished with a three-hitter and an 8–1 win—a win in which Ruth homered and knocked in three runs and Gehrig drove in two.

It is here worth noting that a pitcher named Johnny Miljus—a Pittsburgh native—might perhaps have found it fortunate that the Yankees had that 3–0 lead entering Game 4 the next day at Yankee Stadium. Had the series been anything but one-sided, his name might yet be spat more than spoken. Because it was in Game 4 that the Pirates played their best game and that Miljus made the sort of history that tends to stick to a man. This history would be recalled 45 years later on a rainy afternoon in Cincinnati and with Bob Moose on the mound.

The score was tied 3–3 going into the bottom of the ninth. Miljus, who enjoyed his best season of seven in the majors that summer with eight wins and a 1.90 ERA out of the bullpen, had been on in relief of Carmen Hill since the seventh—the inning the Pirates had tied the score on a sacrifice fly by Paul Waner. The Yankees loaded the bases with no one out, but Miljus battled. He struck out Gehrig and Meusel. It brought Lazzeri to the plate. Miljus' first pitch was a ball. If only his second could have been so mundane. Instead, he threw a pitch so wild that catcher Johnny Gooch barely got his glove on it. The ball caromed toward the Pirates dugout. Yankees runner Earle Combs bounded home with the game-winning and series-clinching run—the only World Series ever to end on a wild pitch. "It was a terrible moment for Pittsburghers…who saw their Buccaneers go down into oblivion as one of the poorest world series teams in the entire history of the classic," Davis wrote.

How poor? The Yankees outscored the Pirates 23–10. The Yankees, led by Ruth who batted .400 with two homers and seven RBIs, outhit them .279–.223. Of the 36 innings played, the Pirates led for only 2½ and never later than the third inning. Lloyd Waner managed to hit .400 to pace the Pirates, and Clyde Barnhart drove in four runs. But they would have needed so much more to beat these Yankees. The Pirates might have been the best team in the National League that year, but the Yankees team that swept them has proved against time to be the best team of any year.

57 They Named a Disease After Him

There had already been symptoms in the spring of 1973. Six times in his first 11 starts he'd failed to make it past the fifth inning. Even hidden in a complete-game win at San Diego in mid-May were six walks and a hit batsman. "It'll take care of itself, I kept telling myself," wrote Steve Blass in his 2012 book, *A Pirate For Life*.

It never did.

During a three-game series in Atlanta in mid-June, the symptoms blossomed into a full-fledged case of the "disease" that would eventually bear his name. He started the series opener. Over 3⅓ innings, he allowed the Braves five runs on eight hits, two walks, a hit batsman, and a wild pitch; a pitching line that could actually have been worse had he not picked off Ralph Garr in the first inning or induced John Oates to ground into a double play to limit the damage to two runs in the second.

Knowing he had a star in trouble, manager Bill Virdon brought Blass back two nights later in the series finale, this time out of the bullpen. What's that about getting back on the horse? What ensued was "a complete meltdown," Blass wrote. "I was no longer just walking guys or hitting batters or getting hit hard. I was throwing the ball in back of hitters and behind their heads. It was just god-awful." His contributions to an 18–3 blowout loss: 15 batters faced in 1⅓ innings, seven runs, five hits, six walks, three wild pitches, and so many questions about where the pitcher had gone that won 78 games from 1968 to 1972 and had pitched a three-hitter and a four-hitter in complete-game victories against the Baltimore Orioles in the 1971 World Series that even today they still get asked.

In 1972, Blass had walked a career-worst 84 batters but in a career-high 249⅔ innings while winning 19 games. In 1973, he

The Pirates' 1971 World Series Game 7 battery of Steve Blass (left) and Manny Sanguillen acknowledge the cheers of the fans at PNC Park on June 21, 2011, during a pregame ceremony celebrating the 40ᵗʰ anniversary of the 1971 World Series championship. (Pittsburgh Post-Gazette, Peter Diana)

again walked 84 but in just 88⅔ innings. He also hit 12 batters and threw nine wild pitches while winning three and losing nine, prompting some people to wonder how he even won the three. The World Series hero not only couldn't win anymore, he couldn't guarantee he would even put the ball anywhere close to the catcher's mitt. And he never would again, a crushing and humiliating end for a pitcher who was only in his early 30s, never had a sore

Life? He Wasn't Kidding

The title of his autobiography is *A Pirate For Life*, and Steve Blass wasn't far off. He was 18 when he left his hometown in Connecticut to sign with the Pirates and has been affiliated with the organization ever since. As of the end of the 2013 season, the clock was at 54 years and counting—one of the longest affiliations with the team of any player in franchise history. He made his professional debut with the organization's Kingsport minor league team in the summer of 1960, made his major league debut in 1964, earned 103 wins and two more in the 1971 World Series in a pitching career that lasted through 1974, became active in the franchise's alumni association and community service projects, then moved into the broadcast booth in 1983, where he's been a staple for 30 years. And through it all, he became not just a Pirate but a Pittsburgher for life—both badges he wears with pride.

"The one thing I've found with Pittsburgh is that if you reach out a foot and a half, people here will reach out 10 miles and a half," Blass said.

arm, and had been so dependable that he made 30-plus starts each of seven seasons from 1966 to 1972. Through that '72 season, his career numbers stood at 100–67 with a 3.24 ERA. God only knows what could have been.

He looked for that pitcher in the bullpen, in the minor leagues, in video, in the bottom of a beer bottle, in hypnotism, in a psychologist's office, and in transcendental meditation. He never found him. It got so bad that his own teammates didn't want to get into the batting cage against him.

Before spring training of 1975 ended, he retired—the first victim of what has become known as Steve Blass Disease, the inexplicable loss of control when throwing a baseball. Others have experienced it since. Pitchers Mark Wohlers and Rick Ankiel. Infielders Steve Sax and Chuck Knoblauch. Even a catcher, Mackey Sasser. As these and other cases have surfaced, Blass—who has since come to grips with what happened and will often pitch just for the joy of it in fantasy camps—has come to expect a call or 20 from reporters around the country, looking for insight and perspective.

He told Ron Cook of the *Pittsburgh Post-Gazette* in 2012 that he always laughed when people talked of other players with control problems having Steve Blass Disease. But he was crying inside. "Many nights, I would sit in this backyard by myself until 3:00 or 4:00 in the morning and keep asking, 'Why is this occurring?' I never had a sore arm. I thought I was going to pitch forever. I just wanted to know why this was happening to me."

What can he tell them?

He knows two things. First, he wouldn't wish what he went through on anyone. And second, "Only two players ever had a disease named after them, Lou Gehrig and me." He has used that line often through the years. It always earns a laugh. And it always beat the alternative—having people feel sorry for him. He lived his dream. Its ending just had a wild twist.

58 Operation Shutdown

It's hard to believe that one player could come to personify two decades of losing baseball—particularly when so many (un)worthy candidates came and went over the 20 seasons from 1993 through 2012 in which the Pirates set the North American professional sports record for continuous years of futility. But one 32-year-old journeyman managed the impossible.

His name is Derek Bell.

The name will make most any Pirates fan put Bell ahead of the likes of Chad Hermansen, Zach Duke, Brant Brown, and Brad

Eldred. All initially embodied hope for a franchise on an epochal search for a season with an 82nd win at its end. All proved false. But none so false to their sensibilities as Bell.

When the struggling, cash-conscious Pirates signed Bell, a veteran with a World Series ring and a couple 100-RBI seasons on his resume, to a two-year, $9.75 million contract between the 2000 and 2001 seasons, manager Lloyd McClendon said the signing would send "shockwaves through baseball." He couldn't have been more correct, though for all the wrong reasons.

In return for the first $5 million, Bell gave the Pirates a .173 batting average, five home runs, and 13 RBIs in 183 plate appearances over 46 games in 2001—none after July 3 because of problems with his left knee. Fans could in some perverse way have been okay with that. After all, by the end of Year 9 of losing, they'd become resigned to disappointment and dashed promise.

What couldn't be forgiven was what he did to earn the remaining $4.75 million. What couldn't be forgotten was what played out the following spring as the Pirates tried to pick up the pieces from a 100-loss season—the worst since their run of losing began. Despite his abysmal 2001 numbers, and despite the fact that he was hitting just .148 through the first half of the exhibition season, Bell was somehow surprised to find out that he was actually competing for the starting job in right field with Armando Rios and Craig Wilson. Rios was coming off a knee injury but had hit 14 homers in the first half of 2001 with the San Francisco Giants. Wilson had batted .310 with 13 homers in less than 200 plate appearances as a part-time player in his first season with the team, and McClendon and general manager Dave Littlefield were trying to find a way to get his bat into the lineup.

"Nobody told me I was in competition," Bell responded to a reporter when asked about the three-way battle in mid-March, just two weeks before Opening Day. "If there is a competition,

Derek Bell strikes out in the third inning against the Detroit Tigers in the home opener at McKechnie Field in Bradenton, Florida, on March 1, 2002, during spring training. (Pittsburgh Post-Gazette)

somebody better let me know. If there is a competition, they better eliminate me out of the race and go ahead and do what they're going to do to me."

What became clearer in the ensuing moments was an incredulity that separated Bell not only from reality but from the rest of the team's failures of that period. In the process, he reserved for all time his own line item in that ledger of red ink.

"If it ain't settled with me out there," Bell continued, "then they can trade me. I ain't going to hurt myself in spring training battling for a job. If it is [a competition], then I'm going into operation shutdown. Tell them exactly what I said. I haven't competed for a job since 1991."

They heard. So did much of the baseball world. Bell never appeared in a Pirates uniform again—or in any other major league uniform. A day after the story overheated talk radio the Pirates reported Bell was out with an injured right groin. He would take therapy at the team's complex, then return to his 54' yacht docked near the Pirates' spring complex in Bradenton, Florida. In the interim, he attempted to paint himself as a victim. "Ever since I came over here, it seems like everybody hates me," he said. It was a disgust he couldn't begin to comprehend. Less than two weeks later, the Pirates released Bell, swallowing the $4.75 million still owed him.

Bell's parting words still resonate: "Just tell them I got in my yacht and rode out into the sunset."

The team's final return on investment was $1,950,000 for each of his five home runs and $361,111.11 for each of his 27 hits. Ultimately, those obscene numbers are how his 11-year career is most remembered. Not the player who won a World Series ring with Toronto in 1992, who once finished fourth in the National League batting race, and who was a member of the vaunted Killer B's lineup in Houston with Bagwell, Biggio, and Berkman.

Just two stinging words: Operation Shutdown.

In a fitting epitaph, one Pittsburgh writer opined, "Bell is the consummate Pirate because he lives on a boat and steals money."

It is why he is alone on the poster of broken promises. Because he didn't even try—or seem to care that he didn't.

59 After Midnight

Games that last 6 hours and 39 minutes tend to have a long shelf life in the memory bank. Games that drag out for 19 innings manage to spark conversation even years after. Certainly, games that begin on one day and end on another find a way of writing themselves into team lore. They are games that begin in reality and always manage to end in absurdity or, at the very least, "like backyard baseball—no rules, just go," said Daniel McCutchen, the night's, er, morning's losing pitcher. On most any other day after most any other game, a losing pitcher would likely be serious-minded, maybe sullen or angry. In the wake of the Pirates' record-setting 4–3 19-inning loss to the Braves on July 26–27, 2011, in Atlanta, McCutchen was heard to say, "It was awesome." Awesome, anyway, in the way camping out in the backyard with only a kerosene lantern to ward off the shadows can be awesome when you're 10.

And as with any good tale told on such a late midsummer night, it even came with a bad guy dressed in black and wearing a mask. Okay, he was really dressed in blue. But black? Blue? At that hour, it's really just a quibble. And it doesn't alter the fact that he cost the Pirates the game. How much more home-plate umpire Jerry Meals cost the Pirates that night became the focus of some debate the rest of that season. But at the very least, even he admitted he cost the Pirates that game at Turner Field.

After Atlanta's Jason Heyward singled in two runs in the bottom of the third to tie the score at three, neither team scored for the next 15⅓ innings during which the better part of the game's 609 pitches and 41 players were used up. By the time the game reached the bottom of the 19th and the clock was pointed toward 2:00 AM, the game had already set a Pirates franchise record for longest by time—breaking the record of 6:12 set against San Diego in 1979. McCutchen had already been on the mound since the 14th inning, and Atlanta's Martin Prado had already managed to go 0-for-9, a feat performed by only 30 men in the live-ball era. Yet what transpired from then on made them footnotes and Meals sports talk fodder for the rest of that summer.

With one out, McCutchen walked Julio Lugo. Jordan Schafer singled him to third, then moved to second on defensive indifference. With his bench and bullpen depleted, Braves manager Fredi Gonzalez had no choice but to let Scott Proctor—Atlanta's eighth pitcher—bat for himself. Proctor fouled off the first pitch, then he swung and missed at the second. If McCutchen could get Proctor, Prado, lugging that oh-fer, was due up next. Sending the game to a 20th inning seemed doable for the Pirates. Then Proctor swung and sent a bouncer toward Pedro Alvarez at third base. Lugo broke for the plate on contact. Alvarez threw home to catcher Michael McKenry. Lugo slid. McKenry, in front of the plate but up the third-base line, applied the tag well before Lugo got near the plate. Thinking Lugo was out, McKenry popped up, looking to see where Schafer was. It was then that he realized Meals had called Lugo safe. McKenry spun around in disbelief even as the Braves' dugout emptied in celebration.

"I saw the tag, but [McKenry] looked like he ole'd him and I called him safe," Meals explained. Only after seeing replays did he realize his mistake. "On one particular replay, I was able to see that Lugo's pant leg moved ever so slightly when the swipe tag was attempted by McKenry. That's telling me…he should have been ruled out."

Meals' *mea culpa* came too late to save the Pirates, who until that trip to Atlanta had been surprising contenders in the National League Central Division after finishing under .500 the previous 18 seasons. The loss began a free fall in which the Pirates lost 12-of-13 games—a death spiral during which they went from being tied for first place to being 10 out in less than two weeks. By the end of the season, their deficit was 24. And while there were any number of bona fide reasons for their collapse, the loss that night in Atlanta—and Meals' role in it—became the Frankenstein for frustrated talk-show callers who didn't know where to stick the business end of their pitchfork but needed to stick it somewhere.

60 The Cobra

Dal Maxvill, a veteran of two World Series championships playing alongside the likes of Bob Gibson and Lou Brock with the St. Louis Cardinals in the mid-1960s, would not have figured to be awed by much after more than a decade in the major leagues. But when a 22-year-old rookie measuring 6'5", 235 lbs., and with a bravado to match walked into the Pirates' clubhouse in the middle of 1973, he was heard to say, "I don't know who he is, but I'm glad he's on our side." The impressive figure was Dave Parker, just up from Triple A. It was the beginning of an 11-year stay that would be defined by the extremes of size. Big talent. Big numbers. Big contract. Big expectations. Big letdown. Big breakup.

The void that Parker walked into that season was also large. Roberto Clemente had been dead less than seven months. Three different players—Manny Sanguillen, Gene Clines, and Richie Zisk—had already been used in right field. Parker joined the mix. By 1975, after platooning with Zisk, he couldn't be kept out of the everyday lineup any longer. Zisk moved to left field, and Parker blossomed in right. He hit .308 with 25 home runs and 101 RBIs as the Pirates won the National League East Division championship. In 1977, he hit .338, won the NL batting championship, and made the first of four All-Star teams in five years. A year later, he hit .334 with 30 homers and 117 RBIs, won his second consecutive batting title, and was named NL Most Valuable Player. By 1979, he had become the first player in major league history to sign a contract that averaged $1 million a season. And, if asked, Parker would have told you he was worth it.

"There's only one thing bigger than me, and that's my ego," Parker told Roy Blount of *Sports Illustrated* before that '79 season. After he hit .310 with 25 home runs and 94 RBIs to help the Pirates win their fifth World Series title that fall, someone told teammate Willie Stargell that Parker had referred to him as his idol. Stargell replied, "That's pretty good, considering that Dave's previous idol was himself."

But, as Dizzy Dean said 40 years before, "It ain't bragging if you can do it." And for five brilliant years, Parker did it. In some ways, he was a super-sized Clemente—the proverbial five-tool player with "Made in Cooperstown" forged into the steel handle of each. He didn't just hit .300 each of those years or account for 851 runs (RBIs plus runs scored minus home runs). He threw out 26 runners in a single season (1977). He earned MVP honors in the 1979 All-Star Game after cutting down a runner at third base and another at home. Three times he had 10 or more triples. Twice he stole 20 bases. "He's one of those rare individuals who come along every 15 or 20 years," Stargell said. "Rare, and unique, and strong." Parker's future seemed so bright that historian Lawrence Ritter, in writing the book, *The 100 Greatest Baseball Players of All Time* with Donald Honig, included Parker even though he was only just reaching his thirties.

The heights to which Parker ascended only made the fall over the next four years so stark and not a little bit tragic. There were injuries. There were issues with weight. There was that brashness that wore well in good times but not so well in bad. And there was cocaine. He began using after the 1979 championship season and did so, he said, until quitting in 1982 because "I felt my game was slipping, and I felt it played a part in it." If so, his epiphany came too late. In 1980, he slipped under .300 for the first time since '74. His power numbers also declined. His numbers fell off still more as injuries limited him to 140 games combined over the next two seasons. About that time the team also began a descent toward lows not seen since the 1950s. Parker, hurting, overweight, and perceived as dogging it, became a whipping boy. Fans booed. Some even threw batteries at him as he stood in right field. "Parker became a villain, the man Pittsburghers loved to hate," Steve Hubbard of the *Pittsburgh Press* wrote.

After a 1983 season in which he hit .279 with 12 home runs and 69 RBIs, Parker had enough and escaped to Cincinnati in free agency. But Pittsburgh was not finished with him. He surfaced as a central figure in the Pittsburgh Drug Trials as they ran their ugly course through the summer of 1985. He was among a long lineup of high-profile players who testified for the federal government in a trial whose stated aim was seven dealers but whose indirect result was to expose the drug problem within the game, within the Pirates' clubhouse, and within the personal life of Pittsburgh's one-time star. The trials renewed old angers. Resentment ran so high that the Pirates took him to court to recoup deferred money still owed him. They settled out of court.

The bitterness of their divorce could hardly have been imagined as a smiling Parker stood back-to-back with Boston's Jim Rice on the cover of *Sports Illustrated*'s 1979 season preview issue, which championed him as the best player in baseball. He would regain some of that mojo in stints with the Reds, Oakland Athletics, and Milwaukee Brewers over the remainder of the 1980s and early '90s. He would finish his career with 2,712 hits, 1,493 RBIs, and 339 home runs. He would even earn another World Series ring with the A's in 1989. But he would never regain the unique status within the game that he once held. And he would never make it to Cooperstown. Never even came close. A player must be named on 75 percent of ballots cast; Parker never appeared on even 25 percent. The drugs? The injuries? The trials? Those years in the early 1980s cost him dearly.

To a lesser degree, they also cost him the chance to fulfill a prophecy made elsewhere in the locker room that day he had so impressed Maxvill. Stargell had hit his 302nd home run the night before to break Ralph Kiner's franchise record, but in talking to reporters he deflected the spotlight. "That man over there," Stargell said, "may break my record in three years." The man toward whom he pointed was Dave Parker. Like the Hall of Fame, it is just another reminder of what could have been when it came to Dave Parker. Could have been and perhaps should have been, but never quite was.

61 The Ultimate Fantasy League Team

The greatest Pirates team of all time never played in Forbes Field or Three Rivers Stadium. It wasn't managed by Danny Murtaugh or Jim Leyland. It never heard the roar of 50,000 fans, yet it is seen by thousands of people every day. It is a team so obvious that it hides in plain sight in downtown Pittsburgh and has done so for more than a decade. Great and overlooked. Bigger than life and just hangin' around. Real and the creation of artist Michael Malle's fan-tastic imagination.

It is the Legends of Pittsburgh mural, a 40' wide by 15' high "team portrait" of 14 Pittsburgh legends selected by the Pirates at the end of the twentieth century and timelessly painted by Malle into a time capsule of the imagination that hangs on the wall of an underpass where Ross Street passes under the Boulevard of the Allies in the city. It is a piece of art that thousands of commuters drive past every weekday morning, yet how many ever take the time to see?

The background is Forbes Field. Yet somehow a bystander swears he hears Shoeless Joe Jackson asking Kevin Costner, "Is this heaven?" The cast of players, lined up and casually posed, stretches from left to right. But not oldest to youngest nor in any way aligned by period or era; instead in the randomness that might be found in a single unit. Honus Wagner stands next to Roberto Clemente, Ralph Kiner next to Clarke. The Waner brothers are next to Murtaugh. Every player is in his prime and ready to play two on a sweet-blue summer afternoon. All are in the uniforms of their day, as meticulously researched by Malle. The mind wonders: Has Clemente flashed back to the modern Forbes Field of 1909 or has Wagner flashed forward to the decaying Forbes of 1960? The soul replies: What does it matter? Here, on this wall, they will never again age as they once did; they will never pass away as they once did. The bystander looks with eyes remembering greatness gone by; the eyes that look back at him do so with a young man's self-confidence of greatness yet to be. The give and take is enduring.

"A little dream we put together," said Malle, a native of Pittsburgh who took three months to paint the original that was then digitally enlarged and mounted on the wall of the underpass in April 2000.

The 14 legends from left to right are Kiki Cuyler, Kiner, Clarke, Max Carey, Paul and Lloyd Waner, Murtaugh, Negro Leagues great and Pittsburgh native Josh Gibson, Arky Vaughan, Willie Stargell, Pie Traynor, Bill Mazeroski, Clemente, and Wagner. Fourteen men. The faces of more than a century of baseball in Pittsburgh. "What this 114 years of tradition is all about," said Pirates owner Kevin McClatchy at the mural's unveiling.

"My pride and joy," Malle said.

And a destination point of any Pirates fan who ever wondered, "What if…"

62 One Mean Lefty

If you sat down and compiled a list of highlights for the Pirates over the course of their first 125-plus seasons in the National League, pitching would not be among them. They've had good pitchers, perhaps some for a time even bordering on great. Yet of the 10 uniform numbers the franchise has retired and hung on the façade of PNC Park, none are pitchers. Likewise, of the 14 Hall of Famers they claim in Cooperstown, none are pitchers.

Yet somewhere in the land that baseball time forgot, in the period before 1900 and the advent of the game's modern era, toiled a left-hander by the name of Frank Killen. He was 6'1", 200 lbs., and reportedly threw so hard that, according to *The Pittsburgh Pirates Encyclopedia*, was one of the reasons the pitcher's mound was moved back to its present 60'6" from home plate.

He was also the only Pirates pitcher ever to win 30 games. And he did it twice.

In 1893, at age 22 and in his first season after coming home from stops in Milwaukee and Washington—he was born in Pittsburgh in 1870—Killen went 36–14 with a 3.64 ERA and 38 complete games. His 36 wins led the National League. Three seasons later, after injuries cut short 1894 and '95, he came back to again lead the National League with a 30–18 record and an NL-best 44 complete games and 432⅓ innings. His 30-win campaign also marks the most recent time a National League left-hander won 30 games.

Certainly, the game Killen played was different. But it also could be argued that no Pirates pitcher dominated his time as Killen did when healthy. Not Deacon Phillipe nor Jack Chesbro. Not Bob Friend nor Vernon Law. Manager Connie Mack claimed that an infected spike wound that left Killen in the hospital for 49 days during the 1895 season cost the Pirates the pennant that season.

Yet for as swift as his ascent was, so was his decline. In 64 starts in 1897–98, he went just 27–34. Late in '98 and still just 27, he was traded to Washington. By age 29 he was out of the majors.

He would eventually operate a hotel on Pittsburgh's North Side and went to his grave in 1939 as not only the last left-hander to win 30 games in the National League, but his 36 wins in 1893 represent the most by a lefty in NL history—marks that still stand regardless of baseball era.

63 So You Left Early?

On a beautiful Saturday afternoon in late July 2001, the Pirates were well on their way to another forgettable loss in what was to become a 100-loss season; it was a season that itself was part of even greater losing, sitting as it did smack in the middle of a historic and embarrassing run of 20 consecutive losing seasons. They trailed the Houston Astros 8–2 in the opener of a day-night doubleheader and were down to their final three outs at the bottom of the ninth inning. About a third of the 32,977 at PNC Park that afternoon had already left, resigned to the fact that loss No. 63 was in the bag. It was a decision that within hours they would regret.

When Aramis Ramirez flied out to left field and John Vander Wal to center, their decision seemed vindicated. One out to go. Houston manager Larry Dierker was content to let reliever Michael Jackson, who had come on to pitch the eighth, finish the game. Closer Billy Wagner certainly wouldn't be needed. Vinny Castilla would dominate the headlines the next day after belting three home runs.

"I counted it as a win," Houston starter Roy Oswalt admitted later.

And why not? With Wagner and his triple-digit fastball backing the bullpen, the Astros had been 49–0 when leading after eight innings that summer.

But a funny thing happened on the way to No. 50. They got hit by a bus crossing the intersection of history and absurdity.

One out to go. Kevin Young doubled. One out to go. Light-hitting Pat Meares homered to left. The score was 8–4 but still only one out to go. No problem, right? Pinch-hitter Adam Hyzdu singled to center. Still no problem, right? Just one out to go. Tike Redman walked. Hyzdu moved to second. Okay. Still ahead. One out to go. Jack Wilson shot a single to left. Score: 8–5.

The buzz in the park built. Dierker had seen enough. Wagner was up, then in. Now it was over, right? Wagner, a small left-hander with a big fastball, was in the prime of a career in which he would save 422 games before retiring in 2010.

And on this afternoon, all he needed was one out. One meek pop-up. One easy grounder to second. One lazy fly to center. Three swings and misses. Any of those. But he got none.

Wagner hit Jason Kendall in the left leg with a pitch. The bases were loaded. What were those fans thinking who had left early? Did they even know? Did they even know that left-handed slugger Brian Giles, who had made the final out of the eighth inning, was somehow getting another at-bat—the potential winning run on an afternoon that had seemed lost 20 minutes before?

"I just thought if we could get him up—you don't want to see Kendall get hit—but I just thought if we could get him up…" Meares said, trailing off into the impossible and unbelievable.

Giles filled in the blank. Against a pitcher who had not given up a home run to a left-handed batter all season, Giles crushed a Wagner fastball. "A line drive that was gone from the instant

Brian Giles rounds the bases after hitting a grand slam to beat the Houston Astros at PNC Park on July 28, 2001. (*Pittsburgh Post-Gazette*, Peter Diana)

barrel met ball," wrote Bob Smizik in the *Pittsburgh Post-Gazette* the following morning. "It screamed into the right-field seats."

If Al Michaels hadn't already coined the phrase, someone surely would have asked, "Do you believe in miracles?" Grand slam. Game over. Pirates win 9–8.

"I was just trying to put it in play and hit it hard," Giles said. "I don't think you ever go up there expecting to go deep. You want to be short to the ball, and he's going to supply the power."

And, oh yes, the Astros never got that one last out. Seven consecutive Pirates batters reached. Seven consecutive Pirates batters scored. The comeback tied a National League record for most runs with two outs in the ninth inning, giving this last-place lineup a spot in the record books next to the 1952 Chicago Cubs who had likewise rallied for a 9–8 win against the Cincinnati Reds on June 29 that season.

Granted, it was only one win. They were still 40–62 when it was over. And they would be 40–63 before the day ended after getting routed in the nightcap 12–3. But as Smizik concluded, "For these few minutes that game didn't seem too important. The Pirates were still 22 games under .500, but in the aftermath of this astonishing victory, who cared?"

64 Hello, Pirates Friends...

Two men arrived in Pittsburgh in 1976, the season after longtime announcers Bob Prince and Nellie King were fired from the Pirates' broadcast booth in a move so controversial it sparked public protests. The first, Milo Hamilton, left after four seasons. The other endured for 33 seasons, surpassing not only Prince but any other man who had worn the moniker "Voice of the Pirates." In fact, Lanny Frattare's tenure with the Pirates is unmatched by all but one broadcaster in the history of Pittsburgh's three major professional sports franchises—one-of-a-kind Steelers sideman Myron Cope, who did Steelers games for 35 seasons. But football on radio was not baseball. Cope never had to be on six months out of every 12. Cope never did more than 5,000 games as Frattare did between radio and television.

Lanny Frattare, the voice of the Pittsburgh Pirates, in the booth at Three Rivers Stadium on September 27, 2000. (*Pittsburgh Post-Gazette*, Peter Diana)

Frattare's career began in 1976 in the heyday of The Lumber Company and ended in 2008 with what some mockingly referred to as the Slumber Company. In between, he gave voice to John Candelaria's no-hitter on a Monday night in August 1976, the Pirates World Series run in 1979, the Jim Leyland/Barry Bonds mini-dynasty of the early 1990s, the Hollywood-esque Francisco Cordova/Ricardo Rincon no-hitter in July 1997, the final games of Willie Stargell, Jim Leyland, and Three Rivers Stadium, the first game at PNC Park, the night in October 1992 when Francisco Cabrera scratched his name into the Pittsburgh sports psyche like a key down the side of a new car, and the first 17 of what would be a record 20 consecutive losing seasons that spanned the late twentieth and early twenty-first centuries.

In that time, he made his mark with a broadcasting-school voice, a consistent delivery, and meticulous preparation. His calls for a home run—"Go ball, get outta here"—and for a Pirates win—"There was no-o-o-o-o doubt about it"—became signatures. His broadcasts rarely devolved into stream-of-consciousness banter or storytelling at the expense of play-by-play. That wasn't him. Despite claiming Prince as a mentor, Frattare was at the opposite end of the broadcast booth from Prince, who wanted to entertain and insert himself into a broadcast as a neighbor and friend might even if it meant failing to call the occasional 6–3 groundout. That was never Frattare. He wasn't Prince, and after a while he seemed to accept that fact of life. How could a man have lasted 33 years in a market that "embraces idiosyncratic announcers" such as Prince and Cope if he hadn't?

"Some broadcasters are great storytellers," Frattare said in a 1995 interview after calling his 3,000[th] game. "I will weave stories into the broadcast, but I will not let that impede my ability to react to a play."

Translation: I am not Bob Prince, never was and never will be. And he might have added, who could be?

It wasn't a fair lot in life. But, paradoxically, it was the cost of doing the thing he most wanted to do. "I remember in my second or third year, I wasn't sure if I was going to get past three years," he said. "It was about then that I realized what a great opportunity I had, and I worried about losing it. I did not want to lose it." And, despite internal tensions within the Pirates' TV broadcast partners in the mid-1990s, he never did.

"When I got here, the chair to the right of the booth, that was the chair that Prince sat in," Frattare said. "[Then] Milo was in that chair at first [when we got here in '76], and when I went into it, that was big for me."

And when he chose to step away from it after the 2008 season, that was big, too. The man who wasn't Bob Prince had put together a body of work that spanned more than three decades and several generations of fans in a job that is traditionally impossible. Mark

Malone was never Terry Bradshaw, Manny Sanguillen was never Roberto Clemente, and Lanny Frattare was never Bob Prince. But the difference between Frattare and the other two was that Frattare lasted and, in his own way, succeeded at one of the toughest roles in professional sports—the next man up after the king is gone.

65 If Not For Him...

Tapping some perverted logic, it could be argued that Pittsburgh sports fans could have been spared the neverending torment of Francisco Cabrera that began late in the evening of October 14, 1992, had pitcher Bob Walk not been so darn good three nights earlier in Three Rivers Stadium. Without Walk's performance, perhaps the Atlanta Braves, already ahead three games to one in the National League Championship Series, would have closed out the Pirates in a disappointing but otherwise mostly forgettable five games. Instead, Walk turned in the performance of his career that, in tandem with a 13–4 rout of the Braves in Game 6, turned the series momentum in the Pirates' favor and thus propelled them toward a date with Cabrera and unforgettable heartbreak in Game 7.

As a rookie with the Philadelphia Phillies in 1980, Walk had started and won Game 1 of the World Series against the Kansas City Royals. With the Pirates in 1990, he started and won Game 1 of the NLCS against the Cincinnati Reds. Yet even with that postseason experience and 92 career wins through more than 400 innings, it was seen as a surprise when, with the season one loss away from being over, Jim Leyland named Walk to start Game 5 instead of Danny Jackson. Primarily a starter from 1988–91, Walk, by then 35, had been moved into a swing role in '92. He appeared in 36 games with 19 starts but only eight after August 1. He went 10–6 with a 3.20 ERA. In just one of his starts had he pitched all nine innings. In fact, he had gone the distance just that once in his previous two regular seasons.

When he walked two of the first four batters he faced that Sunday night, many in the home crowd of 52,929 would have doubted his chances of lasting a few innings let alone nine. Yet when he got Sid Bream to line out to third to end the inning, it would be the only inning in which the Braves had more than one runner on base. The Pirates scored four times in the bottom of the inning thanks to back-to-back-to-back RBI doubles by Barry Bonds, Jeff King, and Lloyd McClendon, and Walk was off on one of the great pitching performances in franchise postseason history.

He didn't allow his first hit until the fourth inning—a double by Bream. He didn't allow a run until the eighth when the Pirates had already built a 7–0 lead. And he didn't leave the game until it was over for just the 14th time in 231 major league starts. What's more, he didn't allow the Braves to entertain any realistic thought of closing out the Pirates after the first inning. He finished with a three-hitter. It not only tied his career low-hit game set 12 years before, but was the lowest-hit game by a Pirates pitcher in the post-season since Nelson Briles tossed his two-hit masterpiece in Game 5 of the 1971 World Series, and it tied Steve Blass' three-hitter—also in the '71 Series—for the second lowest-hit game in franchise postseason history.

"He was outstanding—absolutely outstanding," said Mike LaValliere, who caught Walk that night.

"Our guys felt if the Pittsburgh Pirates ever had a chance to stay alive, Bob Walk gives us that chance," Leyland said. "I think our guys felt, 'We've got a guy out there that we'd want to be in a [fox] hole with. And Walkie came through with flying colors."

He returned hope where there had not been much. At least for a few more days, anyway. And, as it turned out, it was the last real hope of any kind felt along the three rivers for the next 20 years.

The Freak Show

To explain the Pirates' 1997 season would be to explain how a 27-year-old career minor leaguer with no past and no future beat a Cy Young contender on a Monday afternoon in July. Or how a team with a total payroll of $9.1 million remained in a pennant race until game No. 160 of 162 in a world in which a recalcitrant slugger from Chicago named Albert Belle made $10 million all by himself. Or how a bubble-blowing T-ball manager somehow made a city believe in all things freaky. Which is to say that there was no explanation then and there is none now other than baseball is a funny game, Slim Whitman sold more than 100 million records, and people enjoy Will Ferrell movies.

The Pirates had lost 89 games the season before and would lose 93 the season after in what would be Years 4 and 6 of a now well-documented North American professional sports record of 20 consecutive losing seasons. But thoughts of such ignominy were far off that summer when home runs were hit at all the right times, a folk hero was plucked out of a T-ball league in Florida, their starting right fielder jumped all the way from Class A to the Opening Day lineup, and a no-hitter on a Saturday night in July might have been penned on the Warner Bros. back lot of 1940s Hollywood.

The roster manager Gene Lamont broke camp with that spring carried 18 players with two years or less of major league experience. The Pirates' highest-paid player was 29-year-old left fielder Al

Martin, who was to make $2.2 million; No. 1 on the Pirates but just No. 178 in the major leagues. It was a team that preseason pundits expected to be a legitimate threat to the 1962 New York Mets' major league record of 120 losses, and not a threat to the Houston Astros for the top of the National League Central Division—albeit a division derisively referred to that year as "Comedy Central" for its lack of muscle, an analysis given credence by the presence of the Pirates near the top of the standings.

On May 9, after shutting out the Atlanta Braves 9–0 behind Francisco Cordova and the fourth homer of the season from 20-year-old right fielder Jose Guillen, who had made the relatively rare jump from Class A to the Pirates primarily because there were few bona fide candidates standing in his way, the Pirates were 19–15 and in first place. On May 14, they wiped out a 9–6 deficit to Colorado by scoring nine runs in the bottom of the eighth inning keyed by a Martin grand slam. By May 25, when Kevin Young hit an eighth-inning grand slam of his own to rally the Pirates to an 8–6 win in Montreal and make them 24–24 and still just a half-game behind the Astros, broadcaster Greg Brown marveled at all the freaky things that were going on in this Pirates season and for the first time used the term "The Freak Show" to describe the team—a moniker that would come to define that season.

Even when injuries and reality seemed to be catching up with them, the Pirates still somehow conjured the unexpected. By midseason, their lone "big" offseason acquisition, a 32-year-old shortstop by the name of Kevin Elster, was long gone with a broken wrist and other players were coming and going with regularity. The injuries opened the door for a 27-year-old shortstop named Kevin Polcovich, who wasn't even among 70 players invited to camp that spring, and a 32-year-old outfielder named Turner Ward, who was out of baseball and coaching his 6-year-old son's T-ball team in Florida when the Pirates signed him to a minor-league contract in late April. They would come to be Freak Show stars. Ward hit .353

with seven home runs and 33 RBIs after being called up in early July and helped the Pirates to a four-game sweep of the Cardinals that sent the Pirates into the All-Star break at 43–43 and in first place in the division. "I didn't expect this in my wildest dreams," Lamont said.

As for Polcovich, general manager Cam Bonifay admitted, "I would not want to go to war for the next seven years with him as our starting shortstop." Yet from mid-May until he was hurt at the end of August, he played the position as if he belonged, hit .273 with four home runs and 21 RBIs, and won one of the more memorable games in a season of memorable games. With the score tied 2–2 in the seventh inning against Phillies ace Curt Schilling on July 21, he pulled a Schilling pitch down the left-field line for a home run and a 3–2 win. "It was very cool—probably the highlight of my career," Polcovich said. "It was just one thing after another that year."

True enough, his home run came nine days after the freakiest of things in that season's list of Freak Show happenings. On July 12, in front of 44,119 at Three Rivers Stadium and after coming out of the All-Star break with consecutive 7–0 and 10–0 losses to the Astros and the descent to the basement that had been expected since April knocking at the clubhouse door, Cordova and Ricardo Rincon combined for not only the most unforgettable game of that season but of most any Pirates season by pitching a 10-inning no-hitter against Houston. The game went 0–0 into the 10th inning before pinch hitter Mark Smith hit a dramatic three-run homer to win it.

"I think people are starting to believe in us and baseball again," Martin said.

No one knew it then, of course, but the middle of July would be the high watermark. Less than a week later, on July 18, the Pirates lost to the Phillies 8–6 while the Astros beat the Expos 2–0. The Pirates fell out of first place. While they would never fall too far behind the Astros—or the Astros get too far out in front by going just 26–28 in August and September—the Pirates would never regain first place. They were 68–68 on August 30. It would be their last time at .500. The Astros went 14–12 in September, and the Pirates went 11–14, including a two-game split against the Astros at Three Rivers in mid-September when a sweep could have pulled them within 1½ games.

"We've got to rub the bottle and hope the genie comes out one more time," Martin said. It didn't. On September 25, while the Pirates were off before playing Houston for what they hoped would be a season-ending three-game showdown in the Astrodome for the division title, the Astros defeated the Chicago Cubs 9–1 to take a four-game lead with only those last three against the Pirates to play. The curtain closed on the Freak Show.

The Pirates lost two of those final three games to finish 79–83 and five games out of first. Polcovich was the last player to leave the dugout that weekend. "My career was a whole lot like our season," he said. "Expectations weren't very high. We were a bunch of over-achievers. It was frustrating at the end. But all in all, it's something I'll cherish forever."

A year later, Polcovich was out of the majors. The magic of that summer dissipated even faster. The Pirates fell back to 69–93 in 1998 and sixth place. The 1997 season had been an aberration, a true freak of baseball nature. It would be 16 years before they again contended in September.

67 Splashdown

When PNC Park opened in 2001, the juxtaposition of its right-field wall to the Allegheny River excited the imagination. Forbes Field had its right-field roof. Three Rivers Stadium had its upper deck. And

PNC Park would have the river, its own home-run hitter's Everest. Yessir, yessir, step right up, knock it in the drink and win a prize—a spot in stadium history. It wouldn't be easy, but one physicist interviewed in the park's early days estimated—after a few calculations—that there could/would be one or two balls hit into the river on the fly each season. It's a good thing rocket science is not baseball, otherwise America might still be trying to land on the moon.

It wasn't until June 2, 2013—in the ballpark's 13th season and in its 1,002nd game—that Garrett Jones became the first Pirate to knock a ball into the Allegheny on a fly. Many had done it on a bounce, but none without first hitting grass or concrete. What's more, he was only the second player overall. Daryle Ward of the Houston Astros was the first, smashing a drive off Pirates pitcher Kip Wells into the water on July 6, 2002. Then nothing for more than a decade.

As seasons came and went and the park began to give up its secrets and idiosyncrasies, fans and players began to realize hitting the river wasn't so much the distance as it was the direction. Longer

An exuberant baseball fan falls out of his boat as he attempts to catch a home run hit in the Allegheny River during the July 10, 2006, Home Run Derby at PNC Park (Pittsburgh Post-Gazette, Matt Freed)

home runs had been hit than the 443' required to find the river, yet they either bounced in or settled on the concourse or grassy bank beyond the stands. A ball would not only have to be hit far enough and high enough, but in the right spot—practically straight down the right-field line, yet just to the left of the foul pole while charting the following mathematical course: 320' down the line, 21' over the right-field wall, 38' high to clear the stands, approximately 80' across the concrete concourse, and approximately 50' beyond—the expanse between the park and the river's edge. And, of course, the swing has to be just right and mighty.

All those tumblers locked into place for Jones as he awaited the pitch from Cincinnati Reds reliever Jonathan Broxton. "I took that one swing that a lot of hitters take when they're trying to hit the ball far and hard," he said. "It doesn't always connect. But everything just felt like it connected into the ball."

It had the look of a home run from the time it left the bat. Its getaway was quick, its trajectory true and swift and skyward. Yet there was some doubt. For his first two or three steps out of the batter's box, Jones could be seen looking after the ball, leaning into fair territory, willing it to stay to the good side of the foul pole. "When it went out it was high. I didn't know if the umpire might call it foul…. There's a fine line," Jones said, "but right spot, right time."

Officially, Jones' home run was listed at 463', the same as Ward's 11 summers before. Of greater importance at the time, it came with two outs in the bottom of the eighth inning and pulled the Pirates into a 4–4 tie against the Reds. The Pirates would go on to win it in the 11th 5–4. In the grand scheme of things, though, the blast will be remembered long after the final score. In the history books and in its re-telling by the 29,407 who witnessed it.

"And, hopefully, when I'm older," Jones said, "I can bring my son to the game and maybe that trivia question will pop up and I can say, 'See, I wasn't lying.'"

68 Dinner With Manny

There are dozens of eateries scattered throughout PNC Park where you can grab a burger and a beer before the game. But only one place brings with every pulled pork sandwich the chance to shake the hand, snap a picture, or get your ticket stub autographed by arguably the most accomplished catcher in Pirates history. For almost as long as PNC Park has been open, Manny's BBQ has been serving up a taste of the past on the park's outer concourse beyond the batter's eye in center field, a lone piece of living history you can talk to any day there's a ballgame. Get in line. Place an order. And meet Manny Sanguillen, sitting near the cash register in a comfortable, high-backed office chair before practically every home game, holding court, Sharpies and trademark smile at the ready. As one-time Pirates trainer Tony Bartirome said, "If you didn't like Manny, then there was something wrong with you!"

He is decades past his prime, he has added a few pounds, and his slow gait belies the qualities that made him Sangy—agility behind the plate, speed on the bases, and a young man's desire to swing at balls no man ever should have thought about swinging at. Time and appearance can make the old forget how good he was, and the young tend not to comprehend. He is not just some old man telling tales and spinning yarns. For a time, he was one of the best catchers in the National League, and his stories have a place both in the park and in any team history. We just forget sometimes.

Consider:

- He played on the 1971 and '79 World Series championship teams. Fans are likely to remember that he hit .379 in the '71 Series against Baltimore and was behind the plate for every inning of those seven games, including Steve Blass' memorable

Catcher Manny Sanguillen on July 3, 1980. (*Pittsburgh Post-Gazette*)

Game 7 victory. Fans are not as likely to remember that, as a role player off the bench, he drove in Ed Ott with the winning run in Game 2 of the '79 Series.

- He made three NL All-Star teams.
- He twice finished third in the National League in batting, hitting .325 in 1970 and .328 in '75.
- Incredibly, as a catcher he finished in the top five in the NL in triples in 1970 (9) and '72 (8).
- His .296 career batting average is fourth-highest for a catcher since World War II.

In addition to the prose, his resume also includes the poetic:

- On Opening Day 1973 against the St. Louis Cardinals—the Pirates' first game since the death of the beloved Roberto Clemente—it was Sanguillen, one of Clemente's best friends, who started in right field in place of the Great One.
- On November 5, 1976, he was traded—along with $100,000— to the Oakland Athletics for their manager. The manager was Chuck Tanner. Sanguillen would play one year in Oakland before finding his way back to the Pirates.

Even then he knew where he belonged. In a Pirates uniform. Part of Pirates history.

69 The Best Way In

Every stadium in America has a way in. An entrance. A gate. A turnstile. Maybe an arch for style. But only PNC Park has a 994' span of suspended steel and inspiration that transcends time as well as a river. Only PNC Park has an entrance so unique that it was built first and the stadium later. It was built 71 years before the first shovel of dirt was turned and six years before the birth of the man for whom it was to be named, to be precise. Only PNC Park has the Roberto Clemente Bridge, a span that reaches out from the city, crosses the Allegheny River, and empties into the stadium's southern gates and concourses. "The best entrance in baseball that doesn't include the bullpen door swinging open and 'Hells Bells' blaring over the loud-speaker," wrote Jim Caple of ESPN.com in 2003. Caple was among the first to proclaim PNC Park the best ballpark in America.

On game days, the bridge is closed to motor traffic, allowing fans coming from the South a leisurely—and normally uncon-gested—walk from the heart of the city to the game. With a clear view of the stadium and at some points a glimpse into it, the bridge is also a popular spot for pictures. But its real genius occurs once fans are inside. It is then that the bridge is transformed from a utili-tarian walkway into a piece of the park itself—a piece of the skyline that to the eye *is* the outfield wall. No home run will ever clear it, but all paint themselves against it.

It is a tribute to the vision of stadium architects that they saw this possibility and embraced it. And it is a tribute to the bridge's architects that it was something worth embracing. Originally known as the Sixth Street Bridge, it is one-third of the "three sisters" bridges built in the city between 1924 and 1932, a time still two stadiums and several city renaissances away from PNC Park. Its twins cross the river at Seventh Street and Ninth Street. The Sixth Street Bridge—the fourth built over this spot on the Allegheny since the mid-nineteenth century—opened in 1928 and incorporated "beautifully modulated crossings" and "stiff eye-bar chains to keep the spans rigid." It and its sisters were modeled after a similar eyebar-chain bridge in Cologne, Germany, and it was named the most beautiful erected in the United States or Canada that year by the American Institute of Steel Construction. Adding to its place in the park's night-game tapestry, the bridge was lit for the first time in 2002.

But use of the bridge was more than an incorporation of design. It was also the site of compromise. When it became apparent in the late 1990s that a new stadium was to be built, there was a move to name it after Clemente—the Pirates Hall of Famer who patrolled right field for the team from 1955 to 1972 and was still the face of the Pirates to several generations of fans. But to do that would have been to do without the $30 million in naming rights the team ultimately received from PNC Bank—$30 million the team needed to help with its share of construction. Allegheny County's decision to step in and rename the bridge after Clemente as park construction began in 1999 was the next best thing. As time has shown, the bridge has become a signature piece of the park every bit as magnificent and unique as Clemente.

70 A Smiling Sadness

If, in the course of the 24 years that had been his professional baseball career to that point, anyone had harbored doubts about who Chuck Tanner was, about the too-good-to-be-true positive energy he exuded, and about the goodness of heart that had managed to ward off the human corruption that the money, fame, and ego of professional sports can inflict, they were silenced on October 14, 1979, and in the days that followed. With his Pirates on the brink of elimination at the hands of the Baltimore Orioles that afternoon in Game 5 of the 1979 World Series, Tanner learned that morning that his mother, Anne, had died from complications of a stroke suffered three weeks before.

Chuck Tanner savors the 1979 World Series championship trophy on his ride home. (*Pittsburgh Post-Gazette*, Edwin Morgan)

It is said that adversity reveals character. Tanner revealed nothing that he had not showed friend or stranger, teammate or player, during his baseball odyssey from Shenango High School standout in New Castle (Pennsylvania) in 1955 to manager of the Pittsburgh Pirates in the late 1970s.

If he considered leaving the team to grieve, Tanner never let on, neither on that October Sunday nor thereafter. He arrived at Three Rivers Stadium that day with his mother on his mind but with a job to do.

"We knew Chuck as our manager, but we also knew how close he was to his family," said Kent Tekulve, the team's closer, in recalling the scene years later. "We knew this was a powerful loss, and we're sitting there in the clubhouse not knowing what to say to the man."

They shouldn't have worried. Tanner gave them the words. He addressed the team that afternoon before Game 5.

"My mother is a great Pirates fan," he told them. "She knows we're in trouble, so she went upstairs to get some help."

"We're all sitting there feeling sorry for him," Tekulve said. "Well, that gives you a focal point. It's still not going to be easy, but all of a sudden all this other stuff didn't seem so important. We could just go out and play ball."

Play ball they did. They won Game 5 that afternoon. And they won the two after that to give the Pirates their fifth World Series championship.

What part Anne Tanner played, well, only God knows. But after the game that night, his mother dead less than 24 hours, a red-eyed Tanner talked with Marino Parascenzo of the *Pittsburgh Post-Gazette*.

Ahead 3–1 in the seventh inning and scratching for insurance with Tim Foli on third and two outs, Tanner recalled begging for his mother's help.

"Don't profane the memory, don't ask in something so meaningless, so transitory, so achingly empty now as a baseball game," Parascenzo wrote. But this was here and now, and this was the World Series. Tim Foli was on third, and Dave Parker was coming up. Parker had given Anne one of her biggest thrills, Tanner recalled, phoning her from New York on her birthday, and now he was up.

"'I kinda looked up,' Tanner said. He would ask now, just this once. C'mon Grandma, here he is. Let him hit it over the Cardinals sign."

Parker doubled. Not over the sign. But the ball did roll up against it.

The Pirates added three more runs in the eighth and won Game 5, 7–1. Two days later, John Candelaria and Tekulve combined on a 4–0 shutout to even the series. Three days later, Willie Stargell and the Pirates became the third team to come back from a 3–1 deficit to win the World Series, and they did it in front of President Jimmy Carter and a subdued Memorial Stadium crowd in Baltimore. Four days later, Chuck Tanner went home to bury his mother.

71 He Did What?

Hard as it was in an unconnected time before 24-hour cable sports and the worldwide web, and decades before the founders of Twitter and YouTube were even born, Ron Necciai, a 6'4", 190-lb. teenager from Gallatin, Pennsylvania, became an overnight national sensation. Ultimately, he would pitch just 12 times in a

Pirates uniform and win only once while losing six before health problems and dumb luck intervened, but it will always and forever be fun to think of what could have been when it came to Ronald Andrew Necciai—what could have been because of what was in the three months before he arrived in Pittsburgh in August 1952. It is a cliché, but his was the picture in *Merriam-Webster* next to the word *phenom*.

Pitching for the Pirates' Class D Bristol, Virginia, team in the Appalachian League the night of May 13, 1952, Necciai achieved the ridiculously impossible—he struck out 27 batters in a nine-inning no-hitter against Welch. Only one Welch out showed up as anything but a K on the scorecard—a groundout to second base in the second inning. Otherwise, all that Welch had to show for its night at the plate was an error, a walk, a hit batsman, and a passed ball on a swinging third strike in the ninth inning that actually gave Necciai the chance to notch strikeout No. 27 one batter later. "After the game, [catcher] Harry Dunlop said, 'Hey, you had 27 strikeouts,'" Necciai recounted. "I just assumed it had been done before. It wasn't till the next morning when the phone started ringing that I understood it hadn't." Not even close. The major league record at the time was 19, and that had been set in 1884. The minor league record had been 25 by Clarence "Hooks" Lott in a Northeast Arkansas League game in 1941. Newspapers and magazines weren't the only ones calling for Necciai's story. *The Ed Sullivan Show* also called.

More than 5,000 fans crammed into Bristol's Shaw Stadium for his next start. Among them was Branch Rickey Jr., son of the Pirates' general manager, on a directive from Dad to see if Necciai was for real. Necciai threw a two-hitter and struck out 24. "He's a miracle," Rickey told a local reporter after the game. Should he have been that surprised? In Necciai's two starts prior to his 27K gem, he'd struck out 20 and 19. Soon thereafter, the Pirates promoted him to Class B Burlington of the Carolina League.

Including a handful of relief appearances, he left Bristol having pitched 42⅔ innings, giving up 10 hits and two earned runs. Put another way, of the 128 outs he recorded in his brief stay, 109 came on strikeouts. Burlington proved more of the same. He struck out 172 in two months.

The elder Rickey could wait no longer. With his Pirates on their way to a 42–112 record—the franchise's worst of the twentieth century—he brought Necciai to Pittsburgh amid great fanfare and expectation and started him against the Chicago Cubs on August 10. Predisposed to stomach ulcers—a malady that would factor into the premature end of his career—Necciai staggered through six innings. He gave up seven runs on 11 hits and, as incredibly as his 27-strikeout performance three months before, struck out only three. Said catcher Joe Garagiola, "[Necciai] was shaking so bad out on the mound, he couldn't see my signals." He made eight more starts for the Pirates that season and also pitched out of the bullpen three times, but major league fans never saw the pitcher that those in Bristol and Burlington witnessed that summer. In six weeks with the Pirates, he was 1–6 with a 7.08 ERA and more walks (32) than strikeouts (31). He never pitched in Pittsburgh again.

Necciai was drafted into the military in 1953, but the ulcers that had long bothered him led to an early discharge in April. He rejoined the Pirates, but in trying to get in shape too quickly hurt his shoulder—a torn rotator cuff 25 years before it became a fixable injury. He tried through 1953, '54, and '55 to rehabilitate the arm that had earned him the nickname Rocket three decades before Roger Clemens, but it never happened. "I was 23 years old, and it was over," Necciai said.

He went on to have a successful business career, lived a life with no regrets about what might have been, and if any regrets did try to creep in around the edges, he could always take solace and comfort in a comment made by no less than the elder Rickey. "There have only been two young pitchers I was certain were destined for greatness, simply because they had the meanest fastball a batter can face. One of those boys was Dizzy Dean. The other is Necciai. And Necciai is harder to hit."

72 It Only Took 57 Years

The Rookie of the Year Award was first handed out in 1947. Yet until Jason Bay more than a half-century later, no Pirates player would win it. Not Roberto Clemente. St. Louis' Bill Virdon won in 1955. Not Willie Stargell. Chicago's Ken Hubbs won in 1962. Not Dave Parker. San Francisco's Gary Matthews won in 1973. Not Barry Bonds. St. Louis' Todd Worrell won in 1986. But in 2004, Bay ended the drought, becoming the Pirates' first—and so far only—National League Rookie of the Year.

Bay was a soft-spoken, 25-year-old left fielder from Trail, British Columbia. He had arrived in Pittsburgh in August 2003 with no small amount of pressure awaiting him, the residue of the deal that brought him and pitcher Oliver Perez to the Pirates from the San Diego Padres. To acquire them, Pirates general manager Dave Littlefield had to trade the popular and productive Brian Giles. Giles, only 32 and still in his prime, had averaged more than 30 homers and 100 RBIs a season in 4½ years in Pittsburgh. Bay, meanwhile, joined his fourth organization in four years and carried with him a suitcase of unfulfilled promise. One writer compared the trade to one that sent Ralph Kiner to Chicago in 1953. The deal certainly did little to polish Littlefield's image with the fan base, such as it was in Year 11 of the franchise's record 20-year streak of losing seasons. "I understand sports," Littlefield said after

Pittsburgh Pirates GM Dave Littlefield (left) congratulates Bucs left fielder Jason Bay after he received the 2004 Rookie of the Year honors in a ceremony prior to the Pirates vs. Milwaukee Brewers game on April 4, 2005, at PNC Park. (Pittsburgh Post-Gazette)

the trade. "[The fans are] not going to wait to judge your decisions. The grades come out the next day."

While his GM grade-point average in his six years with the Pirates more closely resembled that of Bluto Blutarski, Littlefield was spot-on with this one. By July 2004—11 months after the trade—a Pittsburgh newspaper columnist wrote that the deal "has the makings of one of the biggest heists in recent baseball history." While the Pirates were on their way to a 72–89 record, Perez was on his way to finishing in the National League's top 10 in strikeouts and earned run average. And Bay, after missing the first five weeks of the season recovering from off-season shoulder surgery, was leading all NL rookies in home runs, RBIs, slugging percentage, and on-base percentage, and he was threatening many of the franchise's rookie batting records.

In July and August, Bay hit .312 with 11 homers and 35 RBIs. He was NL Rookie of the Month in June, July, and September. On September 19, he hit his 24th home run to break the Pirates' single-season rookie home-run record shared by Ralph Kiner and Johnny Rizzo. On September 29, Bay knocked in three runs against the Phillies to give him 82—the most by a Pirates rookie in 64 years. Despite going just 2 for his last 26, he finished the season hitting .282 with 26 home runs, 82 RBIs, and a .550 slugging percentage. And he did that damage in only 411 at-bats.

Although San Diego shortstop Khalil Greene was believed to be a serious threat to Bay, when the Rookie of the Year voting was announced November 8, it was Bay in a runaway. He received 25 first-place votes and 146 points to Greene's 7 and 108. "I probably didn't think [winning the award] was possible," Bay said. "I just wanted to establish myself in the big leagues."

He accomplished that, too. Over the next 3½ seasons—until he was traded to the Boston Red Sox at the 2008 trade deadline—he hit .281 with 110 home runs and 358 RBIs and made two

National League All-Star teams. And Giles? He never again realized the numbers he put up with the Pirates. In his six full seasons with the Padres, he averaged .278, 13 home runs, and 66 RBIs.

73 Calling Mr. Blackwell

Do a Google request for the worst/ugliest/what-were-they-thinking uniforms in baseball history and the Pirates' mix-and-match togs of the late 1970s invariably appear on any top 10 list of shame. Those teams are fortunate they were as good as they were or the critiques might've made even Mr. Blackwell feel bad for them. It's hard to knock the all-yellows for making Dave Parker look fat when he's being presented the 1979 All-Star Game MVP. And it's absolutely gauche to take a shot at Willie Stargell's mix-and-match black-and-yellows when he's jumping into a World Series victory mash-up.

Those Pirates do have a ready-made excuse for why they wore this explosion of color and stripes (horizontal and vertical), this expansion of double knit and polyester. It was the 1970s. Enough said. The Pirates were not alone in sartorial bad taste. It was the era of leisure suits, open collars, cowboy hats, and mood rings. When compared to the eyeballs being scarred in other major league outposts in the second half of the decade, it could have been worse. Much worse.

"The '70s were certainly the dark days in baseball uniform history," wrote ESPN.com in its "End of the Century" project in the late 1990s. The Indians sported an all-red uniform that Boog Powell said made him look like "the world's largest blood clot." The San Diego Padres wore a combination of brown and mustard that

Bert Blyleven pitches for the Pirates in 1979. He won 34 games for the Pirates and two more in the postseason in three seasons with the team from 1978 to 1980. (*Pittsburgh Post-Gazette*, Darrell Sapp)

Stargell Stars

While the Pirates uniforms of the late 1970s have been consistently panned through the years, the pillbox hats with their horizontal stripes provided the perfect field for a player of those days to display his Stargell Stars—a gold star the team captain presented to players for various on-field achievements during the Pirates' run to the 1979 world championship. The idea that might have on the surface seemed more kindergarten than major league carried the weight of God in that clubhouse because of the man who awarded them. They said as much about the stature of the giver as the accomplishment of the recipient.

"We fought for those stars," said Bill Robinson, who played for the Pirates from 1975 to 1982. "Those were precious."

So precious, that upon Stargell's death in 2001, adorned on the funeral clothes of many who'd come to say goodbye were single gold Stargell Stars.

left players wondering if they should have been asking customers if they wanted fries with that in one of owner Ray Kroc's McDonald's outlets. And oh, those poor Chicago White Sox. It was criminal what owner Bill Veeck did to the likes of Wilbur Wood, Jorge Orta, and Chet Lemon. He put them in a throwback/beer-league softball outfit that featured knee-length shorts, white knee-high socks, and shirts with open necks and collars—wide collars.

By comparison, the Pirates' uniforms of the time were relatively sedate. After all, it's hard to make black too garish. Fans just never knew what Pirates team—literally—they were going to see each night. From 1977 to 1985, the players' lockers contained some or all of the following: black, yellow, and white pinstriped jerseys; black, yellow, and white pinstriped pants; two different pillbox hats; two different sets of stirrup socks; and two different undershirts. At the height of their mix-and-match frenzy, they utilized 18 different combinations.

The pinstripes were retired after the 1979 World Series, and by 1985 the effects of the '70s finally wore off and the team reverted to basic white and gray. The pillbox hat was the last item to go. It had been brought in during the 1976 season as part of America's bi-centennial celebration and baseball's part in the nation's history. While other participating teams such as the Reds and Phillies discarded it after that one season, the Pirates kept it as part of their new-look uniforms. It lasted until 1986 when, at last, the pendulum of baseball clothing swung back toward a long-lost quality—taste.

74 The Press Box

Before there was Twitter and the 24-hour news cycle and ESPN, before there was television and even radio, there was the baseball beat writer. He is almost as old as the game itself. He has for more than a century marked its wins and losses, painted its stars, captured its hopes, and conveyed its misses. The Pirates have had their share of memorable scribes, but only one can be found on the rolls at Cooperstown. Charley Feeney, a newspaper lifer and transplanted New Yorker who covered the Pirates from 1966 to 1986 for the *Pittsburgh Post-Gazette*, received the J.G. Taylor Spink Award in 1997 and acknowledgment at the Baseball Hall of Fame. Previous winners included Damon Runyan, Grantland Rice, Red Smith, and Jim Murray. Feeney found himself almost embarrassed to be thrust among the men considered the giants of the profession.

"I always looked at myself as a utility infielder in our business," Freeney said. "The next thing you know, they're going to be putting Tommy Helms in the Hall of Fame." He intended for the joke to be on himself. When he later realized his brush of

Former Post-Gazette *baseball writer Charley Feeney in the baseball press box at Three Rivers Stadium. Date of photo unknown.* (*Pittsburgh Post-Gazette,* Joyce Mendelsohn)

deprecation painted Helms, an infielder of modest offensive skills for four teams from 1964 to 1977, he called Helms to apologize. It spoke to his fairness. Not that he shied from a fight. "On a scale of 1 to 10 with 10 being a great relationship, I probably had a 4 with [Roberto Clemente]. I told that to [Bill Mazeroski] one day and he said, 'Pally, you'd better make that a 3.'" But he never went looking for one. To him, everyone was "Pally."

His career spanned Joe DiMaggio to Willie Stargell, Willie Mays to Dave Parker, Leo Durocher to Chuck Tanner. It lasted from New York baseball in all its 1950s glory to Pittsburgh and all its mid-1980s scandal. He was in the Polo Grounds when Bobby Thomson hit "The Shot Heard 'Round The World" in 1951 and in Baltimore's Memorial Stadium when Willie Stargell homered in Game 7 to rally the Pirates past the Orioles in 1979.

He was not the writer of those previous Spink recipients. But writing, Feeney knew, was only part of the job. "He always told me, 'Not all of us can be great writers, but we can all hustle,'" said Ron Cook, who Feeney befriended when Cook was just a 17-year-old starting out in the business and who years later would champion Feeney's case before the Spink voters. "[He] taught all of us a passion for the newspaper business," said Cook, who grew from that 17-year-old kid to become a columnist for the *Pittsburgh Post-Gazette*. "He loved baseball. He loved his job. But most of all, he loved newspapers."

The record will show that in his 20 years in Pittsburgh, he covered six division champions, two World Series winners, and three Hall of Famers in Roberto Clemente, Bill Mazeroski, and Stargell.

And, oh yes, Tommy Helms, too.

75 The Next Great One

Andrew McCutchen was 14 years old and an eighth-grader when he not only played on the Fort Meade (Florida) High School varsity but hit .591. He was 18 when the Pirates tagged him as the hope for the future and selected him in the first round of the 2005 draft. He was 22 when they traded away an All-Star center fielder to bring him to the major leagues. He was 22 years, 9 months, and 22 days old and in his 51st major league game on August 1, 2009, when he became just the 10th player in Pirates history to homer three times in a game. He was 24 when he made his first All-Star team. He was 25 when Pirates brass had seen enough to sign him to the second-richest contract in franchise history—$51.5 million over six years—before spring training in 2012. He was 26 when he led the Pirates to their first winning record and first postseason berth in 21 years and led himself to the brink of the 2013 National League Most Valuable Player Award.

Is it any wonder that descriptions of McCutchen, a 5'10", 190-lb. center fielder, focus not just on his arm, his bat, his glove, his speed, and his power—the proverbial five tools—but also on his maturity, his poise, his confidence, his character, and his ability to play beyond his years? In 2009, he addressed the anger and resentment that surrounded the trade of popular center fielder Nate McLouth, which had made it possible for his callup to the majors, by going 2-for-4 with three runs scored in his big-league debut and by hitting in 18 of his first 20 games. In 2012, with the weight of that fat new contract in his wallet, he raised his batting average from .259 to .327, his home-run output from 23 to 31, his RBIs from 89 to 96, his on-base percentage from .364 to .400, and finished third in MVP voting. In 2013, facing criticism that he hadn't done enough to help the Pirates avert a late-season collapse in 2012 that saw them lose 36 of their final 52 games to finish under .500 for the 20th year in a row, he hit .339 with 11 homers, 35 RBIs, and a .441 OBP after the All-Star break to help the Pirates finish 94–68 and qualify for the postseason for the first time since 1992.

"He has a wonderful combination of speed and power, the best this city has seen in a player other than Barry Bonds in the past quarter-century," *Pittsburgh Post-Gazette* columnist Ron Cook wrote when McCutchen signed his milestone deal in 2012. His invocation of the Pirates' two-time MVP, who they'd been unable to keep for financial reasons after the 1992 season, was not the first time the name had come up when it came to McCutchen. The Pirates scout who first saw McCutchen said, "[Andrew] could be Pittsburgh's baseball savior, the next Barry Bonds," according to a lengthy profile by J. Brady McCullough before the 2013 season. The numbers through their first five seasons would also seem to beg the comparison.

McCutchen	Category	Bonds
734	Games played	717
.296	Batting average	.265
103	Home runs	117
379	Runs batted in	337
459	Runs scored	468
162	Doubles	156
30	Triples	26
125	Stolen bases	169

This is not to say that McCutchen will go on to hit 762 career home runs or win a record seven MVPs as Bonds did before retiring. But is it taking too great of a leap to predict that if this same 100-things exercise were carried out again in 2023 that McCutchen would be appreciably higher on it after 15 seasons than he is after five? Is it too much of a stretch to point out that Bonds won his first MVP at the end of his fifth season, the same year McCutchen won his first? For now, though, McCutchen is at No. 75 on this all-time list as much for the symbolism of the placement as anything else—a number that equates to the diamond. Diamond wedding anniversaries. Diamond jubilees. And, in his case, the diamond of the Pirates system, the gemstone in their renaissance.

76 Bring Your Camera

There are more than 250 statues of baseball players in the United States. Four stand watch in all their bronze and larger-than-life greatness over each of the four main gates at PNC Park. Like the Kauffman's Clock for shoppers Uptown, they are meeting points for fans attending games on the North Shore. They are also some of the most popular spots for those wanting to take pictures of their day at the ballpark. They are, on one level, reverential places where parents can pose their children next to their childhood heroes or themselves pose with the images of their own baseball memories. They are, on another level, testaments to the franchise's place in the history of baseball and Pittsburgh for more than 125 years. They represent the very best of the Pirates and have been shaped and erected not en masse as some newer teams that have attempted to manufacture history, but slowly over time, each with its own place, each with its own history, each cast in a certainty that its meaning is not temporary but lasting like the bronze to which it is committed.

They are, in order of dedication:

Honus Wagner: April 30, 1955—The first great Pirate, he starred from 1900 to 1917 and then became a fixture in Pittsburgh

Ken Morell (left) takes a picture of his sons, Rob and Andy (right) all from Seattle, in front of the Roberto Clemente statue in front of PNC Park on March 28, 2011. In town for their annual trip to the 'burgh to see the Penguins play hockey, they stopped by the park to look around. (Pittsburgh Post-Gazette, John Heller)

upon his retirement. His statue originally stood near Forbes Field but has moved as the team's homes have moved, first to Three Rivers Stadium outside Gate C and then to PNC Park, where it is located at the park's home-plate entrance. It depicts him at the completion of his swing and stands atop a pedestal that features admiring children. Within the base is a hermetically sealed scroll that lists the names of every donor who helped make the privately funded statue possible.

Roberto Clemente: July 8, 1994—He went from star to legend in 18 years as the Pirates right fielder from 1955 to 1972, a career that ended prematurely in a New Year's Eve 1972 plane crash. His statue was dedicated as part of All-Star Game festivities at Three Rivers Stadium in 1994. Like Wagner's, his statue was moved to PNC Park in 2001 and stands outside the center-field gate and just a few steps off the bridge that bears his name. It captures him starting off from home plate following yet another line drive and stands on a base that contains soil from his native Puerto Rico, Forbes Field, and Three Rivers Stadium. Encircling it are 16 spaces where Clemente's career is detailed. Only 15 are filled in. The 16th remains empty, a reflection of a career that was never completed.

Willie Stargell: April 7, 2001—The greatest slugger in Pirates history, he hit 475 home runs from 1962 to 1982, won two World Series rings, and defined the spirit of one of the most beloved Pirates teams in franchise history—the 1979 "We Are Family" team. While the statue depicts him just on the brink of unleashing one of his thunderous swings, it is also a reminder of one of the sadder season openers in Pirates history. On April 9, 2001—the day PNC Park opened and two days after an unveiling ceremony that Stargell was too weak to attend—he died at age 61.

Bill Mazeroski: September 5, 2010—He is the author of the greatest moment in Pittsburgh sports history when, on October 13, 1960, he became the only man in baseball history to end a World

Series Game 7 with a home run—a dramatic shot off Ralph Terry of the New York Yankees that gave the Pirates an improbable 10–9 win and an equally improbable world championship. His hat-waving trip around the bases that October afternoon is captured outside PNC Park's right-field gate.

Eight other statues can also be found within the gates of PNC Park—the powerful hands of Ralph Kiner in the concourse behind the left-field bleachers and those in honor of Pittsburgh Negro League greats Cool Papa Bell, Oscar Charleston, Josh Gibson, Judy Johnson, Satchel Paige, and Smokey Joe Wood in Legacy Square just inside the left-field gate—but the four at the gates were Pirates for their entire careers. And, in bronze, they will be so forever.

77 202 Still the Number

On the afternoon of September 20, 1924, Wilbur Cooper pitched all 11 innings of a 5–4 win at Brooklyn's Ebbets Field against Dazzy Vance and the Robins for his 20th win of the season and the 202nd of his Pirates career. Nearly 90 years later, the number 202 still stands atop the Pirates' career pitching charts. Five days later, he pitched his 263rd career complete game in a 5–4 loss to the New York Giants. It, too, still sits up there, unchallenged and unlikely ever to be. One month later, at age 32, he was traded to the Chicago Cubs along with Charlie Grimm and Rabbit Maranville for Vic Aldridge, George Grantham, and Al Niehaus in one of the biggest trades of the 1920s.

"Cooper was arguably the greatest pitcher in Pittsburgh Pirates history," David Cicotello wrote in his story on Cooper for the Society of American Baseball Research's biography project. The counter argument is that the Pirates historically have never been a franchise of great pitching. Of the 13 Pirates in Cooperstown who played at least five seasons with the team, none are pitchers. Still, famed sportswriter Grantland Rice once wrote of Cooper that he was "the greatest pitcher in organized baseball"—quite a tribute considering that Cooper's contemporaries included Hall of Famers Christy Mathewson, Grover Cleveland Alexander, and Walter Johnson.

That Cooper, a 5'11" left-hander with pinpoint control, never joined them in Cooperstown is viewed as one of the Hall's great oversights. When he retired after a major league career that lasted from 1912 to 1926, Cooper owned the most wins of any left-hander in National League history (216 including 14 with the Cubs) and sported the lowest ERA of any NL left-hander with at least 3,000 innings (2.89). The latter number still stands. In addition to wins and complete games, he also ranks in the top 10 in Pirates history in starts (369), innings pitched (3,199), earned run average (2.74), shutouts (33), and strikeouts (1,191). So greatly valued was Cooper's left arm that in 1919, during a span from 1917 to 1924 in which he never won fewer than 17 games and four times won 20, New York Giants manager John McGraw offered the Pirates $75,000 for Cooper.

Yet not only did he never make the Hall, he was never even seriously considered. In all his years of eligibility on the writers ballot, he never received more than 4.4 percent of the vote. Cooper came to accept his fate.

"I would die a happy man if they voted me into the Hall of Fame," Cooper wrote in a letter to the *Pittsburgh Post-Gazette* late in his life. "But if they don't, I will understand. Once people get my age, people understand a little more about things than they did when they were younger."

His lack of a plaque in Cooperstown, however, does not take away from the fact that his 202 wins are one of the oldest-standing franchise wins records in baseball history. Only Mathewson's record of 372 with the Giants from 1900 to 1916 and Eddie Plank's record of 284 with the Athletics from 1901 to 1914 pre-date Cooper's 202 that he locked in that afternoon against Brooklyn in 1924.

78 A Work of Art

"Darn-dest game I ever saw" was the recurring comment in the Pirates clubhouse in the early morning of August 13, 1966. It was 1:30 AM and players, sportswriters, and fans were still attempting to sort out the game that had just played out in Cincinnati's Crosley Field—the sort of game that at 8:00 PM no one expects to see and that as midnight passes no one ever forgets. The sort that separates itself from so many of the 162 that mean something only for purposes of the standings.

Pirates 14, Reds 11. Played out over 13 innings and 4 hours, 22 minutes, it was not one of the many.

The two teams combined to set a National League record with 11 home runs. The star of the game played for the losing team. The Pirates led six different times, the Reds three. Manny Mota ultimately decided the game for the Pirates on a two-run single to left field in the top of the 13th inning, part of a three-run inning for which—amazingly on this night—the Reds had no answer.

Such was not the case in the ninth, 10th, and 11th innings—all innings in which the game could have ended. All innings in which it didn't. And all somehow finding at their epicenter the decision made by Reds manager Dave Bristol to put a young outfielder named Art Shamsky into left field as part of a double switch in the top of the eighth inning. Three years later, Shamsky would earn a

214

World Series ring with the Miracle Mets of 1969. On this night, though, he carved out a story that is told better by grandfathers than by resumes.

The Pirates carried a 7–6 lead into the bottom of the eighth inning when Shamsky, a left-handed batter, came to the plate for the first time in the game. Al McBean was on the mound for the Pirates. A runner was on first. Shamsky, who despite having just 33 hits to that point in the season had 12 home runs, drove a McBean pitch out to right to put the Reds up 8–7. His night was only just beginning.

Now down by a run going into the ninth, the Pirates found magic of their own in pinch hitter Jerry Lynch. Lynch hit a Don Nottebart pitch for a tying home run and set the stage for extra innings.

The Pirates struck first when Willie Stargell hit his 27th home run of the season off Nottebart in the top of the 10th for a 9–8 lead. With Elroy Face on the mound in relief, the Pirates had to like their chances. Shamsky didn't agree. Up for the second time, he again sent a drive hurtling into the right-field stands. Game tied 9–9.

The teams would go to the 11th. Again the Pirates scored first when Bob Bailey, who had already homered twice, hit a two-run double off Billy McCool. But Shamsky was due up in the bottom of the inning. Harry Walker had already seen what Face could do against Shamsky. He brought in Billy O'Dell to face him with two outs and a runner on. On this night, it didn't matter. Shamsky homered again, pulling it just inside the foul pole, to tie the score at 11. Four innings played, three home runs.

"It was just one of those days when everything I did was right," Shamsky said later.

Unfortunately for the Reds, he couldn't pitch. After a scoreless 12th that allowed everyone to take a collective breath, Matty Alou singled off McCool, Bailey reached on an error, and Roberto Clemente was intentionally walked to get to Mota. He promptly shot a ball into left field to score Alou and Bailey for what proved to be the winning runs.

In the bottom half of the 11ᵗʰ, Tommy Sisk got Chico Cardenas to ground into a game-ending double play. That was a good thing in more ways than one. The Pirates won, and Shamsky never got to bat again.

79 Let's Play Three

While every baseball fan knows what happened at Forbes Field the afternoon of October 13, 1960, not as many know what happened there the afternoon of October 2, 1920. In its own way, it was equally unique. Had that eternal baseball optimist, Ernie Banks, been alive, he'd have been beside himself. Let's play two? Heck, let's play three! The Pirates that afternoon played host to the last tripleheader in major league history.

With four games left in the 1920 season, the Pirates trailed third-place Cincinnati by 3½ games. The Reds were in Pittsburgh for a three-game weekend series, after which they had one game left vs. St. Louis while the Pirates finished with one vs. Chicago. Four Pirates wins and four Reds losses would give the Pirates third place in the National League. A hollow victory? Not in 1920, when the second- and third-place teams shared in the World Series till.

The series opener, scheduled for Friday, October 1, was rained out. With a doubleheader already scheduled for Saturday and both teams scheduled to play elsewhere on Sunday, Mother Nature would seem to have locked up third place for Cincinnati. But Pirates owner Barney Dreyfuss would not go down so easily. He proposed a tripleheader for Saturday. Reds manager Pat Moran "sensibly, if not sportingly, refused," wrote A.D. Suehsdorf of the Society for American Baseball Research. Dreyfuss then turned to National League President John Heydler. Heydler sided with Dreyfuss. Three games in one day was not without precedent. On September 1, 1890, Brooklyn had hosted the Pirates (then known as the Alleghenies) for three, and on September 7, 1896, Louisville and Baltimore did the same.

Needing to win them all, Pirates manager George Gibson sent out the best he had for a noon start in Game 1, 24-game winner Wilbur Cooper, along with a lineup that included future Hall of Famers Max Carey and Pie Traynor. But the day was unseasonably cold for so early in October. Cooper couldn't warm to the occasion. The Reds scored one run in the first, one in the second, then knocked Cooper out of the game with six runs in the third inning. Any drama that might have built during that historic afternoon was quickly sucked out of Forbes Field. The Pirates, who had led 3–2 after the second inning, never threatened again. The Reds went on to win in a rout 13–4.

Games 2 and 3 became little more than a good workout for the two teams. Moran sat his regulars and filled his lineup with pitchers and bench players. Gibson did much the same. Despite a mixed bag of a lineup, the Reds won the second game 7–3. The Pirates came back in the Game 3 to win 6–0 in a game shortened to six innings by darkness. Of some note in a lost day for the Pirates, Jughandle Johnny Morrison, who would win 25 games for the Pirates in 1923, earned his first major league win in the abbreviated nightcap, and third baseman Clyde Barnhart got a hit in all three games to make him the only player in major league history to hit in three games in a single day.

None of that trivia altered the teams' reason for being there that afternoon. The Reds would finish third and because of that earn $10,744.14 to divvy up; the Pirates got nothing other than the distinction of having hosted the last tripleheader in major league history.

80 For My Son

By the time Rob Mackowiak arrived at PNC Park that mid-Friday afternoon for a twi-night doubleheader against the Chicago Cubs, it had already been the most amazing day of his life. At 11:12 that morning—May 28, 2004—his wife, Jennifer, had given birth to their first child, Garrett Matthew Mackowiak, 8 lbs., 5 oz.. What happened the rest of the evening in front of a near-sellout crowd would leave him, both teams, and the 37,806 fans who witnessed his performance wondering if God didn't have an angel working for Steven Spielberg.

What other explanation was there for what Mackowiak did when he stepped to the plate in the bottom of the ninth inning of the opener? The score was tied 5–5, the bases were loaded, and he had done nothing in his first four at-bats from the No. 5 spot in the batting order. The only reason he had been given much of an opportunity to play so far that season was because Chris Stynes wasn't hitting and Raul Mondesi had mysteriously gone home to the Dominican Republic.

It was as if they were making way for this moment. This night. He took ball one from Cubs reliever Joe Borowski. Mackowiak swung through his second pitch. "I just tried to regroup," he said. Then ball two. "I tried to hit it hard somewhere. There's so much adrenaline going." He swung again and in the time it took for bat to meet ball, PNC Park became the setting for a DreamWorks production. The ball carried—going, going, gone into the seats in right-center field. As he rounded first and headed for second, he pumped his right fist into the air. The blue hospital bracelet dangled from his right wrist. His son was now about nine hours old. Had that really just happened? It had. It was a walk-off grand slam for Garrett Matthew's dad, and the Pirates won 9–5.

"That's not supposed to happen to a guy like me," said Mackowiak, who as a 53rd-round draft pick in 1996, had to scratch his way up just to get to the major leagues.

Makes a person wonder, then, how Spielberg would go about explaining that—impossibly—Mackowiak's day wasn't yet finished. After a long day, he wasn't in the starting lineup for Game 2. However, after being called on as a defensive replacement in the seventh inning first in center field and then at third base with the Pirates down 3–2, he eventually found himself at the plate in the

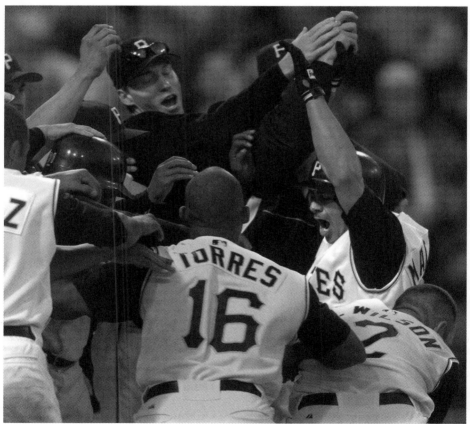

Rob Mackowiak hits a walk-off grand slam in the bottom of the ninth off Cubs reliever Joe Borowski to beat the Cubs in the first game of a doubleheader at PNC Park on May 28, 2004. (*Pittsburgh Post-Gazette*, Peter Diana)

bottom of the ninth with the Pirates now down by two, a runner on first, and Cubs reliever LaTroy Hawkins on the mound.

Hawkins delivered. Cue the timpani, strings, and French horns. (And, yes, this really happened.) Mackowiak, the blue bracelet still on his wrist, swung and hit a tying two-run homer, and not just anywhere but into the same section of seats where he'd hit his grand slam just hours earlier. An inning later, Craig Wilson hit a walk-off home run of his own to give the Pirates a sweep. But in the grand scheme of the day and night, it was almost anticlimactic (if any walk-off home run can be ho-hummed).

"My lucky day," Mackowiak said later.

Wilson, the overlooked Game 2 hero, was more creative in his description of the improbable to which he'd just been part. "Good friend has a kid. Goes deep twice in a night. Two walk-off homer victories. Pretty good night," Wilson said. "Some of us are going to be talking to the doctor to see if we can have kids now, too."

Mackowiak would have had no problem with that. But Garrett Matthew was all his. "It's still kind of hard to believe," he said the next day in referencing that last Friday in May. But he wasn't referring to the home runs. The part that was so amazing? "I'm a father." A father with a story to tell Garrett's kids one day. Whether or not they believe Grandpa is another story.

81 What's Next?

As the 2013 season ended, Gerrit Cole had been 23 for less than two months and a major leaguer for not quite five. There is no way of knowing his future; no way of knowing if by the time, say, the 2033 season ended if this pitcher, who resembled Roger Clemens both in build and demeanor, would be the one who will knock Wilbur Cooper and Bob Friend from atop the franchise's all-time pitching charts. Just as there is no way of knowing if he will be the next Ron Necciai or Zach Duke or any of the other pitching supernovas in Pirates history.

This much was in the books, though: In the Pirates' first foray into the postseason since 1992, Cole was as much the stud down the stretch as the team envisioned when it selected him first out of UCLA in the 2011 draft. From his June 11 debut through the end of August, Cole had teased, winning his first four starts—the first Pirates rookie to do so in more than a century—while going 6–7 with a 3.80 earned run average. But from September 1 until the lights went out on the best Pirates season in two decades with a loss to the St. Louis Cardinals in Game 5 of a best-of-five first-round playoff series, he was their best pitcher. He made seven starts, won five, and posted a 1.88 ERA. Five of those starts followed a loss; four times he won.

When the Pirates went into Texas on September 9, lugging a season-high four-game losing streak and showing signs of feeling the stretch-run heat after getting swept by the division-leading Cardinals, Cole stared down Rangers ace Yu Darvish for seven innings and won 1–0 in a game that also carried with it the parallel pressure of being the one that secured the Pirates their first winning season in 21 years. On September 19, while trying to avoid a four-game sweep by West Division also-ran San Diego and at very least maintain an edge for home field in a postseason wild-card scenario, Cole struck out 12 during six innings in a 10–1 win. Then in the National League Division Series, with the Pirates in a 1–0 hole to St. Louis after dropping Game 1—a game in which veteran A.J. Burnett was tagged for seven runs in the third inning of a 9–1 rout—Cole went out in Game 2 and limited the Cardinals to one run and two hits in six innings in a 7–1 victory that pulled the Pirates even.

However, nothing he did in those first months so announced his arrival or earned him so much baseball "street cred"—a term manager Clint Hurdle pulled out after Cole's performance against Darvish—as when Hurdle was forced to choose his starter for the winner-take-all Game 5 in St. Louis. The choice was between Cole and his 20 major league starts and the 14-year veteran Burnett and his 378. Hurdle chose Cole. As testament to Cole's growth and presence, no one questioned the choice.

"The competitive edge that he takes to the mound is visible," Hurdle said. "The emotion that he pitches with…that's special and that can be significant. He respects everything. He fears nothing."

In winning Game 2, Cole was already just the third Pirates rookie to win a postseason game. In earning the Game 5 start, he became the first Pirates rookie to start a deciding game since Babe Adams in the 1909 World Series. It also made him only the third No. 1 overall draft pick to start in any deciding game. "The first dream for everybody I'm sure is to get to the big leagues," Cole had said after an August win, "and the second dream is to [play in big games]." For a franchise that hadn't even been in the playoffs in 21 years, there was none bigger.

There was also no storybook ending. Cole pitched well but not as well as Game 2. With a runner on base in the second inning, he hung a curveball that David Freese hit for a two-run homer. The 2–0 lead would be more than enough working margin for Cardinals ace Adam Wainwright and an insurmountable hole for a Pirates offense that managed just two runs in the last two games of the series. Cole pitched three more innings. He allowed two more hits. He struck out five. And speaking to the pitcher he had become, he escaped a one-out, second-and-third jam in the fourth by inducing a groundout and then coming back against Freese—the hitter who had gone deep against him—and struck him out. When Cole was lifted an inning later, one long-time national baseball writer tweeted, "Gerrit Cole won't win tonight, but he left his mark on this series. 11 IP, 5 hits, 10 K. He'll be fun to watch for a long, long time." The question that dangled tantalizingly in the ether—how fun and how long?

82 In the Beginning

With a little imagination and the help of several sabermetricians, fans can stand on the spot of earth where Cy Young once pitched a baseball and wander the area between third and second that Honus Wagner called home for half his career. They can stand at home plate and imagine what Fred Clarke or Ginger Beaumont might have seen as they dug in against Young under the very same piece of sky on a long ago October afternoon, and they can try to envision what a sight it must've been to see a ballgame spill over—literally— into the Allegheny River.

Lost for decades after the 1920s, Exposition Park—the home of the Pirates from 1891 to 1909 and, of greater import, the site of the first World Series game to be played in a National League park on October 6, 1903—lives again, albeit among parked Subarus, Dodges, and SUVs. In 1995, an engineer with a passion for baseball by the name of Dan Bonk, along with three other members of the Society for American Baseball Research (SABR), plotted the long-lost park's dimensions using old maps and what landmarks remained from the early 1900s.

Today, their findings are noted in a parking lot between Heinz Field and PNC Park on Pittsburgh's North Side—more precisely in the lot nearest the intersection of General Robinson Street and Tony Dorsett Drive. There, home plate and the three bases of the wooden, rickety ballpark that could hold 16,000, are painted on

223

the spots where the original bases would have been when Wagner and the Pirates met Young and the Boston Americans in Games 4, 5, 6, and 7 of the first World Series. "We felt we'd discovered a lost treasure," Bonk said. And because they did, a bit of history was restored and its grounds can now be walked by fans.

Not that there is much to see. It's still, to the twenty-first century eye, just a parking lot, gray and cracking and blemished by oil leaks. But there is something special in knowing just where Wagner would have readied himself for a pitch by Deacon Phillippe or where the fabled Tinker to Evers to Chance would have whipped the ball around the infield when the Cubs were in town. There is something wondrous, like a visit to an old battle-field, of what memories and stories lie in the strata below.

What might give the mind's eye its greatest challenge, though, is picturing how the Allegheny River would have crept onto the outfield grass when its waters were running high in a time when the land sat lower and the rivers ran freer and before engineers worked their magic on both. It wasn't the rare occurrence, either. The river so routinely overspilled its banks that the outfield was often referred to as Lake Dreyfuss after Pirates owner Barney Dreyfuss. During a doubleheader on July 4, 1902, the waters rose even as the Pirates played Brooklyn in a holiday doubleheader. At some point, a ground rule was made up on the spot—any ball that hit the water was a single. Ridiculous when imagined through the prism of the modern game, but no more so than in that first World Series when Dreyfuss—not wanting to lose a single fan's ticket money— jammed the overflow crowd into roped-off areas of the outfield. Apparently, hitting a fan is worth more than hitting water; players were awarded not singles but ground-rule triples for balls hit into the crowd—a contributing factor to the 25 triples that were hit in the series that year, a series record that still stands.

The Pirates would play in the park for six more years before moving into modern concrete-and-steel—and dry—Forbes Field in the middle of the 1909 season. Exposition Park played host to its final game June 29, 1909, an 8–1 Pirates win vs. the Chicago Cubs in which Lefty Leifield outpitched Mordecai "Three Finger" Brown and Dots Miller knocked in four runs. And in the moments after Leifield struck out Cubs catcher Jim Archer for the final out, local musician Charles Zieg, also known as "The Commodore," lifted his bugle to his lips and blew "Taps."

An era was dead—and so nearly forgotten.

83 A Key Player

As the Riddler might have posed to Batman: Riddle me this, holy cowled one. Who is the only person to play for the Pirates, the Penguins, and the Steelers? Here's a hint: He played for as many as 35 million fans in his career, died in 2009, and has yet to miss a Pirates home game. Impossibly confused? Confused impossibly? There actually is an answer. Really, there is. And his name is Vince Lascheid, whom one writer aptly dubbed Pittsburgh's "sports organist laureate." For most of the period from 1970—the year Three Rivers Stadium opened—to 2005, he was stadium organist for the Pirates and/or the Penguins with a couple of years at Steelers games thrown into the mix along the way.

Other teams had organists, but Lascheid, who once toured with Tex Beneke and the Glenn Miller band after World War II and then developed a following in small Pittsburgh clubs through the 1960s, was credited with being the first to marry songs to athletes in ways that were at the same time witty, "pretty corny, and some…real groaners," Lascheid admitted. Before the age when ballplayers picked their own metal-edged musical introductions and ballparks opted for loud and louder recorded music, fans came to appreciate and expect Lascheid's organ commentaries. During his tenure, he provided the soundtrack to a lifetime of games and seasons. He became so ingrained in the stadium experience for fans that the Penguins inducted him into their Hall of Fame in 2003, and the Pirates presented him with their Pride of the Pirates award in 2005.

"Pittsburgh without Vince Lascheid," wrote one writer in 1996, "seems no more right than Pittsburgh without those two teams."

Dodgers first baseman Steve Garvey, he of the rugged good looks (and he knew it), never saw the humor in being serenaded by the Miss America theme when he'd come to the plate at Three Rivers. When Jesus Alou once struck out with the bases loaded, Lascheid let loose with a joyful "What A Friend We Have in Jesus." The great Roberto Clemente earned "Jesus Christ Superstar." When Viagra became popular, product pitchman Rafael Palmeiro received a short burst of "Pop Goes The Weasel." And proof that not all musical puns are come by easily, he was at the top of his game for Baltimore's Benny Ayala in the 1979 World Series when he came up with Tony Orlando's "Tie A-Yala Ribbon" for an Ayala at-bat.

"Some of his stuff, you really had to think," said Tom McMillan, a Penguins official. "It was clever."

"He really enjoyed what he did, and he never cared for the limelight," Kent Tekulve said. "That's what made him a special part of the organization for a long time."

A part so special that it has endured even after his death in 2009. Club president Frank Coonelly vowed, "When our fans hear organ music at PNC Park, it will continue to be Vince Lascheid for years to come." True to his word, when it comes time for the seventh inning stretch, it is a Lascheid recording of "Take Me Out to the Ballgame" that fans sing along with. When they hear the three-note rally cry "Let's Go Bucs," they are three notes tapped out by Lascheid during a time when he was as much a part of the Pittsburgh stadium experience as Clemente and Stargell.

Public address announcer Tim DeBacco (left) and audio engineer Ken Javorski work behind the scenes to deliver music and announcements on Thursday, August 8, 2013, during the Pirates' home game against the Miami Marlins. There is no longer an organ at PNC Park, but the sounds of the late Pirates' organist, Vince Lascheid, were recorded before his death and are now broadcast at PNC Park. "What you're hearing is the sound of our longtime organist, Vince Lascheid," DeBacco said. (Pittsburgh Post-Gazette, Julia Rendleman, Elizabeth Bloom)

84 An Afternoon of Stars

Pittsburgh has played host to seven World Series. It has been home to Honus Wagner and Roberto Clemente, to Ralph Kiner and Willie Stargell and Pie Traynor. Yet it has never had so much star power within in its hands as it did the afternoon of July 7, 1959—the date of the second of five All-Star Games that Pittsburgh has hosted since the game became a midsummer staple in 1933. Of the 50 players on the two rosters, 21 went on to be enshrined in the Hall of Fame. Of the 18 starters, nine ended up in Cooperstown. Tickets ran $2.20 for a bleacher seat and $6.60 for a lower level reserved seat. Scalpers wanted $30. Even Vice President Richard Nixon showed up. He threw out the ceremonial first pitch and then stayed in his box seat near the first-base dugout until the final out for a game at a time when the leagues still held on to the remains of early twentieth-century rivalries and fraternization between the two was still a dirty word.

Neither he nor any of the 35,277 fans who filled Forbes Field that Tuesday afternoon likely went away disappointed. For six innings, National League pitchers Don Drysdale and Lew Burdette dueled American League counterparts Early Wynn and Ryne Duren. Drysdale, a hard-throwing terror for the Los Angeles Dodgers and the NL starter, struck out four in three hitless innings. Duren, who came on in relief of Wynn in the fourth for the AL, was nearly as effective, striking out four and allowing just one hit in his three innings. Home runs accounted for the only scoring. Milwaukee third baseman Eddie Mathews connected off Wynn in the first inning for the NL; Detroit outfielder Al Kaline hit one off Burdette in the fourth for the AL.

And so the game went into the seventh inning at 1–1. The rest of the game would play out like some kid's idea of the 1950s ultimate fantasy league game. Batting in the bottom of the seventh for the NL, Ernie Banks led off with a double off Jim Bunning. Del Crandall drove in Banks to break the tie with a single to center. The Pirates' own Bill Mazeroski—still 15 months from becoming a legend—then knocked in Crandall for a 3–1 NL lead.

Had the game ended there, it would have been a perfect day for the hosts. Mazeroski would have contributed an RBI, and Pirates closer Elroy Face stood to be the winner after pitching a perfect seventh inning, including strikeouts of Harmon Killebrew and Luis Aparicio. But baseball is nine innings, not seven. Face, The Baron of the Bullpen, came back out for the eighth. He retired Frank Malzone and Minnie Minoso easy enough on pop-ups that never left the infield. But he would never get that third out. Nellie Fox singled to center. Face walked Harvey Kuenn. Vic Power singled in Fox, and after Ted Williams walked, Gus Triandos drove in both Kuenn and Power for a 4–3 AL lead. The perfect Pirates storyline would not be written. NL manager Fred Haney brought in Johnny Antonelli to replace Face. After walking Roy Sievers, he finally stopped the bleeding for the NL by getting Sherm Lollar to pop out.

Now ahead, American League manager Casey Stengel brought in his own Yankees ace, Whitey Ford, to protect the one-run lead. He failed miserably, much to the delight of a thrilled pro-NL crowd. Ken Boyer singled to open the eighth and, with Hank Aaron and then Willie Mays due up, Pirates shortstop Dick Groat sacrificed Boyer to second. Aaron promptly singled to center to drive in Boyer and tie the score at 4–4. Mays, 3-for-3 in previous All-Star Games against Ford, then made it 4-for-4 by smoking a shot to the wall in right-center field for a triple, driving in Aaron all the way from first with what proved to be the winning run after Don Elston shut down the AL in the ninth.

Not only did the NL win, but the stirring narrative it wrote along the way left the fans in a festive mood. At least until they tried to exit the stadium and many—particularly those using the gate near the left-field bleachers—found themselves held up so that VP Nixon and his party could leave. "It was a toothpaste tube, teeming with humanity," according to the *Pittsburgh Post-Gazette*. The scene prompted one disgruntled fan to exclaim, "Hell, he's only another citizen." If only he knew how true those words would ring on another summer day in another time.

85 Dr. Strangeglove

His would have been one of the great nicknames in Pirates history had Dick Stuart still been with them when it was coined. Certainly top 10, up there with Big Poison, Little Poison, and The Deacon. But the fact is that the Pirates traded Stuart to the Boston Red Sox in November 1962 and *Dr. Strangelove or: How I Learned to Stop Worrying and Love the Bomb*—the black, Cold War comedy starring Peter Sellers—was not released until January 1964, or 29 errors after Stuart booted his last for the Pirates. Yet he cannot be ignored. While he did not receive the nickname in a Pirates uniform, he most certainly earned it in one.

Stuart played 502 games at first base for the Pirates from 1958 to 1962. In those 502 games, he committed 90 errors, leading National League first basemen each season. It makes one pause and wonder how poor of an outfielder he must have been that early in his career that the Pirates moved him to first base to hide his defensive shortcomings.

Teammate Gene Freese remembered a game in which Stuart had already botched three grounders. When a fourth came his way, he managed to field it cleanly only to flip the ball down the right-field line when he went to wave off the pitcher running over to cover the bag.

Stuart was aware of his deficiencies with glove on hand, yet apparently he didn't care. He even laughed at himself. At one time, he had a vanity license plate for his car that read "E3."

"I know I'm the world's worst fielder," Stuart once said, "but who gets paid for fielding? There isn't a great fielder in baseball getting the kind of dough I get paid for hitting." An ironic statement considering the other half of the right side of the infield during Stuart's time in Pittsburgh was a guy named Mazeroski.

For the record, the Pirates paid Stuart $20,000 in 1961 and $30,000 in '62. And the Red Sox, Phillies, and Mets paid him even more after he was dealt away. For all the jokes about his fielding, Stuart could hit. He once hit 66 homers in a minor league season;he hit 27, 23, and 35 for the Pirates from 1959 to 1961; and he would hit a career-high 42 for Boston (to go with 24 errors) in the season of 1964 when he earned the Dr. Strangeglove moniker.

He also authored a home run that those who remember Forbes Field understand best of all just how great a wallop it was. But for those who never saw a game there, center field was so deep and spacious at the old park that the Pirates stored the batting cage in its deepest part in right-center field. After all, no one ever had or would hit it there.

No one ever did. Or would. Except on June 5, 1959. That day, Stuart hit a sinker ball from Cubs pitcher Glenn Hobbie that cleared the batting cage on its way over the wall, an estimated 500'home run. Stuart later called it one of his best shots. Hobbie, for his part, was thankful that Stuart had not hit the ball lower or "I might not be here to talk about it." Manager Danny Murtaugh and former third baseman Pie Traynor, both of whom had seen a lot of games in the stadium, agreed it was the longest ball hit at Forbes.

Yet it is neither that blast nor the other 227 home runs he hit for which Stuart is best remembered. It is not even that he was the answer to the trivia question: "Who was on deck when Mazeroski hit his home run in 1960?" Instead, it is for what he couldn't do—field, catch, or throw. And for the telltale nickname his fielding earned him for all time:

Dr. Strangeglove or: How I Learned To Stop Worrying About My Defense And Love The Big Fly.

86 Now You See Him...

A season earlier, Turner Ward, a bubble-blowing journeyman out-fielder from Alabama, had written a small chapter for himself in Pirates history. He had contributed a career year to the Freak Show team of 1997, a team that improbably challenged the Houston Astros for a National League Central Division title into the last week of the season despite a payroll that was the lowest in baseball at just more than $10 million.

In 192 plate appearances after being called up in July, Ward had hit .353 with seven home runs and 33 RBIs. He played hard and had a knack for delivering the key hit or RBI in the big moment. In many ways, he became the poster boy for an overachieving team that had not contended for much of anything since Barry Bonds left for San Francisco five years earlier.

Ward came across as the sort of player who would run through walls for his team, and the fans loved him for it.

Who could have known where that would lead him on this afternoon at Three Rivers Stadium on May 3, 1998. The Los Angeles Dodgers were in town and Ward, starting in right field, would do something out there that even the great Roberto Clemente never did.

He ran through the right-field wall. Quite literally. Quite completely. Quite through.

Already down 9–0 in the top of the sixth inning, the Pirates were well on their way to a forgettable Sunday afternoon loss when, with one out and runners on first and third, Dodgers All-Star catcher Mike Piazza stepped in to face Pirates reliever Elmer Dessens. Dessens delivered, and Piazza drove a ball to deep right. Ward ran back.

From that moment, the game became anything but forgettable.

The ball was carrying. Ward, his back to home plate, was running all out. Nine runs down? Hrmmph. He hit the warning track and, as *Pittsburgh Post-Gazette* columnist Bruce Keidan wrote the next morning, "He ignored the warning." He stuck up his glove, catching the ball an instant before he hit the wall.

There was still time to stick out an arm to absorb some of the coming impact. Instead, he brought his throwing hand into his glove to make sure the ball didn't get jarred loose.

"[The ball] stayed put," Keidan wrote. "The wall didn't."

The outfield wall consisted of a layer of padding that could be seen. Behind the padding was a frame of wood at top and bottom, with vertical slats spaced at intervals of 4'. Panels of fiberglass filled the spaces between the slats.

Ward hit the wall at full speed. He hit it just right. He hit the padding. The padding separated. Then one of the fiberglass panels blew up "like a clap of thunder." And then he was gone from sight like Alice through a major league looking glass, the padding falling mostly back into place to cover where he'd just been.

"I felt something strange when I hit the padding, and the next thing I knew I was on the other side of the wall," Ward recalled.

"I knew I was going to be on the highlight reels for the rest of my life," Piazza said.

Almost forgotten as players, coaches, managers, media, hot dog vendors, and the 18,674 in attendance that afternoon tried to wrap their heads around what they'd just seen—including Ward—the ball and play were still live. The runner on third had scored easily, but the runner on first had tagged and was still alive.

To the amazement of all, Ward emerged through the padding and, despite a bruised arm and a stunned sense of time and place, he threw—make that meekly lobbed—the ball back in the direction of the infield to keep the runner from advancing beyond second.

"I actually thought for a split second about throwing the ball over the fence onto the playing field," Ward said later, "but I thought they'd rule it wasn't a catch."

Crazy are the things that go through your head—or fall out of them—in the seconds after you've just run through a wall.

The runner held at second. Time was called. After being checked by trainer Kent Biggerstaff and manager Gene Lamont,

Turner Ward wears a rainbow-colored wig thrown into the dugout by a fan during a rain delay against the Cincinnati Reds. (*Pittsburgh Post-Gazette*)

Ward left the game. His forearm had a 2" bruise, but otherwise he was physically none the worse for wear. "I think I'm in better shape than the wall," he said later.

The crowd gave him a standing ovation. He turned to Biggerstaff as they walked. "I did catch it, didn't I?"

87 A Trip to the Museum

The Pirates have been around longer than rock-and-roll, the airplane, and Elvis. Those last three have their own museums. The Pirates do not. However, not more than a mile from PNC Park, the Pirates are a cornerstone of the next best thing. Within the walls of the Senator John Heinz History Center in Pittsburgh's Strip District is the Western Pennsylvania Sports Museum. And within its 20,000 sq. ft., the history of the franchise lives on in twenty-first-century interactive glory, dominating the better part of the first of the museum's two floors.

The players: Honus Wagner to Andrew McCutchen. The homes: Exposition Park to PNC Park. The voices: Rosey Rowswell to Lanny Frattare. The games: The first World Series to the first decade on the Internet. All are there in one form or another and presented in such a way that fans will be whisked back in time by touchstones of the team's past, then through time as they follow its growth from Barney Dreyfuss's dream to those played out by the latest group of Pirates.

In one respect, it might be better than a Pirates museum because the Pirates are not the story tellers. Stories told about you, after all, are often better told by someone else. In this case, the museum falls under the umbrella of the history center and a champions committee. That notion is brought home not long after entering. Among the first stops is the overture space—an open theater area every visitor comes to after emerging from a tunnel and a locker room. A larger screen dominates one end; smaller screens line the side walls. The room darkens. Music and narration build from the dark and from the past. Screens light up. Memories play. Hairs rise on the back of the neck. Wagner waits to bat. Pirates long dead flicker around a stadium long built over. Bill Mazeroski homers. Roberto Clemente drives hit No. 3,000 into the left-center field gap, and Pops lofts a home run long into a dark October night.

But there is also championship boxing at Forbes Field. There is Tony Dorsett running to the Heisman Trophy and Mario Lemieux making a goalie look foolish. There is Roger Kingdom hurdling toward Olympic gold and Franco Harris galloping into an immaculate legend. Chip Ganassi kisses the bricks at Indy just as many Steelers kiss the Lombardi Trophy. In and out. Left side, then right. Bob Prince's voice, then Mike Lange's. Cheers from Three Rivers Stadium echo off the roof of the Civic Arena. How high is too high?

By themselves, the Pirates' flashbacks would likely induce the same sensory reaction. But sewn together into the best of all sports that a century-plus has to offer, a visitor sees the Pirates' greater contributions to the whole of Pittsburgh's sports tapestry. And it's not on the fringes, but an integral piece of the cloth—one the franchise began to sew long before there was a Steelers Nation or a Stanley Cup. It's a fact that two decades of losing and cultural irrelevance in the late twentieth and early twenty-first centuries might have diminished—a fact a generation that never knew a world without cellphones or reality TV might have never known.

But it was so. The succeeding artifacts are evidence. The pitching rubber that Ralph Terry toed moments before Maz became a legend. A ticket stub from the first game at Forbes Field. Pie

Traynor's 1925 World Series pin. Willie Stargell's bat. Andrew McCutchen's uniform. Steve Blass's glove. The Gunner's voice. Frankie Gustine's dream. Every Pirates baseball card you had as a kid (or wished you had).

"Every artifact tells a story," said history center president and CEO Andy Masich when the museum opened in 2004.

And the Pirates have had their share of stories. Actually, they've had more than their share.

88 Go Ahead, Top This

Hank Aaron hit 755 home runs and held baseball's all-time record for 33 years, yet it was Aaron who said, "the triple is the most exciting play in baseball." If so, then no player was more exciting throughout baseball in 1912 than John Owen "Chief" Wilson. On April 13, in the Pirates' second game of the season, Wilson, a 28-year-old outfielder in his fifth season, tripled off Cardinals pitcher Bill Steele in the second inning of a game in St. Louis. By the time the season ended six months later in Cincinnati, his count stood at 36.

Thirty-six triples.

The number broke by 11 the previous modern-era record of 25 set in 1903 by the player who was synonymous with the three-base hit in the early twentieth century, Detroit's Sam Crawford. It broke by five the professional baseball record of 31 set by Dave Orr of the American Association's New York Metropolitans in 1886 and equaled by Heinie Reitz of the National League's Baltimore Orioles in 1894. And it set a so-far unreachable major league record that no player since has even remotely approached it. Only two single-season major league records have stood longer: batting average (Nap Lajoie, .426 in 1901) and pitching wins (41 by Jack Chesbro in 1904).

Yet at 6'2" and 185 lbs., Wilson was not particularly fast as most would associate with a big triples hitter. Rather, in a day of cavernous ballparks and still a few years before Babe Ruth re-imagined the home run in the mind of the game, Wilson was, by definition of the day, a slugger. He didn't so much drive the ball into gaps as he knocked it over outfielders' heads into that area between a team's last line of defense and fences that, in the case of Forbes Field, ranged up to 460' from home plate. A year earlier, he'd hit 12 home runs—a Pirates record that stood until 1925—and driven in a National League best 107 runs.

Of Wilson, a story in *Sporting Life* that summer read, "Chief Wilson's three base shots are entitled to be credited as one of the wonders of 1912. Best of all, few of the smashes have struck in front of fielders. They have been all over their heads or between the fields, all juicy jams. Ask any pitcher if Wilson hits a high ball hard."

Fans at Forbes Field got into his unprecedented triples binge, even in a season in which National League batters smacked 684 of them—a record that, like Wilson's, still stands. Anything else became a disappointment, such as when Wilson "attempted to triple, but tapped the pellet a trifle too hard and floated it over the right field wall." Disappointment? In a home run? It was another time—of pellets and juicy jams, apparently. It was the year of Chief Wilson.

He would not have another year like it. In fact, he played just one more season with the Pirates and then three with the St. Louis Cardinals before fading from baseball entirely. In those four years, he wouldn't hit 36 triples combined. That one year still stands, though. And, with smaller parks the norm and home runs having long since become the juicy jam of our day, there is a good chance the record will stand for all time.

89 The Ultimate Penalty

Officially, 11 players, including Dave Parker, Keith Hernandez, and Lonnie Smith, were penalized by Major League Baseball as a result of the Pittsburgh Drug Trials of 1985. Most came back from the hit to their careers, and most were able to clean up their lives and their images. Parker made three more All-Star teams. Hernandez batted .310 with 83 RBIs to help the Mets win the 1986 World Series. Smith was voted the major league Comeback Player of the Year in 1989. The irony is that the player who ultimately paid the greatest price was not penalized at all by commissioner Peter Ueberroth.

Rod Scurry, a 29-year-old left-handed pitcher from Reno, Nevada, was the Pirates first-round draft pick in 1974—No. 11 overall—out of Procter Hug High School. "When I first saw him, I said, 'Nobody can hit his curveball,'" Pirates manager Chuck Tanner said. "He's better than this league." Scurry's curve, in fact, reminded him of Sandy Koufax. "That's why I thought he'd be one of the best in relief I ever managed." Still, Scurry couldn't crack the Pirates roster until 1980. In retrospect, the timing of his success couldn't have been worse.

As testimony in the '85 trials revealed, cocaine was the recreational drug of choice in society as the 1980s dawned, and it had found its way into the bowels of Three Rivers Stadium. While prevalent throughout the major leagues, its hold was no stronger than in Pittsburgh—the perceived epicenter of the sport's problem based on the publicity generated by the trials. For as strong as the drug's hold was, Scurry was that weak and susceptible to it. The mix was toxic.

In 1982, Scurry had 14 saves and a 1.74 ERA. It would be the best season of his career. His numbers fell off in 1983, and in early April 1984 it was announced that he had entered a drug reha-bilitation facility. It was only the first of Scurry's links to cocaine. After completing his rehab program, he was activated in May and went 5–6 with a 2.53 ERA, but also failed to show up for a game in Philadelphia and was suspended for not following his aftercare program.

As the 1985 season careened toward the team's second consecu-tive last-place finish and the trials in September, Scurry was the first player directly linked to the investigation of drug use in baseball when in August he was identified as the customer of a man who had pleaded guilty to selling cocaine. It came out that one night during a game, Scurry had gone looking to buy cocaine. It came out that he'd purchased cocaine as many as 20 times in 1982–83. He testified before the grand jury, though he was not among the 20-plus players called as witnesses in the trial that September of Curtis Strong and six other men who were actually the ones on trial.

Scurry was done as a Pirate. Even before the final post-mortems on the trials were written, general manager Joe L. Brown announced on September 13 that the Pirates had sold Scurry to the New York Yankees. "With the public and media attention Rod has received here, it would be difficult for him to have the kind of success he's capable of having if he were to stay with the Pirates," Brown said.

He never found that success. The Yankees released him. The San Francisco Giants traded him. Finally, on December 21, 1988, the Seattle Mariners let him go. Scurry was out of baseball for good at age 32 and with just 19 wins and an addiction to cocaine to show for that Sandy Koufax–like curveball. Three days after his release by the Mariners, Scurry was arrested for possession and use outside a known crack house in Reno. While he may have never found success on the mound, he always found cocaine.

Not quite four years later, on the night of October 29, 1992, Scurry stood outside his house in Reno. Police were there. Scurry claimed there were snakes inside his house, crawling on him and biting him. He wouldn't—or couldn't—calm down. Police attempted to handcuff him. He became agitated and violent. They scuffled. Then he stopped breathing. He never returned home. He was taken to a hospital and spent the next week on life support. The man who was never officially punished as a result of the Pittsburgh Drug Trials seven years before died November 5, 1992. He left behind a wife and two children. The official cause of death was listed as a heart attack—a cocaine-caused heart attack.

90 The Doctor Was In

George "Doc" Medich came by his nickname naturally. By summer, the right-hander from nearby Aliquippa, Pennsylvania, was a major league pitcher who would win 124 games in his career, including eight for the Pirates in 1976. By winter, he was George Medich, Pitt pre-med student.

He was 27, five years a major league pitcher, and 15 weeks from becoming Dr. George Medich as the Pirates opened the '76 season in Philadelphia's Veterans Stadium. With Medich pitching 7⅓ innings in his Pirates debut after being acquired from the Yankees in the offseason for Dock Ellis, Willie Randolph, and Ken Brett, they won the opener on Saturday in 11 innings. A day later, they were an hour from Game 2 when Medich's worlds convulsed and converged in the stands of The Vet.

A 73-year-old man was having a heart attack in a seat near the field. Medich was walking past. "I've been around enough to know the signs," Medich said. Bluish lips, flushed face, and no chest movement.

Medich climbed into the stands. Someone told Medich that the man had a pulse, but Medich could not detect one. He thumped the man's chest. He breathed air into the man's lungs. He compressed his chest. Air. Compressions. Air. Compressions. One observer guessed he worked for at least 20 minutes until paramedics arrived. Many elementary school children would come to know CPR (cardio pulmonary resuscitation) by the end of the twentieth century, but in 1976 its ins and outs were still mostly a mystery outside the medical field.

The man was alive—albeit barely—when he was wheeled from the seating area, but he would be dead 30 minutes later. A stroke and four previous heart attacks likely curtailed his chances. And Medich wasn't certain how long the attack had been in progress before he arrived.

It didn't matter. Medich had to try until he couldn't try any longer. "That's the bottom line...helping people," he told Phil Musick of the *Pittsburgh Press*.

"Someone mentioned that the drama of death had reduced the art of throwing a baseball to insignificance," Musick wrote.

Medich, who had seen the point from both ends, responded, "Matter of perspective," he said. "It's a different kind of pressure, seeing someone die in your hands."

91 Chester, Oliver, Hanna, and Saul

Arguably, not since the days of the Green Weenie have fake food products been so popular at Pirates games. Even the jaded eye will, if only for a moment and because it forgets it's jaded, pay attention between the bottom of the fifth inning and top of the sixth when

The Pittsburgh Pierogies mix it up with the Pirate Parrot during their race on August 28, 2003, during the Pirates-Marlins game. (Pittsburgh Post-Gazette, Matt Freed)

Chester, Hanna, Saul, and Oliver make their entrance at PNC Park on game days. Milwaukee has its sausages. Washington has its presidents. And Pittsburgh has the Great Pittsburgh Pierogi Race N'at, a "race" of four human-sized stuffed dumplings, including one who swings a mean purse and another who holds his own despite being too geeky to have much chance in the real world.

The name is an apparent homage to both Pittsburgh's roots as a destination for Eastern European immigrants in the late nineteenth and early twentieth centuries and to a dialect that has become identifiable with Western Pennsylvania. The pierogi is a dumpling traditionally stuffed with potato filling, sauerkraut, ground meat, or cheese, then baked or fried in butter with onions, giving rise to racing names Cheese Chester, Oliver Onion, Sauerkraut Saul, and the dear, departed Potato Pete. As for the "N'at" that grammatically has no business being at the end of the race name anywhere but in Pittsburgh among Yinzers—as in Where Yinz Goin'?—it is an extender commonly utilized at the end of a sentence when there's nothing more to be said yet when silence (or a period) is, um, well, like, ya know, not an option.

Because of that, while racing presidents might possibly work outside the Washington Beltway, racing pierogies would seem out of place away from the three rivers. There, the races have lasted for nearly two decades, first in the final two years at Three Rivers Stadium (1999–2000), now at PNC Park (2001–present). They race at every home game between the bottom of the fifth inning and top of the sixth, always the same so that fans, particularly those with children, know not to go out for a hot dog or take a bathroom break. Fans have their favorites. Children giggle. Some older fans even throw down a friendly wager as the stuffed pillows make their way around the outfield warning track. Funny how by the end of the season all four are virtually tied in wins going into the final race, but, since Las Vegas has never been involved, federal authorities have never been called in.

It's fun and all Pittsburgh. And who among Yinzers by birth and Yinzers by choice didn't take some silent joy the night in 2009 when—in a rare out-of-town matchup against the four presidents from D.C.—Potato Pete came out of nowhere to drop "Teddy Roosevelt" with a flying tackle and allow Sauerkraut Saul to race home with victory for the hometown pierogies...and for Pittsburgh?

92 The Kid Falls

Many fans in Three Rivers Stadium that Sunday afternoon swear they heard Jason Kendall's right ankle blow out. Too many, including players on both sides, saw it and wish they hadn't. "I'm still nauseous," said Milwaukee Brewers first baseman Mark Loretta after the game. The play was reminiscent of a $1 million racehorse breaking down at full gallop—beautiful and majestic one moment, and pitifully lame and flailing the next.

"I have never seen an injury quite like it," Pirates team physician Dr. Jack Failla said. Local television stations would come under fire for what they showed and how often they showed it. Letters to the editor in local newspapers questioned news judgment and good taste in the pictures that ran the next morning. It was that bad, the 21st most gruesome injury in sports history, opined website Bleacher Report more than a decade later. Still, Kendall, known as "The Kid" from the time he cracked the lineup at age 21, said it was good baseball.

Milwaukee pitcher Steve Woodard had set down the first 13 Pirates he faced the afternoon of July 4, 1999, including seven by strikeout. Kendall was the second batter up in the fifth inning. The Pirates trailed 3–0. Kendall, fifth in the National League in batting at .333, went to the plate looking to jump-start the offense more than break up a no-hitter when he made a fateful decision. He opted to bunt. It was a perfect bunt down the third-base line. Kendall charged from the batter's box. Brewers third baseman Jeff Cirillo ran in on the ball. Kendall picked up speed. Cirillo barehanded the bunt. Kendall neared first. Cirillo threw. Kendall didn't lunge, but drove full speed through the bag. Cirillo's throw popped

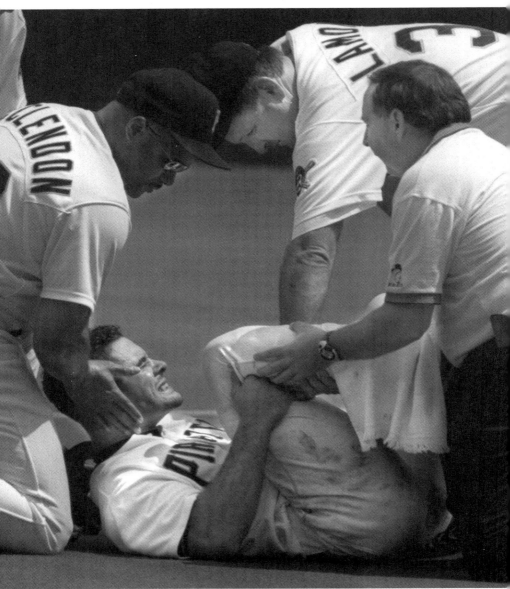

Pirates hitting coach Lloyd Mclendon, manager Gene LaMont, and trainer Kent Biggerstaff (right) attend to Jason Kendall after he broke his right ankle trying to bunt for a single in the fifth inning of a game against the Brewers on July 4, 1999. (*Pittsburgh Post-Gazette*, Bob Donaldson)

into Loretta's glove. Kendall's right foot hit the outside corner of the base. It bent awkwardly, and it popped, too.

"I looked down and saw the bone sticking out of my sock," Kendall said. "I took another step and thought, *This isn't too smart,* so I went right down on my back."

"His foot was pointing one way and the bone was the other way," Loretta said.

The lower leg flopped uselessly until the team trainer could reach him and hold it. A towel was put over the leg as much to protect Kendall from seeing it as to those sitting and standing near him. The ankle was not broken but dislocated; the bone was effectively turned upside down. It didn't matter. Kendall's season was finished.

The question that hung out there as limply as his foot: was his career finished, too? After all, he was a catcher—the most demanding position physically in baseball and one that requires the ankles and feet to support the body in a crouch as many as 150 times a game. He was only 25, but "few who watched him writhe in agony...thought Kendall would come back the same player in 2000. If at all," wrote Paul Meyer of the *Pittsburgh Post-Gazette.* "I didn't think there was any way," Pirates Hall of Famer Bill Mazeroski said.

Kendall defied them all, though. He beat every odd, slayed every doubt. When the Pirates took the field to open the 2000 season—274 grueling days of rehabilitation after an injury comparable to the broken leg suffered by Joe Theismann on *Monday Night Football* in 1985 that ended his career—Kendall was in the lineup batting leadoff...and catching. Amazing? Not as amazing as the fact that he would not only catch regularly that season, but that no catcher in the National League would catch more. He played 147 games behind the plate; he started 145. What's more, he batted .320, hit a career-high 14 home runs, became the first Pirates catcher to score 100 runs (112), stole 22 bases, and started—at catcher—for the National League in the All-Star Game.

In fact, he would go on to play 11 more seasons, set the Pirates' franchise record for games caught (1,205), and finish his career with 2,025 games played at the position—fifth-most in major league history—by the time he retired in 2010 at age 36. Not bad for The Kid whose career hung by a few frayed ligaments one horrific Sunday afternoon more than a decade before.

"I hope," Kendall joked one day during his comeback in early 2000, "I'm not remembered as [just] the guy who put his foot on backward."

93 Holy Moises

The 1994 All-Star Game at Three Rivers Stadium "is considered by most die-hards as one of the best All-Star Games ever played," according to *Baseball Almanac*. It featured five lead changes, a game-tying home run in the bottom of the ninth, and it ended on a play at the plate—one of only six contests to be decided on the game's final play. It might also be the one All-Star Game that seems as if it was never played. It was, of course. July 12, 1994. Despite the 59,568 who were there and the 50 million fans who watched on television, it might require a Google search just to be sure.

Even as Pittsburgh played host to its fourth Midsummer Classic, the specter of a work stoppage that would historically lay waste to the last third of the season and the World Series lurked just outside the gates. For as good as the game was, the memory of it tends to get lost in the dust storm of lawsuits, ill will, financial data, failed mediation, court dates, and fan outrage that blotted

Tony Gwynn celebrates after scoring the winning run in the bottom of the 10th after a hit by Moises Alou on July 12, 1993. (*Pittsburgh Post-Gazette*, Peter Diana)

out the sun over the next nine months. In any other summer, the All-Star Game would have fed into the season's second half and the race to October. That summer, it fed into an abyss and its unfinished business is what is most remembered. Would Tony Gwynn have hit .400 as he was threatening to do? Would the future of the Montreal Expos have been different had they been allowed to play out a season in which they had the best record—and best team—in baseball? Would Matt Williams, with 43 home runs and two months to play, have been the one to break Roger Maris' single-season home run record four years before Mark McGwire?

The shame of it is that the American and National League put on a dramatic show that night, worthy of Ted Williams' three-run, walk-off homer in 1941, Stan Musial's game-ender in '55, and Pete Rose famously bowling over Ray Fosse to score the winner in 1970.

After twice trailing in the game, the American League appeared headed to a seventh consecutive All-Star win after scoring three runs in the sixth and three more in the seventh to take a 7–5 lead. The National League went down quietly in the seventh and eighth innings.

AL manager Cito Gaston called on hulking right-hander Lee Smith, then the closer for the Baltimore Orioles and the major league saves leader with 29, to pitch the ninth. Due up for the NL: Marquis Grissom, Craig Biggio, and a pinch-hitter for Randy Myers, the NL pitcher. Smith walked Grissom, but Biggio forced him at second. To bat for Myers, NL manager Jim Fregosi had to choose between Jeff Conine and Fred McGriff. He opted for the lefty-swinging McGriff.

"I was hoping Jim [Fregosi] had used him earlier," Gaston joked later.

As he stepped in, McGriff was in the midst of a streak in which he had hit at least 30 home runs every season since 1988. Smith got ahead in the count. One ball. Two strikes. McGriff fouled off several pitches. Then Smith delivered a fastball away. McGriff swung. "All I was thinking was, *Let it go, be aggressive.*" He hit it square. And he hit it well. It ended up in the center-field seats for a game-tying two-run homer. Teammate Greg Maddux gushed, "To sit there for three hours…you have to be special to do what he did."

What transpired an inning later proved special, too. After reliever Doug Jones escaped an American League threat in the top of the 10th to preserve the 7–7 tie, the National League gave fans something not seen in nearly a quarter-century. Tony Gwynn led off the National League's half of the inning with a single to center field off Jason Bere. Moises Alou, who had replaced Barry Bonds in the ninth, was due up next. As a one-time Pirates prospect, Alou had recorded his first major league hit at Three Rivers in 1990. "That was something I'll never forget," he said. He would never forget the next few minutes, either.

Alou rifled a Bere pitch toward left-center field. Neither left fielder Albert Belle nor center fielder Kenny Lofton were going to flag it down. "As soon as he hit it, I took off," Gwynn said. The ball short-hopped the wall. Pirates manager Jim Leyland, coaching third base for the NL, waved him home even though the stocky Gwynn was easily the most speed-deficient player in the NL lineup. "Coming around third I had my doubts," Gwynn said.

AL shortstop Cal Ripken Jr. delivered a strike to catcher Ivan Rodriguez. Gwynn slid. "I saw Rodriguez catch the ball, but I barely got my foot in. When [home plate umpire Paul Runge] called me safe, I about lost it." So did his teammates. So did the thrilled crowd, which was treated to the first home-plate finish to an All-Star Game since Rose-Fosse in 1970. In 2013, *Bleacher Report* rated it the 37th greatest moment in All-Star Game history.

94 The Man From "Z"

Some things, like the movie that inspired it, are difficult to explain. For more than a decade, it was a mostly ignored hand gesture in a largely obscure movie perhaps best known for giving Ashton Kutcher his big-screen breakthrough. Then one day, one station's programming schedule, one major league team's season schedule, and one television set in Atlanta all happened to align like a set of cosmic tumblers to the vault door of one of life's great mysteries and out stepped a connection between the long-suffering Pirates and their fans not seen since the Green Weenie in the 1960s.

The Pirates of 2012–13 had a hit sign, a bunt sign, a steal sign, a stop sign, and, after a four-game series against the Braves in Atlanta in April 2012, a Zoltan sign—a gesture made with the hands by extending them in front of the body, turning the left hand palm out, the right hand palm in and touching the two at the tips of the thumbs, thereby forming the letter Z. By all accounts, second baseman Neil Walker was the first to start goofing with it.

"We were watching [television] in the clubhouse, and there was nothing we wanted to watch," he said. "We saw *Dude, Where's My Car?* And guys were like, 'Oh, we haven't seen this in a while.' So we watched it."

Among the many oddball characters in a movie whose title betrayed the depth of its plot—"two potheads wake up from a night of partying and can't remember where they parked their car"—is Zoltan, the leader of a cult of geeks obsessed with outer space. The cult's "secret" sign is the hand-scripted Z.

"It was just so terrible and stupid," Walker said. But it was terrible and stupid in that good-bad sort of way. Walker started flashing the "Z" when the Pirates made a big play or got a big hit. A few others did the same. In its infancy, it was a bonding experience. But few outside the club noticed.

That changed a week later. The Pirates were down to the Washington Nationals 4–3 in the bottom of the ninth on a Tuesday night in mid-May with their slumping catcher, Rod Barajas, at the plate. Barajas was 0-for-3 and had yet to hit a home run or drive in a run since signing a $4 million contract in the offseason. What he did next not only jump-started a run to the top of the standings but invited the fans along for the ride. The 36-year-old catcher with no homers pulled the first pitch he saw

Hal Sparks, the actor who played Zoltan in Dude, Where's My Car?, *gives the Zoltan sign to fans before the start of the game against the Cubs on July 25, 2012. Sparks threw out the first pitch.* (Pittsburgh Post-Gazette, Matt Freed)

down the line and into the seats just inside the left-field foul pole for a game-winning, two-run homer.

As Barajas rounded third base and headed for home, every player on the Pirates bench waited for him at the plate. They weren't just waiting, though. They were also flashing the "Z." Barajas laughed, and he flashed back. Cameras captured the moment. It made highlight shows. It appeared in the next day's newspapers. But what was it? What did it mean?

With one swing of the bat, Barajas revealed the man, the myth, the cellophane-wrapped legend that was to be Zoltan.

What began as an inside joke among overgrown kids became a sensation that enveloped the team and its fans. With the players flashing the "Z" after every big hit and fans giving it back to them from the stands and T-shirt vendors slapping hands onto every shirt that didn't have buttons down the front, and the media trying to find new ways to define the undefinable, the Pirates that had not had a winning season since 1992 suddenly began to win. They had been four games under .500 before Barajas' home run. By the end of May they were back to .500 then played .633 ball over the next two-plus months to find themselves at 63–47 on August 8. The original Zoltan also known as actor/comedian Hal Sparks even showed up for a game and threw out the first pitch. Naturally, the Pirates won.

That they collapsed into a 20th consecutive losing season that year was never blamed on Zoltan. His powers, after all, rested more on the offensive side. He couldn't do much about a tired and frayed pitching staff or prevent Cincinnati Reds pitchers from throwing at Pirates batters.

Even as they lost, the players remained faithful to the "Z," and so did the fans. And when the Pirates finally did end that long run of losing a season later, the hands were right there with them. After a big hit. In the stands. On shirts. Still as inexplicable as the fact that the movie that gave it to the Pirates somehow earned nearly $47 million at the box office.

Did it make a difference? As manager Clint Hurdle said after Barajas' home run that night in May 2012, "You can't be looking for tangible evidence all the time to make things right."

95 Tip the Sax Man

As surely as the statues of Clemente, Stargell, Wagner, and Mazeroski can be counted on to be at their posts, "The Sax Man" can be counted on to be at his usual spot halfway across the Clemente Bridge—the gateway between downtown Pittsburgh and

PNC Park and across which thousands of Pirates fans find their way to the park on game days. Before and after. Rain or shine. Win or lose (and he's played "Taps" after a lot of losing). Playing in 10- or 15-second bursts. Playing for change. Playing because he likes music and he likes sports and he once upon a time found out he could make a living standing on the bridge and blowing a tune into an old saxophone that long ago was separated from its shine. Playing for so long, it could be argued, that he's played more games at PNC Park than anyone since it opened in 2001.

Reggie Howze would like to hear his "Sax Man" persona referred to in such fashion. At one time, he would have hoped it would have been as the next Tony Pena or Manny Sanguillen. As a kid growing up in Pittsburgh's Hill District, Howze played several sports, but it was as a catcher that he dreamed his dream, carrying it as far as attending one of the Pirates' open tryouts at Three Rivers Stadium in the mid-1980s. There might have been as many as 400 hopefuls that day. He didn't make it. If he had, he might've found himself farther up on this list.

As it is, he still made the cut. Why? Because as managers and players and seasonal hopes came and went in the early days of PNC Park, Howze became a constant. Is it a stretch to imagine he'll be longer remembered by fans who regularly heard him blow on the bridge than will the likes of come-and-gone Pirates such as J.R. House, Yamid Haad, or Bruce Aven? Is it too difficult to imagine that thousands of fans have thrown fifty cents or a buck in his case at some time over the years and found it money better spent than the millions the team gave to Derek Bell or Matt Morris? If it were, Howze would have moved on long ago. Instead, he's been there from Opening Day through fan appreciation day for as long as the park has been open. "I kind of equate it to Cal Ripken. I've got a streak going," he said.

One moment he's playing the theme from *Rocky*, the next he's riffing on Cleveland because he spied someone with a Browns

Reggie Howze, also known as the Sax Man, playing on the Roberto Clemente Bridge before the Pirates home opener against the Los Angeles Dodgers on April 5, 2010. (Pittsburgh Post-Gazette, Bill Wade)

jersey. That bleeds into the first few lines of "Here We Go Steelers," from which he bounces into a sports headline of the day, which caroms back to the sax and the da-da-da, da-da-da of ESPN's *SportsCenter* and then a promise that the Pirates have a better chance of winning, or not losing, or not getting rained out, if you tip The Sax Man. Anyone gotta high-five for The Sax Man? As the patter goes, tipping The Sax Man has been known to cure losing streaks, guarantee sweeps, help Andrew McCutchen's dreadlocks grow, and, in a few cases, help troubled marriages before he plays the last note of Stevie Wonder's "Isn't She Lovely."

It's a melding of sports with the music that has set him apart from other buskers who show up for a while but have never remained. Perhaps because they never had the patter and they never had the love.

"I like baseball, and I like this horn," he said. "I've found a niche, and it works. I use everything that I can to connect with people.

"Some days it's 98 degrees and I'm on the bridge blowing. I'm always blowing. In fact, I might end up dying on the bridge."

And in memoriam he would ask but one thing—a day's always better when you tip The Sax Man.

96 A Big Hurt

Officially, the longest home run hit at Three Rivers Stadium was 483' into the upper deck in left field by Philadelphia's Greg Luzinski off Pirates pitcher Don Robinson on April 18, 1979. Officially, Willie Stargell hit the most home runs into its far reaches, owning four of the nine balls hit into the 600 level of the stadium that was the Pirates' home from 1970 to 2000. But those who were there July 11, 1994, know that they saw the longest ball ever hit there. It didn't actually count for anything. But it wasn't a work of fiction, either, only legend.

Ken Griffey Jr. won the first of his three All-Star Home Run Derby titles that afternoon, but it was one monster shot by Frank Thomas, a 6'5", 275-lb. first baseman for the Chicago White Sox who had once played football for Auburn and would go on to hit 521 (real) career home runs, that provided the day's takeaway moment. Considering the afternoon Griffey had, it needed to have been on par with a swing not seen since Paul Bunyan cleared the North Woods. Of the seven home runs Griffey hit, five landed in the upper deck in right field, including one measured at 512'. Thomas managed just one. And it wasn't even the one that dropped the stadium's collective jaw.

The one entrenched in memory didn't even reach the upper deck but instead hit off a banner hanging on its façade. What made it so impressive was that the part of the façade where the banner hung was nine sections over from the left-field foul pole. "That one would have gone to the Civic Arena," said Pirates assistant coach Rich Donnelly, referring to Pittsburgh's one-time arena that stood one river and about 10 blocks southeast of Three Rivers. The distance attached to the bomb was 519', or 36' longer than Luzinski's in-game record.

Donnelly pitched to seven of the eight participants that day and admitted to trying to give up the longest batted ball in stadium history. With Thomas' blast, it was mission accomplished.

That said, his blast shouldn't have come as a total shock. Thomas, nicknamed "The Big Hurt" for his menacing power, was hitting .383 at the All-Star break that year with 32 home runs and 78 RBIs, and he was on pace to become the first player in history to hit .350 with 50 homers and 150 walks in a season that was cut off at the knees by a labor stoppage. It was a season so good that when asked how to pitch to him that year, one American League manager remarked that the best way was to "throw it 10' in front of the plate and hope he doesn't hit it on the first hop."

His magnificence also prompted Gregg Jefferies, a National League All-Star and witness to Thomas' shot, to propose a modification to derby rules. "Frank Thomas is just too big," he said. "If you're over 260 lbs., there should be a rule—that you have to play football."

97 Sausage Brat Out the Wurst in Him

"...It's practically standing still now...Get this, Charlie; get this, Charlie! It's crashing! It's crashing terrible! Oh, my! Get out of the way, hot dog, please!...Italian Sausage is falling on the dirt track around the stadium. And all the folks agree that this is terrible; this is the worst of catastrophes in the world...it's...cr---ashing...oh! Four or five feet into the sky...and it's a terrific crash, ladies and gentlemen. It... hot sausage, and it's in flames now...Oh, the meat products! And all the sausages screaming around here...Ah! It's...it...it's a...ah! I...I can't talk ladies and gentlemen. Honest; it's just lying there, a mass of smoking sausage..."

—How the late Herbert Morrison of WLS Radio
(or "Les Nessman" of WKRP in Cincinnati, for that matter)
might have called the Milwaukee Brewers'
sausage race the night of July 9, 2003

Randall Simon, a 28-year-old first baseman from Curacao and a ballplayer with no priors when it comes to encased meat parts, hit 10 home runs and drove in 51 runs in just more than half a season for the Pirates in 2003. Yet it was a seemingly innocuous swat to the chef's hat of a racing sausage mascot for which—for better or, um, wurst—he will likely be most remembered. As grown-up kids are wont to do, his intention was to make his buddies laugh. What he got that night of July 9, 2003, was a trip to jail (in handcuffs), a fine, a suspension and, incredibly, enough notoriety over the ensuing few days to make it seem as if Lizzie Borden had risen from the grave wielding a Louisville Slugger and was clubbing baby pigs.

The Pirates and Milwaukee Brewers were tied 1–1. The game in Miller Park was headed to the bottom of the seventh inning. Per tradition, out came the Brewers' four racing sausages—four volunteers sporting top-heavy, 7'3" mascot costumes each representing a different type of packed meat product—for their nightly race around the ballpark. As they made their way past the Pirates' dugout, Simon—standing at the dugout rail and packing a bat—took a short swing at the hat of the Italian sausage. The Italian, worn by 19-year-old Mandy Block, lost her balance and fell…right into the path of the hot dog, worn by Veronica Piech. Down she went, too.

At that point, the incident was at most a clip for *SportsCenter* with injuries requiring little more than a squirt of Bactine and a kiss from Mom to make it all better. "I think just because I'm so small and it's such a big costume that I tumbled. And the reason I couldn't get up right away is because I couldn't get up," Block said. But then, someone turned the script over to Harold Pinter, and this odd little cast of characters became preposterously linked (sorry) for all time.

Milwaukee County sheriff's deputies reviewed video. Newscasts in Milwaukee bannered it as bacon, er, breaking news at 11:00. Simon's night at the pork ended not only with him wearing the collar at the plate but also handcuffs in the back of a police car (though there were unconfirmed reports of him being taken away in a patty wagon) on the way to Milwaukee County Jail.

260

Back at the stadium, one Brewers executive vice president, who shall remain nameless to protect the bombastically stupid, described Simon's actions as "an insane act of a person whose conduct is unjustifiable.... It sickened me to see it." Upon hearing that, witnesses who had maintained their hold on reality hurried back to review video in search of the shooter on the grassy knoll they must have missed. Oh, the absurdity!

Whether the editors in Taipei, Taiwan, were attracted by a meaty story or by its (over)reactionary sizzle, news organizations there and around the world picked up the summer tale. By all accounts, none—thankfully—took it as seriously as the aforementioned Brewers VP. A sampling: "Wurst is over for Simon"—*Taipei Times*. "Sausage links Simon to infamy"—*San Jose Mercury News*. "Beef is over"—*Pittsburgh Post-Gazette*. "He shouldn't get the electric chair, but at least the electric skillet"—*Houston Chronicle*.

Oh, the verbal carnage!

In addition to equal amounts mortification and public humiliation, Simon wound up with a $432 fine for disorderly conduct, a $2,000 fine from Major League Baseball, and a three-game suspension.

And Block? Just 19 and a college student, she may have exhibited the most seasoning of any of the principals. Headlines? Fame? Police? Celebrity? Microphones? Cameras? "It just seems ridiculous. It's like a big sausage getting hit by a bat causes all this controversy." Her incredulity was evident.

Then, in a statement that cut through the gristle to perhaps the incident's one truism—it's one momentary glimpse into God's plan—she explained simply:

"I'm just a sausage running a race."

Oh, the humanity, indeed.

98 Seriously?

Mining the full depth of his insight, Nuke LaLoosh stared intently into a TV reporter's camera near the end of the film, *Bull Durham* and pontificates, "Sometimes you win, sometimes you lose...and sometimes it rains." But a rainout in the Houston Astrodome, baseball's first indoor stadium and the so-called Eighth Wonder of the World when it opened in 1965? As Charley Feeney wrote in the next day's *Pittsburgh Post-Gazette*, "Honest to goodness, it really happened."

Tuesday night, June 15, 1976. The Pirates and Houston Astros were scheduled for a 7:35 PM first pitch in the second game of a three-game series. Instead, as 7:35 came and went, the teams sat around tables near second base—in uniform, though shower shoes were more the fashion that night than spikes—eating steak and fried chicken and wondering where this night might rank among the most absurd moments in their careers.

It had begun raining that morning. But for a baseball player in Houston in those days, weather didn't matter. The Astros had played indoors for more than a decade. Management didn't even bother to include a rain-check policy on ticket stubs. What would be the purpose? This was no ordinary rain, though.

By the time the Pirates boarded their chartered bus for the 8–10 minute ride from their hotel to the Dome, flooding was already being reported, and cars were being abandoned. Players saw a manhole cover elevating 6' off the ground, the result of overtaxed sewers and drains. And that 8–10 minute ride? It turned into 30.

But they made it, as did the Astros. Perhaps they were lucky. Floodwaters in some areas near the dome were 5' deep. In the players' parking lot, cars sat in 4' of water. Because the Astrodome sat 45' below ground level, the lower ramps and entries were also under water. Most stadium workers couldn't get through. Neither could fans who thought about thumbing their nose at the weather and getting out to see a ballgame. "It was like a tropical storm. It was raining hard, and it just kept coming down," Mike Acosta, Astros historian, recounted in a 2009 story in the *Houston Chronicle*.

By 6:00 PM, Astros management called the game. The teams were there. The field was playable. But little else about the night was right, including the line that appeared in the major league standings the next morning: Pittsburgh at Houston, ppd. So why not have dinner on the field, a surreal scene witnessed by 45,000 empty seats in what for one night was the world's largest company picnic shelter? Folding tables were set up near second base, and Astrodome management had the grills fired up.

The announcement of the postponement was made by Astros public relations director Don Davidson. "I'm not even going to try to make it to my car," Davidson said. "I'm staying in the dome tonight." To which *Pittsburgh Press* writer Russ Franke pointed out, "Nobody can blame him for playing it safe. Don Davidson is 4'4" tall."

Sometime after 10:00 PM, Pirates players were told the bus was available to take them back to their hotel. Most of the 10½ inches of rain that fell on Houston that day had fallen. Still, the bus driver had to do some on-the-fly navigation through the city streets before reaching his destination. And when he did? The Pirates' traveling party applauded. It had been that kind of night.

99 An Adopted Son

By his own admission, Frankie Gustine was never a great player. He was a middling "plugger" on perennially second-division Pirates teams of the 1940s. He made three All-Star teams but was just a .265 career hitter who never hit .300 or more than nine home runs or drove in more than 67 runs in any of 10 seasons with the Pirates. Yet he wove himself into the fabric of the franchise, its fans, and the city like few outsiders had or have. He was born in Hoopeston, Illinois, but after arriving in Pittsburgh at 19, Gustine lived the life of a Pittsburgher and 'burghers loved him for it.

When traded to the Chicago Cubs in December 1948—part of a four-player deal that netted the Pirates catcher Clyde McCullough and pitcher Cliff Chambers—sportswriters of both Pittsburgh daily newspapers lamented his departure. "He'll leave behind him a lot of good baseball and a lot of good friends," wrote Vince Johnson of the *Post-Gazette.* "[Manager Billy] Meyer's colorful ballplayer won the affection of Pittsburgh fans simply because he gave the best that he had in every game he played." Middling pluggers hardly merit such fanfare unless they have some quality that transcends the stat sheet of the mostly average.

Perhaps it manifested itself in his comments to Johnson after his trade. "I am going away with the feeling that I made more friends than enemies," Gustine said. Then he added that he planned to continue to make Pittsburgh his home. He was a man of his word. Although he played in two more major league seasons, one in Chicago and one in St. Louis, the kid from Illinois never left Pittsburgh. He might never have been a great player, but he would be a great ex-Pirate.

In 1951, he opened Frankie Gustine's Restaurant in the Oakland section of the city. He raised money for the city's Children's Hospital. He coached basketball, first at Waynesburg College from 1949 to 1951—while still in the majors—and then at Point Park College from 1962 to 1968. He coached baseball at Point Park from 1968 to 1975. He was involved in the development of several motels and restaurants. He was so deeply ingrained in the city and its baseball team that when legends Honus Wagner and then Pie Traynor died, Gustine was asked to be a pallbearer.

Yet it was his restaurant, three blocks from the home-plate entrance to Forbes Field, where arguably all of Gustine's worlds came together—a common ground between his past and his present and between the players and the fans. Think *Cheers*, where everybody knows your name. More often than not, he was on hand to welcome anyone who came through the door. It became a gathering place for Pirates memorabilia, fans, players, and sportswriters for more than three decades—arguably one of the more important Pirates landmarks of a generation not involving actual baseball. While the Gustine name has been off the front door since 1982, the bar and restaurant (Hemingway's) that succeeded it still has much of the Gustine look to it.

So large had his footprint become by the time he died of a heart attack in 1991—nearly 52 years after he first put on a Pirates uniform—that his passing merited space on the editorial page of the *Pittsburgh Press*. Its first line proved a fine epitaph: "It would be a rare Pittsburgher, indeed, who wouldn't at least know the name of Frank Gustine, if not the man."

100 September 9, 2013: Dawn of a New Day

After 7,634 days, the final out of the game in which "It" ended certainly did not lack for symbolism. Neil Walker was seven years old the night Sid Bream slid past Mike LaValliere to deny the Pirates the 1992 National League pennant and set off the franchise on what would be the longest streak of losing in the history of North American professional sports. He was a Pirates fan that night. And living in suburban Pittsburgh where his family had settled after Tom Walker's six-year major league career ended in 1977, Neil grew up a Pirates fan. Elementary school. Middle school. A standout three-sport career at Pine-Richland High School. A Pirates fan still.

The bond took on a new dimension on June 7, 2004, when the Pirates made him their first-round pick in that year's major league draft. He began as a catcher then moved to third base. But by the time he settled into the Pirates' lineup in the middle of 2010, he was a second baseman. And it was there that just before 10:30 PM on September 9, 2013, he fielded a ground ball off the bat of Texas' A.J. Pierzynski and threw to first baseman Gaby Sanchez for that last out of the game that ensured the Pirates their first winning season since that night when he was seven.

Final score: Pirates 1, Texas Rangers 0.

Site: Rangers Ballpark in Arlington, Texas.

Winning pitcher: Gerrit Cole.

Losing pitcher: Yu Darvish.

Pirates record: 82–61.

Until that night, the closest they had come in any of the 20 seasons of losing was 79 wins, achieved in 1997 and again in 2012. With this win, though, even a cynic hardened by the unbelievably long run of failure would not be able to figure out a way they could still lose 82 games, or even 81, in a season made up of 162. Even a seven-year-old knew the arithmetic was indisputable.

"To be part of this group that has righted the ship...is pretty significant," Neil Walker said. "The fact that I've lived and breathed Pirates baseball since I can remember, being a baseball fan since I was five or six years old, it holds a little more significance to me."

He knew what it was to have seen Derek Bell go into Operation Shutdown and up-and-coming Aramis Ramirez traded away on a desperate Tuesday night and previous first-round hopes like John Van Benschoten, Bryan Bullington, and Chad Hermansen come and go like so many broken dreams. He knew what it was to have seen the Pirates fall 30 games under .500 by the All-Star break and what 8,600 fans inside cavernous Three Rivers Stadium looked and felt like on a Monday night in April.

They were images Cole and the rest of the Pirates had heard about but "we don't really understand," he said. He had lived in California his entire life until being selected No. 1 out of UCLA by the Pirates in 2011, and he had only just made his major league debut on June 11 of that season—well after the momentum toward ending the streak had found legs. Perhaps it was just as well that he lacked the full weight (or was it wait?) of 20 years as he went to the mound in Texas. A short memory couldn't have hurt in trying to best Darvish, who that season had twice flirted with no-hitters and had five times struck out at least 14 in a game. For a Pirates team that had lost a season-high four in a row after winning its 81st game on September 3 in Milwaukee and had managed only two runs and seven hits in its previous two games, facing Darvish on a steamy night in Texas hardly seemed like the formula for 82.

But against those odds, Cole—in pitcher's parlance—dealt. Armed with a biting curveball and a fastball that consistently hit the mid-90s, Cole matched Darvish zero for zero and even out-Darvished him by striking out nine in seven innings to Darvish's six. Yet the Pirates' offense didn't fare much better against Darvish than it had in losing four in a row. The night took on the feel of a game in which one run could be as good as 10. Who would crack first? The Pirates provided the answer in the seventh inning. After Andrew McCutchen struck out and Justin Morneau grounded out, the game seemed destined to go scoreless into the eighth. But then Marlon Byrd, acquired just two weeks before from the New York Mets, lashed a double into the left-field corner. Six pitches later, Pedro Alvarez, like Walker and Cole a one-time first-round draft pick, lined a double to left-center that scored Byrd. Just like that, the Pirates led 1–0.

And 1–0 was how it would stay as relievers Tony Watson and Mark Melancon finished what Cole had started 2 hours and 24 minutes before...or 7,634 days before, depending on your perspective. Either way, it ended on the eve of a future that for the first time in 20 years did not include The Streak. It was the sort of future that had been promised practically since the night Walker was seven.

Sources

Chapters

1. 3:36 PM, October 13, 1960

Biederman, Lester J. "Pirate champs 'team of destiny.'" *Pittsburgh Press*, October 14, 1960.

Dvorchak, Robert. "50 years later, Maz's home run is bigger than ever." *Pittsburgh Post-Gazette*, September 5, 2010.

Dvorchak, Robert. "Maz blinded by spotlight he likes to avoid." *Pittsburgh Post-Gazette*, July 11, 2006.

Jaffe, Chris. "The 10 greatest Game Sevens in World Series History." hardballtimes.com, January 21, 2008.

Mazeroski, Bill. "Game winner gave 'cold chill' to Maz." *Pittsburgh Press*, October 14, 1960.

McNamara, Jack. "City bats cleanup in Series." *Pittsburgh Press*, October 14, 1960.

Schoenfield, David. "The greatest game ever played." ESPN.com, October 13, 2010.

Williams, Joe. "Pirate win biggest in Pittsburgh since General Forbes' day." *Pittsburgh Press*, October 14, 1960.

2. The Perfect Loss

Biederman, Lester J. "Pirates Tried Hard To Win For Haddix." *Pittsburgh Press*, May 27, 1959.

Biederman, Lester J. "Greatest Game Ever Pitched." *Pittsburgh Press*, May 27, 1959.

Dvorchak, Robert. "Flawless Game, Absurd Ending." *Pittsburgh Post-Gazette*, May 24, 2009.

"Famous Non-Victory." *Pittsburgh Post-Gazette* editorial, January. 10, 1994.

Retrosheet.org

3. National Pride: The First World Series

Anderson, Shelly. "Cy Young found old magic as Boston rallied to win title." *Pittsburgh Post-Gazette,* June 3, 2003.

Anderson, Shelly. "Last time they met, Boston won it all." *Pittsburgh Post-Gazette*, June 1, 2003.

Anderson, Shelly. "Pirates owner took a swing at idea to make money." *Pittsburgh Post-Gazette*, June 2, 2003.

Baseball Almanac

"Champs and Boston in first game." *Pittsburgh Press*, October 6, 1903.

"Pittsburg and Boston ready for the fray." *Pittsburgh Press*, October 1, 1903.

4. The Great One

Batz, Bob. "On his first CD, organist-for-all-seasons Vince Lascheid plays 'em as he sees 'em." *Pittsburgh Post-Gazette*, March 17, 1996.

"Clemente set for Hall." *Associated Press* and *Pittsburgh Post-Gazette*, January 4, 1973.

Dvorchak, Robert. "Clemente still held in awe." *Pittsburgh Post-Gazette*, July 13, 2006.

Smizik, Bob. "Roberto gave everything he had." *Pittsburgh Press*, January 2, 1973.

5. Power Before Pops

Associated Press story, April 9, 2001.

Collier, Gene. "Farewell, Pops." *Pittsburgh Post-Gazette*, April 10, 2001.
Mandel, Ken. "Stargell's Star a Lasting Tribute." mlb.com, June 25, 2003.
Retrosheet.org

6. The First Dynasty
Baseball Almanac
Baseball-Reference.com
Finoli, David, and Bill Ranier. *The Pittsburgh Pirates Encyclopedia*. Sports Publishing, LLC, 2003.
Kovacevic, Dejan. "Pirates Dreyfuss voted to Hall." *Pittsburgh Post-Gazette*, December 4, 2007.
Pittsburgh Pirates media guide
"Realm of the Rooter." *Pittsburg Press*, October 6, 1902.
"The Best Teams in Baseball History." *Baseball Prospectus*, July 28, 1998.

7. New Year's Day 1973
"1972: A matter of record." *Pittsburgh Press*, January 4, 1973.
Breton, Gabriel. "Tragedy evokes tears, disbelief here." *Pittsburgh Post-Gazette*, January 2, 1973.
"Clemente dies in plane crash." *Pittsburgh Post-Gazette* & *Associated Press*, January 2, 1973.
Clemente tributes flow from country." *Pittsburgh Post-Gazette* & *Associated Press*, January 3, 1973.
Feeney, Charley. "The great Roberto died caring for others." *Pittsburgh Post-Gazette*, January 2, 1973.
Livingston, Pat. "The greater loss." *Pittsburgh Press*, January 2, 1973.
McHugh, Roy. "Roberto left own imprint on times." *Pittsburgh Press*, January 2, 1973.
McLean, Don. "American Pie." Universal Music Publishing Group.
"Musick, Phil. "The Great One: Most of all, he was human." *Pittsburgh Press*, January 4, 1973.
Smizik, Bob. "Roberto gave everything he had." *Pittsburgh Press*, January 2, 1973.

8. Who the Heck is Francisco Cabrera?
Baseball Almanac & *Pittsburgh Tribune-Review*, May 25, 2003.
Baseball-Reference.com
Meyer, Paul. "Heartbreaker." *Pittsburgh Post-Gazette*, October 15, 1992.
Meyer, Paul. "That horrible half inning." *Pittsburgh Post-Gazette*, October 16, 1992.
Rushin, Steven. "Unbelievable," *Sports Illustrated*, October 26, 1992.

9. The First Legend
"Death claims Honus Wagner, 81." *Pittsburgh Press*, Decmeber 6, 1955.
"Death takes baseball idol of millions." *Pittsburgh Press*, December 6, 1955.
Baseball Almanac
"President Eisenhower writes to his idol." Seth.com.
McKittrick, Rosemary. "The house that Wagner built." *Pittsburgh Post-Gazette*, July 10, 1994.

10. KDKA Goes Live
Baseball Library.com
Bohn, Michael K. "Radio and sports was the first wireless revolution." *McClatchy Newspapers*, April 17, 2011.
"Celebrating 90 years of radio broadcasts." *St. Louis Post-Dispatch*, October 19, 2011.

ExplorePAHistory.com

Folkart, Burt A. "Nation's first baseball broadcaster." *Los Angeles Times*, March 18, 1986.

Phillysportshistory.com

Retrosheet.org

11. 1960: A Love Affair

"Big crowd hails team downtown." *Pittsburgh Post-Gazette*, September 26, 1960.

Bouchette, Ed. "A round of '60." *Pittsburgh Post-Gazette*, July 2, 2000.

Dvorchak, Robert. "Joe L. Brown: September 1, 1918–August 15, 2010." *Pittsburgh Post-Gazette*, August 17, 2010.

Langosch, Jennifer. "1960 Bucs symbolized Pittsburgh's revival." MLB.com, June 18, 2010.

"Long drought ends for Pirates, fans." *Pittsburgh Press*, September 26, 1960.

Maraniss, David. *Clemente: The Passion and Grace of Baseball's Last Hero*. New York: Simon & Schuster, 2006.

Smizik, Bob. "Pirates stirring excitement, but they can't match the 1960 champs." *Pittsburgh Press*, July 22, 1990.

12. Turn on the Lights

Brooks, Tim and Earle Marsh. *The Complete Directory to Prime Time Network TV Shows (9th ed.)*. New York: Ballantine Books, 2007.

"Bucs Take Different Approach; Hurlers Get Down To Business." *Pittsburgh Press*, October 14, 1971.

Christine, Bill. "Orioles Feel The Pinch." *Pittsburgh Press*, October 14, 1971.

Feeney, Charley. "Bucs Win, 4–3, To Even Series." *Pittsburgh Post-Gazette*, October 14, 1971.

"It's Luke vs. Pat Under The Lights." *Pittsburgh Press*, October 13, 1971.

13. The Whole Pie

Emert, Rich. "Letter perfect." *Pittsburgh Post-Gazette*, July 23, 2000.

Forr, James. "Pie Traynor." Society for American Baseball Research Biography project.

Leonard, Vince. "Pie Traynor: End of a radio era." *Pittsburgh Press*, April 5, 1966.

"Pie simply 'The Best.'" *Pittsburgh Press*, March 17, 1972.

"Pie's sudden death great shock to all." *Pittsburgh Post-Gazette*, March 17, 1972.

"Pirate immortal Pie Traynor dies." *Pittsburgh Post-Gazette*, March 17, 1972.

Schrum, Rick. "Books throw good hooks on Pie and The Deacon." *Pittsburgh Post-Gazette*, May 3, 2010.

14. Kissed By The Gods

Baseball-Reference.com

Blass, Steve, and Erik Sherman. *Steve Blass: A Pirate for Life*. Chicago: Triumph Publishing, 2012.

Feeney, Charley. "We're the champs." *Pittsburgh Post-Gazette*, October 18, 1971.

McHugh, Roy. "Pitching did it." *Pittsburgh Press*, October 18, 1971.

15. The Curse of Barry Bonds

Baseball-reference.com

Chass, Murray. "Giants make investment: $43 million in Bonds." *New York Times*, December 6 1992.

Cook, Ron. "Clemente great, but Bonds better." *Pittsburgh Post-Gazette*, February 23, 1993.

Newhan, Ross. "Bonds on hold until ownership is settled." *Los Angeles Times*, December 7, 1992.

"Pirates say they can't afford not to trade Bonds." *Associated Press* & *Los Angeles Times*, December 4, 1991.

Robinson, Alan. "The Curse of Barry Bonds." *Associated Press* & *The Seattle Times*, August 7, 2007.

Rubino, Robert. "Curse of Barry Bonds about to lift after 20 years." *The Press Democrat*, August 24, 2013.

Smizik, Bob. "Unpopular fact: Bonds best Pirate." *Pittsburgh Press,* May 2, 2001.

16. Big Poison & Little Poison

Baseball-Reference.com

Biederman, Lester J. "A born hitter, Paul surprised even Clemente." *Pittsburgh Press*, August 31, 1965.

Chapin, Dwight. "Penning a story on the Poison brothers." *San Francisco Chronicle*, April 1, 2003.

"Death strikes out Paul Waner at 62." *Pittsburgh Press*, August 30, 1965.

Pittsburgh Pirates media guide

Upchurch, Jay C. "Waner brothers took baseball skills from family farm to Hall of Fame." *Oklahoma Gazette*, July 4, 2007.

17. What Couldn't He Do?

Baseball-Reference.com

Louisa, Angelo. "Fred Clarke." Society of American Baseball Research Biography Project.

Pirates media guide

Welsh, Regis M. "Fred Clarke dies, former Pirate Pilot." *Pittsburgh Press*, August 15, 1960.

18. An Even 3,000

Abrams, Al. "Was robbed of 3,000, Clemente says." *Pittsburgh Post-Gazette*, September 30, 1972.

Smizik, Bob. "Roberto gets 3,000[th], will rest till playoffs." *Pittsburgh Press*, October 1, 1972.

19. He Had Us All the Way

Finoli, David, and Bill Ranier. *The Pittsburgh Pirates Encyclopedia*. Sports Publishing, LLC, 2003.

Kohnfelder, Earl. "Prince lauded as broadcaster, human being." *Pittsburgh Press*, June 11, 1985.

O'Brien, Jim. *We had 'em all the way*. James P O'Brien Publishing, 1998.

20. Mecca

McCollister, John. *The Good, The Bad and the Ugly Pittsburgh Pirates*. Chicago: Triumph Books, 2008.

Kirkland, Kevin. "Fans relive joy of Pirates' 1960 World Series win." *Pittsburgh Post-Gazette*, October 10, 2008.

O'Neill, Brian. "Once upon a time in Forbes Field, a ball cleared a wall." *Pittsburgh Post-Gazette*, October 14, 2008.

Dvorchak, Robert. "Mazeroski's homer still a winner." *Pittsburgh Post-Gazette*, October 14, 2009.

Shribman, David. "Bottom of the ninth." *Pittsburgh Post-Gazette*, October 10, 2010.

Dvorchak, Robert. "Game 7 'still feels like it happened yesterday." *Pittsburgh Post-Gazette*, October 14, 2010.

21. T-206
Associated Press story, September 6, 2007.
Associated Press story, October 27, 2010.
Nuckols, Ben. "Nuns' Honus Wagner card goes to new buyer." *Associated Press*, December 20, 2010.
Wagner, Bill. "Ask Babe: Why does Honus Wagner baseball card attract such big bucks?" *Scripps Howard News Service*, September 11, 2013.

22. The Best Ballpark in America
ABCNews.com
CBS Morning News
Caple, Jim. "PNC Park is a grand slam compared to other ballparks." espn.com & *Pittsburgh Post-Gazette*, September 14, 2003.
Silver, Nate. "Ranking baseball's best ballparks." *New York Times*, May 29, 2011.
Smith, Claire. "Phillies look and learn from PNC Park." *Philadelphia Inquirer*, July 21, 2001.
Smizik, Bob. "PNC Park a diamond in rough season." *Pittsburgh Post-Gazette*, September 27, 2001.

23. The First Championship
Baseball Almanac
Baseball-reference.com
Dvorchak, Robert. "The Good Old Days." *Pittsburgh Post-Gazette*, April 5, 2009.
Pittsburgh Pirates media guide

24. The One-Man Show
Baseball-Reference.com
Corbett, Warren. "Ralph Kiner." Society for American Baseball Research Biography Project.
Meyer, Paul. "Going, going...but never forgotten." *Pittsburgh Post-Gazette*, April 7, 2003.
Pirates media guide
Shrum, Rick. "The good, ol' boys of summer." *Pittsburgh Post-Gazette*, May 2, 2004.
Smizik, Bob. "Brush with history." *Pittsburgh Post-Gazette*, September 1, 1998.

25. No. 712, No. 713 and No. 714
Creamer, Robert. *Babe: The Legend Comes To Life*, New York: Simon & Schuster, 1974.
Dvorchak, Robert. "Ruthian Moment For Fans." *Pittsburgh Post-Gazette*, May 25, 2010.
Retrosheet.org

26. The Magnificent 7
Feeney, Charley. "Stennett 7-Hits Cubs, 22–0." *Pittsburgh Post-Gazette*, September 17, 1975.
Feeney, Charley. "Stennett Sets Mark As Bucs Crush Phils." *Pittsburgh Post-Gazette*, September 18, 1975.
Retrosheet.org

27. The First All-Black Lineup
"The All-Black Lineup." Blogspot.com, February 25, 2008.
Markusen, Bruce. "Remembering The All-Black Lineup." Bruce Markusen's Cooperstown Confidential blog, September 1, 2009.
Vascellero, Charlie. "Bucs broke ground with first all-minority lineup." MLB.com, September 1, 2011.

28. Astro-Naught
Buccofans.wikispaces.com/Pirates+Payroll+History
Cook, Ron. "A weird gem for Cordova." *Pittsburgh Post-Gazette*, July 13, 1997.
Dvorchak, Robert. "Cordova Zeroes In." *Pittsburgh Post-Gazette*, October 21, 1997.
Kovacevic, Dejan. "Calm After The Storm." *Pittsburgh Post-Gazette*, July 14, 1997.
Meyer, Paul. "Pirates 'Freak Show' Hit Zenith With July No-Hitter." *Pittsburgh Post-Gazette*, July 10, 2007.
Smizik, Bob. "Astro-naught." *Pittsburgh Post-Gazette*, July 13, 1997.

29. Train Derailment
Baseball Almanac
Baseball-Reference.com
Finoli, David, and Bill Ranier. *The Pittsburgh Pirates Encyclopedia*. Sports Publishing, LLC, 2003.
Kovacevi, Dejan. "A great story worth retelling." *Pittsburgh Post-Gazette*, June 28, 2005.
Retrosheet.org

30. 8 For 8
Biederman, Lester J., and Chester L. Smith. All game reports and columns published in *Pittsburgh Press*, May 19–30, 1956.
Biederman, Lester J. "Record blast caps Friend's six-hit, 6–0 win over Cards." *Pittsburgh Press*, May 24, 1956.
Biederman, Lester J. "Fines 'made' Bucs." *Pittsburgh Press*, May 25, 1956.
Biederman, Lester J. "Brown early fulfilling promise to Dale Long." *Pittsburgh Press*, May 28, 1956.
Biederman, Lester J. "32,000 cheer Long's record No. 8." *Pittsburgh Press*, May 29, 1956.
Biederman, Lester, J. "Dale humble in midst of glory." *Pittsburgh Press*, May 29, 1956.
Biederman, Lester J. "The other side of Dale Long." *Pittsburgh Press*, May 30, 1956.
Smith, Chester L. "Long clout stirs fans." *Pittsburgh Press*, May 25, 1956.
Smith, Chester L. "Now we can all relax." *Pittsburgh Press*, May 30, 1956.
"Long, Wall traded." *Pittsburgh Post-Gazette*, May 2, 1957.

31. Good Morning and Goodbye
Collier, Gene. "Let's not forget Stargell." *Pittsburgh Post-Gazette,* April 7, 2011.
Collier, Gene. "Wilver Dornel Stargell, 1940–2001." *Pittsburgh Post-Gazette*, April 10, 2001.
Cook, Ron. "Pirates family mourns death of beloved Pops." *Pittsburgh Post-Gazette*, April 10, 2001.
Cook, Ron. "Stargell touches 'em all." *Pittsburgh Post-Gazette*, April 15, 2001.

32. The Original Pirate
BaseballLibrary.com
Baseball-Reference.com
Finoli, David, and Bill Ranier. *The Pittsburgh Pirates Encyclopedia*. Sports Publishing, LLC, 2003.
Potter, Chris. "Why is our baseball team called the Pittsburgh Pirates?" *Pittsburgh City Paper*, August 14, 2003.

33. Pops' Night
Baseball-Reference.com
Donovan, Dan. "Whew, it's over! Bucs are champs." *Pittsburgh Press*, October 18, 1979.

Feeney, Charley. "Battlin' Bucs beat 'em." *Pittsburgh Post-Gazette*, October 18, 1979.

Fimrite, Ron. "Two champs from the city of champions." *Sports Illustrated*, December 24, 1979.

Musick, Phil. "Pops Stargell drives to MVP and new car." *Pittsburgh Post-Gazette*, October 18, 1979.

34. How Long Was It?
Baseball-reference.com
Pingdom.com
Stark, Jayson. "The Pirates' epic journey to win No. 82." ESPN.com, September 10, 2013.

35. One Sweet Night
Baseball-Reference.com
Feeney, Charley. "Candy no-hits Dodgers; 1ˢᵗ modern Buc here." *Pittsburgh Post-Gazette*, August 10, 1976.
Fink, David. "Candy bar night a sweet affair." *Pittsburgh Post-Gazette*, August 10, 1976.
Smizik, Bob. "Candy bars LA from hit column." *Pittsburgh Press*, August 10, 1976.

36. Twenty-one Years in the Making
Brink, Bill. "Rolling on the river." *Pittsburgh Post-Gazette*, October 2, 2013.
Cook, Ron. "Liriano has place in Pirates history." *Pittsburgh Post-Gazette*, October 2, 2013.
Kepner, Tyler. "In October, showcasing a thriving sport that's not football." *New York Times*, October 6, 2013.
Majors, Dan. "Bucs fans bask in their contribution to victory." *Pittsburgh Post-Gazette*, October 2, 2013.
O'Neill, Brian. "Bucs gone wild." *Pittsburgh Post-Gazette*, October 2, 2013.
Stark, Jayson. "A special night in Pittsburgh." ESPN.com, October 2, 2013.

37. Who the Heck Uses the Word Gloamin'?
ESPN.com
John Thorn's OurGame Blog on mlblogs.com
Merriam-Webster.com
Pittsburgh Post-Gazette, September 29, 1938.
Traditionalmusic.co.uk

38. The Old Irishman
"A tough act to follow." *Sports Illustrated*, April 10, 1972.
Baseball Library.com
Dvorchak, Robert. "Murtaugh receives another shot at the Hall." *Pittsburgh Post-Gazette*, November 29, 2009.
Murtaugh, Danny, The Baseball Page.com.
Smizik, Bob. "The fans speak: Mazeroski leads voting on Pirates All-Century team." *Pittsburgh Post-Gazette*, September 19, 1999.
Terrell, Roy. "Danny and the Pirates." *Sports Illustrated*, March 16, 1959.
Walton Hroncich, Colleen. "Pirates legend Danny Murtaugh is in my Hall of Fame, at least." *Pittsburgh Post-Gazette*, December 7, 2007.

39. Under Cy-zed
Baseball-reference.com
Chass, Murray, "Drabek breaks the bank and arbitration mark." *New York Times*, February 15, 1991.

"Drabek wins Cy Young Award." *Associated Press* & *New York Times*, November 15, 1990.
Meyer, Paul. "'He's a real rare guy.'" *Pittsburgh Post-Gazette*, November 15, 1990.
"'That's real nice,' says Law of award." *Associated Press* & *Pittsburgh Post-Gazette*, November 3, 1960.

40. September 1985: The Drug Trials
Cook, Ron. "A terrible time of trial and error." *Pittsburgh Post-Gazette*, September 29, 2000.
Finder, Chuck. "Trying times." *Pittsburgh Post-Gazette*, June 11, 1995.
Fink, David. "Players penalized for drug ties." *Pittsburgh Post-Gazette*, March 1, 1986.
Hubbard, Steve. "Players can't hide scars six years after drug trials." *Pittsburgh Press*, June 2, 1991.

41. High and Right
Baseball Almanac
Blagden, James. *Dock Ellis & The LSD No-Hitter*, animated short. Features audio from interview with Ellis for National Public Radio by Donnell Alexander and Neille Ile, 2008.
Brothers, Eric. "Dock Ellis and The Electric Baseball Game." *High Times*, August 1987.
Hruby, Patrick. "The Long Strange Trip of Dock Ellis." ESPN: Outside The Lines.
Retrosheet.org
Smizik, Bob. "Ellis: I pitched no-hitter on LSD." *Pittsburgh Press*, April 8, 1984.
Witz, Billy. "For Ellis, A Long Strange Trip To A No-Hitter." *New York Times*, September 4, 2010.

42. Wild Heartbreak
Feeney, Charley. "Reds Dethrone Bucs, 4–3, With Heroics in 9th." *Pittsburgh Post-Gazette*, October 12, 1972.
Smizik, Bob. "Man or Superman?" *Pittsburgh Press*, October 12, 1972.
Smizik, Bob. "Wild Pitch Capsizes Bucs, Wrecks Dynasty." *Pittsburgh Press*, October 12, 1972.
"The Strike That Bounced." *Associated Press* & *Pittsburgh Post-Gazette*, October 12, 1972.

43. The Forgotten Pioneer
Baseball-Reference.com
Bouchette, Ed. "'Little Man' took big step." *Pittsburgh Post-Gazette*, May 15, 1997.
Hernon, Jack, "Bucs kayo Roberts in 8th to win opener, 4–2." *Pittsburgh Post-Gazette*, April 14, 1954.
Shrum, Rick. "One of a kind." *Pittsburgh Post-Gazette*, April 25, 2004.
Singer, Tom. "Roberts broke Bucs' color line admirably." MLB.com, February 2, 2012.

44. Hall of Tears
Cook, Ron. "Maz's Moment." *Pittsburgh Post-Gazette*, August 6, 2001.
Cook, Ron. "Second to none." *Pittsburgh Post-Gazette*, August 6, 2001.
Langosch, Jennifer. "Emotional Mazeroski honored with statue." MLB.com, September 6, 2010.
Stark, Jayson. "Mazeroski hits home run with emotional induction." ESPN.com, August 6, 2001.

45. Move Over, Babe
Baseball-reference.com
Christine, Bill. "Robby Snaps Out Of It Just In Time." *Pittsburgh Press*, October 4, 1971.

Feeney, Charley. "Bucs Even It As Robertson Hits 3 Homers." *Pittsburgh Post-Gazette*, October 4, 1971.
"Fellow At First Nasty—Fox." *Associated Press* & *Pittsburgh Post-Gazette*, October 4, 1971.

46. Jim Who?
Collier, Gene. "It's a dream come true for ex-coach." *Pittsburgh Press*, November 21, 1985.
Cook, Ron. "Leyland's epilogue: 'You captured my heart.'" *Pittsburgh Post-Gazette*, September 26, 1996.
Hertzel, Bob. "Leyland's decision from heart." *Pittsburgh Press*, January 23, 1992.
Meyer, Paul. "Leyland counts 1,500 blessings." *Pittsburgh Post-Gazette*, August 13, 1995.
Meyer, Paul. "The long goodbye." *Pittsburgh Post-Gazette*, September 26, 1996.
Smizik, Bob. "Leyland gets the call from Pirates." *Pittsburgh Press*, November 21, 1985.
Smizik, Bob. "Can Leyland succeed in a job built for failure." *Pittsburgh Press*, November 22, 1985.
Smizik, Bob. "Pirates fans to Leyland: Thanks for the memories." *Pittsburgh Post-Gazette*, September 26, 1996.

47. The Other Game
Collier, Gene. "The slugger." *Pittsburgh Post-Gazette*, October 20, 1996.
Emery, Rich. "Lore of the game." *Pittsburgh Post-Gazette*, July 8, 2001.
Finder, Chuck. "Black & Golden." *Pittsburgh Post-Gazette*, July 9, 2006.
Finder, Chuck. "Going, going, gone…and not forgotten." *Pittsburgh Post-Gazette*, October 18, 1998.
Finder, Chuck. "Pirates will put history on display." *Pittsburgh Post-Gazette*, June 27, 2006.
Finder, Chuck. "On the road with Satch & Co." *Pittsburgh Post-Gazette*, July 9, 2006.

48. Der Bingle
Baseball-Reference.com
Bingcrosby.com
Crosby, Bing. *San Diego Reader*.
Oye, Jon. "A Bing Crosby Primer." Contemplations on Classic Movies and Music blog.

49. The Rickey Dinks
Finoli, David, and Bill Ranier. *The Pittsburgh Pirates Encyclopedia*. Sports Publishing, LLC, 2003.
"Foul ball." *The Allegheny Bulletin*, October 14, 1992.
Shrum, Rick. "The Rickey Dinks." *Pittsburgh Post-Gazette*, June 24, 2001.

50. Angels in the Forbes Field Outfield
TV.com/shows/the-twilight-zone
Vancheri, Barbara. "Original 'Angels' Conjured Up Lots of Fanfare, Some Controversy." *Pittsburgh Post-Gazette*, July 3, 1994.

51. I'll Walk Home
Associated Press story, October 5, 1989.
Hoover, Bob. "Rooker makes it across home plate." *Pittsburgh Post-Gazette*, October 18, 1989.
Mandel, Ken. "Rooker puts aching foot in mouth." MLB.com, June 10, 2003.
Meyer, Paul. "Bucs blow 10-run lead, 15–11." *Pittsburgh Post-Gazette*, June 9, 1989.
Stark, Jayson. "Rooker did some talking, now he'll do some walking." *Philadelphia Inquirer*, August 1, 1989.

52. The Baron of the Bullpen
Abrams, Al. "Sidelight on Sports." *Pittsburgh Post-Gazette*, September 2, 1968.
Baseball-reference.com
Biederman, Lester J. "Face ties record, bought by Tigers." *Pittsburgh Press*, September 1, 1968.
Cook, Ron. "Saving Face." *Pittsburgh Post-Gazette*, August 15, 1999.
Robinson, Alan. "When Elroy Face went 18–1." *Associated Press* & *Los Angeles Times*, August 13, 1989.

53. Save of the Century
Barnes, Tom. "Owner says grip on Bucs is solid." *Pittsburgh Post-Gazette*, August 9, 1996.
Collier, Gene. "McClatchy deals are no surprise." *Pittsburgh Post-Gazette*, September 1, 1996.
Collier, Gene. "McClatchy fulfills mission impossible." *Pittsburgh Post-Gazette*, February 14, 1996.
Collier, Gene. "McClatchy had opportunity to reverse dynamics." *Pittsburgh Post-Gazette*, July 8, 2007.
Cook Ron. "McClatchy disappointed, but undaunted." *Pittsburgh Post-Gazette*, May 28, 1996.
Cook, Ron. "Youth will be served." *Pittsburgh Post-Gazette*, September 22, 1996.
Halvonik, Steve. "McClatchy calls rumors of rift exaggerated." *Pittsburgh Post-Gazette*, January 13, 1996.
Halvonik, Steve. "Who will go?" *Pittsburgh Post-Gazette*, August 27, 1996.
Keidan, Bruce. "Chapter IV: The local hero." *Pittsburgh Post-Gazette*, September 1, 1996.
Keidan, Bruce. "Chapter V: The tide turns." *Pittsburgh Post-Gazette*, September 1, 1996.
Keidan, Bruce. "Chapter VI: The eleventh hour." *Pittsburgh Post-Gazette*, September 1, 1996.
Keidan, Bruce. "Major Pirates investor to sell out his share." *Pittsburgh Post-Gazette*, August 8, 1996.
Keidan, Bruce. "McClatchy's financial coalition." *Pittsburgh Post-Gazette*, September 1, 1996.
Kovacevic, Dejan. "Nutting becomes Pirates cleanup hitter." *Pittsburgh Post-Gazette*, January 13, 2007.
Meyer, Paul. "Mired in another losing season, Bucs passed the bucks." *Pittsburgh Post-Gazette*, July 24, 2003.
Nelson Jones, Diana. "Boy wonder." *Pittsburgh Post-Gazette*, April 14, 1996.
"Poor moves dampen McClatchy's charm," September 5, 1996.
Smizik, Bob. "New stadium is priority for league and McClatchy." *Pittsburgh Post-Gazette*, February 14, 1996.
Smizik, Bob. "Pirates savior hurting franchise." *Pittsburgh Post-Gazette*, September 19, 1996.

54. Flat-Out the Best
Baseball-Reference.com
Feeney, Charley. "Briles blanks 'em; Bucs 1 up." *Pittsburgh Post-Gazette*, October 15, 1971.
Jordan, Jimmy. "Briles' secret weapon: Control." *Pittsburgh Post-Gazette*, October 15, 1971.
Leggett, William. "Some kind of comeback." *Sports Illustrated*, October 25, 1971.
Retrosheet.org
Stahl, John. "Nelson Briles." Society for American Baseball Research Biography Project.

55. Hit Masters
Baseball Almanac
Erion, Greg. "Debs Garms." Society for American Baseball Research Biography Project.
Sportslistsoftheday.com
Tarpey, Neil. "Matty Alou: A Giant Among Pirates." *The Times-Standard*, November 4, 2011.

56. Murdered
"Balls and strikes." *United Press International*, October 5, 1927.
Baseball Almanac
Davis, Ralph S. "Babe Ruth stands in class all alone." *Pittsburgh Press*, October 9, 1927.
Davis, Ralph S. "Wild pitch ends series." *Pittsburgh Press*, October 9, 1927.
Davis, Ralph S. "Yanks win opener, 5–4." *Pittsburgh Press*, October 5, 1927.
Davis, Ralph S. "Yankees win third." *Pittsburgh Press*, October 7, 1927.
White, Paul W. "Yanks superior strength should give them edge." *United Press International*, October 4, 1927.

57. They Named a Disease After Him
Blass, Steve, with Erik Sherman. *Steve Blass: A Pirate for Life*. Chicago: Triumph Books, 2012.
Cook, Ron. "A man's story worth telling." *Pittsburgh Post-Gazette*, May 6, 2012.
Retrosheet.org

58. Operation Shutdown
Baseball-Reference.com
"Bell Could Miss Two Weeks With Groin Injury." *Pittsburgh Post-Gazette*, March 22, 2002.
Dvorchak, Robert. "Bad Ring To It." *Pittsburgh Post-Gazette*, March 27, 2002.
Dvorchak, Robert. "Pirates Finally Part With Bell." *Pittsburgh Post-Gazette*, March 30, 2002.
Dvorchak, Robert. "The Bell Goes Off." *Pittsburgh Post-Gazette*, March 18, 2002.

59. After Midnight
Brooks, Matt. "Pirates fall to Braves." Washingtonpost.com, July 27, 2011.
Cox, Chris. "Marathon game rewrites record books." MLB.com, July 27, 2011.
Odum, Charles. "Braves beat Pirates 4–3 in 19 innings." *Associated Press*, July 27, 2011.
Retrosheet.org
Sanaerino, Michael. "Ump called out for 19th-inning flub." *Pittsburgh Post-Gazette*, July 28, 2011.

60. The Cobra
Baseball-Reference.com
Blount, Roy. "A loudmouth and his loud bat." *Sports Illustrated*, April 9, 1979.
Feeney, Charley. "A young and old Pirate." *Pittsburgh Post-Gazette*, July 13, 1973.
Hubbard, Steve. "Players can't hide scars six years after drug trials." *Pittsburgh Press*, June 2, 1991.
Hubbard, Steve. "Top dog." *Pittsburgh Press*, June 19, 1990.
"They Said It." *Sports Illustrated*, April 28, 1980.

61. The Ultimate Fantasy League Team
Fuggetta, Emily. "Missing mural of baseball greats will rise again." *Pittsburgh Post-Gazette*, July 10, 2010.

Thomas, Mary. "Pittsburgh baseball legends enshrined on downtown mural." *Pittsburgh Post-Gazette*, April 6, 2000.

62. One Mean Left
Baseball Almanac
Baseball-Reference.com
Finoli, David, and Bill Ranier. *The Pittsburgh Pirates Encyclopedia*. Sports Publishing, LLC, 2003.
"Killen, Old Pirate Pitcher, Is Dead." *Pittsburgh Press*, December 4, 1939.

63: So You Left Early?
Dvorchak, Robert. "What a blast." *Pittsburgh Post-Gazette*, July 29, 2001.
Smizik, Bob. "Giles helps Pirates grind out victory." *Pittsburgh Post-Gazette,* July 29, 2001.

64. Hello, Pirates Friends…
Finder, Chuck. "Frattare shares his stadium memories." *Pittsburgh Post-Gazette*, September 28, 2000.
Meyer, Paul. "From lounge DJ to the voice of the Pirates." *Pittsburgh Post-Gazette*, May 21, 1995.
Modoona, Bill. "Frattare enthusiastically plays the position he has been assigned." *Pittsburgh Press*, July 8, 1990.
Smizik, Bob. "Brown, Frattare become co-No. 1s." *Pittsburgh Post-Gazette*, September 22, 2006.
Smizik, Bob. "Frattare reflects on tough call to quit the booth." *Pittsburgh Post-Gazette*, October 8, 2008.
Smizik, Bob. "Frattare retires." *Pittsburgh Post-Gazette*, October 2, 2008.

65. If Not For Him…
Baseball-Reference.com
Meyer, Paul. "Bonds, Walk, keep Bucs alive," *Pittsburgh Post-Gazette*, October 12, 1992.
Retrosheet.org

66. The Freak Show
Baseball-Reference.com
Dvorchak, Robert. "A baseball season to cherish and cheer." *Pittsburgh Post-Gazette*, October 21, 1997.
Dvorchak, Robert. "First place at the break." *Pittsburgh Post-Gazette*, October 21, 1997.
Dvorchak, Robert. "Pirates fans, meet the first-place team." *Pittsburgh Post-Gazette*, October 21, 1997.
Dvorchak, Robert. "The uphill climb comes close." *Pittsburgh Post-Gazette*, October 21, 1997.
Meyer, Paul. "Pirates 'Freak Show' hit zenith with July no-hitter." *Pittsburgh Post-Gazette*, July 10, 2007.
Meyer, Paul. "Why the Pirates didn't win their division title." *Pittsburgh Post-Gazette*, October 21, 1997.
Retrosheet.org

67. Splashdown
Finder, Chuck. "What are the odds of hitting a home run with an Allegheny splashdown?" *Pittsburgh Post-Gazette*, April 15, 2001.
Inside Pirates Baseball, Episode 12. Root Sports, 2013.

68. Dinner With Manny
Baseball-reference.com
Hurte, Bob. "Manny Sanguillen." Society of American Baseball Biography Project.

69. The Best Way In
"7th Inning Stretch: Take me out to the ballgame." *Pittsburgh Post-Gazette*, April 7, 1999.
Barnes, Tom. "Now it's Clemente's bridge," *Pittsburgh Post-Gazette*, August 6, 1998.
Barnes, Tom. "The city celebrates." *Pittsburgh Post*-Gazette, April 5, 1999.
Caple, Jim. "PNC Park is a grand slam compared to other ballparks." ESPN.com & *Pittsburgh Post-Gazette*, September 14, 2003.
Flinn, Stephen. "Clemente Bridge: Too much or too little?" *Pittsburgh Sports Report*, September 1998.
Grata, Joe. "Clemente Bridge spans space, time." *Pittsburgh Post-Gazette*, August 9, 1998.

70. A Smiling Sadness
Feeney, Charley. "Blyleven, Rooker combine in victory." *Pittsburgh Post-Gazette*, October 15, 1979.
Feeney, Charley. "Red-hot Bucs crack scoreless duel in 7th." *Pittsburgh Post-Gazette*, October 17, 1979.
Kovacevic, Dejan. "Chuck Tanner: July 4, 1928–February 11, 2011." *Pittsburgh Post-Gazette*, February 12, 2011.
Parascenzo, Marino. "Tanner turned to 'Grandma' for strength to stop Orioles." *Pittsburgh Post-Gazette*, October 15, 1979.

79. He Did What?
Jordan, Pat. "Kid K." *Sports Illustrated*, June 1, 1987.
Perry, Thomas K. "Ron Necciai: The man who struck out everybody." *The Blue Ridge Country*, April 22, 20009.
"Ron Necciai." Baseball-Reference.com, biographical information.

72. It Only Took 57 Years
Baseball-Reference.com
Cook, Ron. "Don't give up on Littlefield yet." *Pittsburgh Post-Gazette*, August 28, 2003.
Dvorchak, Robert. "Bay's window." *Pittsburgh Post-Gazette*, October 4, 2004.
Dvorchak, Robert. "Pirates' Bay Rookie of the Year." *Pittsburgh Post-Gazette*, November 9, 2004.
Dvorchak, Robert. "Pirates win, Bay ties mark." *Pittsburgh Post-Gazette*, September 12, 2004.
Dvorchak, Robert. "The deed is done." *Pittsburgh Post-Gazette*, August 27, 2003.
Meyer, Paul. "New Pirates players ready and willing to make contributions." *Pittsburgh Post-Gazette*, August 28, 2003.
Meyer, Paul. "Prize package Bay starting to make push." *Pittsburgh Post-Gazette*, July 2, 2004.
Smizik, Bob. "Bay appears to be real deal." *Pittsburgh Post-Gazette*, July 17, 2004.
Smizik, Bob. "Bay's the best, but award hardly a lock." *Pittsburgh Post-Gazette*, September 18, 2004.

73. Calling Mr. Blackwell
"1970s uniforms." Heritagesportsart.com.
Baseball-Reference.com
Dzurilla, Eddie. "The 10 worst of all time." *Bleacher Report*, May 15, 2010.
Mindspring.com

"The ugliest baseball uniforms of all time." Faniq.com/blog.
"Top 10 ugliest baseball uniforms of all time." TopTenz.com.
"Worst uniforms." ESPN.com, December 23, 1999.

74. The Press Box
Cook, Ron. "Baseball's hall calls." *Pittsburgh Post-Gazette*, October 24, 1996.
Cook, Ron. "'Pally' gets the call." *Pittsburgh Post-Gazette*, August 3, 1997.
Cook, Ron. "There's no better friend than Feeney." *Pittsburgh Post-Gazette*, August 3, 1997.
"Q&A: Charley Feeney" *Pittsburgh Post-Gazette*, May 29, 2006.

75. The Next Great One
Baseball-reference.com
Cook, Ron. "Investment analysis." *Pittsburgh Post-Gazette*, March 6, 2012.
Cook, Ron. "McCutchen is worth watching." *Pittsburgh Post-Gazette*, June 23, 2009.
Kovacevic, Dejan. "McCutchen debut adds spark atop order." *Pittsburgh Post-Gazette*, June 5, 2009.
Kovacevic, Dejan. "McCutchen wallops three homers." *Pittsburgh Post-Gazette*, August 2, 2009.
Kovacevic, Dejan. "Pirates trade All-Star McLouth." *Pittsburgh Post-Gazette*, June 4, 2009.
McCollough, J. Brady. "Stay humble, remember your faith." *Pittsburgh Post-Gazette*, March 31, 2013.
Sanserino, Michael. "With McCutchen signed, focus now shifts to Walker." *Pittsburgh Post-Gazette*, March 6, 2012.

76. Bring Your Camera
Hoffman, Benjamin. "Baseball statues aplenty, many of them in unexpected places." *New York Times*, March 6, 2013.
Pittsburgh Pirates media guide

77. 202 Still the Number
Abrams, Al. "Arley Wilbur 'Coop' Cooper." *Pittsburgh Post-Gazette*, August 8, 1973.
"All-time winningest pitchers by team." Nashvillegman, hubpages.com.
Baseball-Reference.com
Cicotello, David. "Wilbur Cooper." Society of American Baseball Research Biography Project.
Pittsburgh Pirates media guide
Wollen, L. H. "Pirates beat Vance at last." *Pittsburgh Press*, September 21, 1924.

78. A Work of Art
Biederman, Lester J. "Pop Gun Shot Wins Pirate Homer War." *Pittsburgh Post-Gazette*, August 13, 1966.
Jordan, Jimmy. "Record 11 Homers Belted..." *Pittsburgh Press*, August 13, 1966.
Retrosheet.org

79. Let's Play Three
Retrosheet.org
Dittmar, Joe. "Teams play tripleheader." BaseballLibrary.com
Schindler, Kevin. "Pirates and Reds play in triple-header." Suite.com, October 3, 2011.
Suehsdorf, A.D. "The last tripleheader." SABR Research Journals Archive.

80. For My Son
Cook, Ron. "Special Night Hits Home." *Pittsburgh Post-Gazette*, May 30, 2004.
Finder, Chuck. "Baby Booms." *Pittsburgh Post-Gazette*, May 29, 2004.
Retrosheet.org

81. What's Next?
Baxter, Kevin. "Gerrit Cole is making the most of an early arrival with Pirates." *Los Angeles Times*, October 10, 2013.
Cook, Ron. "No reason to doubt Cole in a playoff situation." *Pittsburgh Post-Gazette*, September 15, 2013.
Sanserino, Michael. "Rookie baffles Padres while Pirates turn up heat on offense." *Pittsburgh Post-Gazette*, September 20, 2013.
Sanserino, Michael. "Worth the wait: Victory No. 82." *Pittsburgh Post-Gazette*, September 10, 2013.
Zeise, Paul. "Young Cole is king." *Pittsburgh Post-Gazette*, August 17, 2013.

82. In The Beginning
Hoover, Bob. "Lost Pittsburgh." *Pittsburgh Post-Gazette*, June 26, 1994.
Nelson Jones, Diana. "City's first ballpark had view and water hazard." *Pittsburgh Post-Gazette*, July 10, 1998.
Nelson Jones, Diana. "Pirates past, future coming alive." *Pittsburgh Post-Gazette*, September 19, 1998.
"Pirates win last game at Expo." *Pittsburgh Press*, June 30, 1909.

83. A Key Player
Batz, Bob. "On his first CD, organist-for-all-seasons Vince Lascheid plays 'em as he sees 'em." *Pittsburgh Post-Gazette*, March 17, 1996.
Batz, Bob. "Vincent C. Lascheid Jr." *Pittsburgh Post-Gazette*, March 21, 2009.
Mayo, Jonathan. "Pirates organist Lascheid dies." MLB.com, March 21, 2009.
Miller, Michael. "The best seat in the house." *Pittsburgh Business Times,* May 24, 1999.

84. An Afternoon of Stars
Baseball Almanac
Johnson, Vince. "City has baseball charm." *Pittsburgh Post-Gazette*, July 8, 1959.

85. Dr. Strangeglove
Associated Press report, December 19, 2002.
Baseball-Reference.com
Dr. Strangeglove or: How I Learned To Stop Worrying About My Defense And Love The Big Fly.
Dvorchak, Robert. "Even With A Strange Glove, ex-Pirate Was Always A Hit." *Pittsburgh Post-Gazette*, December 20, 2002.

86. Now You See Him …
Baseball-Reference.com
Keidan, Bruce. "No Cruise Control." *Pittsburgh Post-Gazette*, May 4, 1998.
Meyer, Paul. "Even The Wall Can't Stop Ward." *Pittsburgh Post-Gazette*, May 4, 1998.
Reid, Jason. "Wall Is No Barrier For Ward." *Los Angeles Times*, May 4, 1998.

87. A Trip to the Museum
Collier, Gene. "A museum to satisfy the most rabid fanmania." *Pittsburgh Post-Gazette*, November 8, 2004.

88. Go Ahead, Top This
Armour, Mark. "Chief Wilson." Society for American Baseball Research Biography Project.
Baseball Almanac
Egan, Timonthy. "Swift and Sharp, Suzuki Sets Mark For Hits In A Season." *New York Times*, October 2, 2004.

89. The Ultimate Penalty
Jaffe, Chris. "20th anniversary: Rod Scurry dies from drugs." *Hardball Times*, November 5, 2012.
"Pirates suspend pitcher Scurry for failing to follow drug program." *LA Times*, June 27, 1985.
Reno-Gazette-Journal, November 8, 1992.
"Rod Scurry, 36, dies." *Associated Press*, November 6, 1992.
"Scurry arrested." *Associated Press*, December 25, 1988.
"Scurry is linked to drug case." *LA Times*, August 20, 1985.
"Yankees acquire Rod Scurry." *Associated Press*, September 14, 1985.

90. The Doctor Was In
"CPR." Wikipedia.com.
Musick, Phil. "The Other Side of Doc Medich." *Pittsburgh Post-Gazette*, April 12, 1976.
Retrosheet.org

91. Chester, Oliver, Hanna & Saul
Bartelby, J. "Pierogi History: Eastern European Dumplings of Dough and Filling." Yahoo.
com. Posted April 26, 2006.
Letteddywin.com
"Steel Town Speak." PBS.org.

92. The Kid Falls
Cook, Ron. "Kendall throbbing with pain, desire to return." *Pittsburgh Post-Gazette*, July 7, 1999.
Meyer, Paul. "Broken hearts." *Pittsburgh Post-Gazette*, July 5, 1999.
Meyer, Paul. "Kendall's dirty uniform is never out of style." *Pittsburgh Post-Gazette*, April 1, 2001.
Meyer, Paul. "One Step At A Time, Paul Meyer." *Pittsburgh Post-Gazette*, February 19, 2000.
Simonich, Milan. "Catcher's recovery 12 weeks off." *Pittsburgh Post-Gazette*, July 6, 1999.
"The 25 Most Gruesome Injuries in Sports History." *Bleacher Report*, February 9, 2010.

93. Holy Moises
Axelrod, Phil. "Nationals thank their lucky stars." *Pittsburgh Post-Gazette*, July 13, 1994.
Baseball Almanac
Berkon, Ben. "The 50 greatest MLB All-Star Game moments of all time." *Bleacher Report*, July 12, 2013.
"Game's rating comes up all stars." *Associated Press*, July 14, 1994.
Meyer, Paul. "Comeback cuts into National debt." *Pittsburgh Post-Gazette*, July 13, 1994.
Robinson, Alan. "Gimpy Gwynn hustles, slides to win game." *Associated Press*, July 13, 1994.
Smizik, Bob. "Fregosi saved a big bopper." *Pittsburgh Post-Gazette*, July 13, 1994.

94. The Man from 'Z'
Brink, Bill. "Not-so-hot Rod wins it in ninth." *Pittsburgh Post-Gazette*, May 9, 2012.
Box Office Mojo
IMDB.com
Majors, Dan. "The power of Zoltan?" *Pittsburgh Press*, July 3, 2012.
Majors, Dan. "Dude, what's the 'Z'?" *Pittsburgh Post-Gazette*, July 4, 2012.
"Pirates powered by sign of the Zoltan." *Associated Press*. Printed in the *Johnstown Tribune-Democrat*, July 13, 2012.

95. Tip the Sax Man

96. A Big Hurt
"Fun facts about Pittsburgh's ballparks." Mindspring.com.
Meyer, Paul. "Griffey unleashes HR power." *Pittsburgh Post-Gazette*, July 12, 1994.
Reilly, Rick. "The big heart." *Sports Illustrated*, August 8, 1994.
Stark, Jayson. "25 Greatest Home Run Derby moments." ESPN.com, July 12, 2010.

97. Sausage Brat Out the Wurst in Him
Dvorchak, Robert. "Sausage swat draws fine, suspension." *Pittsburgh Post-Gazette*, July 12, 2003.
Finder, Chuck. "Overdone sausage incident gave media plenty to chew on." *Pittsburgh Post-Gazette*, July 17, 2003.
Meyer, Paul. "Simon faces battery charge." *Pittsburgh Post-Gazette*, July 10, 2003.
Meyer, Paul. "Simon's sausage beef is over." *Pittsburgh Post-Gazette*, July 11, 2003.

98. Seriously?
Hoffman, Ken. "Astros Made History With A Rainout." *Houston Chronicle*, June 17, 2009.
Feeney, Charley. "Bucs Rained Out in Astrodome." *Pittsburgh Post-Gazette*, June 16, 1976.
Feeney, Charley. "An Unscheduled Feast In Dome." *Pittsburgh Post-Gazette*, June 17, 1976.
Franke, Russ. "Rain Turns Dome Into Picnic Shelter." *Pittsburgh Press*, June 16, 1976.

99. An Adopted Son
"1940s Pirate Frank Gustine Dies In Iowa." *Pittsburgh Press*, April 2, 1991.
Baseball-Reference.com
"Frank Gustine, 1921–1991." *Pittsburgh Press*, April 4, 1991.

100. September 9, 2013: Dawn of a New Day
Hawkins, Stephen. "Pirates' 1–0 win at Texas clinches winning season." *Associated Press*, September 10, 2013.

Sidebars

We Are Family
Copyright: Lyrics © EMI Music Publishing, Sony/ATV Music Publishing LLC, Warner/
Chappell Music, Inc.
People Magazine, November 5, 1979

Following Grandpa
Baseball Library.com
Baseball-Reference.com
ExplorePAHistory.com

Thanks, Roberto
Robinson, Alan. "A rookie thanks Clemente for saving father's life." *Associated Press* & *USA
Today*, September 2, 2010.
Singer, Tom. "Living legacy: Walker carries spirit of Clemente." MLB.com, January 13,
2013.
Wallner, Jeff. "A Press Box View: Clemente's death brought life to Pirates' Walker."
Blogspot.com.

Go figure
Baseball-Reference.com
Corbett, Warren. "Ralph Kiner." Society of American Baseball Research Biography Project.

With this World Series ring...
Allan, William. "Oriole-tamer Bruce Kison copters, jets to wedding." *Pittsburgh Press*,
October 18, 1971.
Jordan, Pat. "End of innocence." *Sports Illustrated*, April 10, 1972.

Double dose of 'Poison'
Retrosheet.org
"Upton brothers hit back-to-back homers for Braves." MLB.com, April 24, 2013.

One last blast
Feeney, Charley. "Thompson leads attack with 4 RBI." *Pittsburgh Post-Gazette*, May 4,
1985.
Weiskind, Ron. "Gunner's comeback: How sweet it was." *Pittsburgh Post-Gazette*, May
4, 1985.

Life? He wasn't kidding
Pirates media guide

Happy holidays?

Forbes' last day
Retrosheet.org

The odd cameo
IMDB.com

Stargell stars
"Stargell was Pirates' inspirational leader in the '70s." *ESPN Classic* & *Associated Press*, April 13, 2001.

Still home
"Baseball history preserved at Pitt." 225.pitt.edu.

Money isn't everything
Pittsburg Press, October 5, 1902.

A left-handed connection
Smizik, Bob. "The fans speak." *Pittsburgh Post-Gazette*
Baseball-reference.com